Green Volunteers

The World Guide to Voluntary Work in Nature Conservation

Green Volunteers
Publications

Green Volunteers
The World Guide to Voluntary Work In Nature Conservation

Editors:	Fabio Ausenda, Erin McCloskey
Cover design:	Studio Cappellato e Laurent srl, Milano
Cover photo:	Volunteer at the Gibbon Rehabilitation Center, Thailand
	Courtesy Rossella Rossi

This Guide is not an annual publication: the password that readers can obtain upon request (see page 6 for details) and the e-mail newsletter which they can join allow the readers to keep the information in this Guide always up to date and to be constantly informed on new opportunities.

Published by: Green Volunteers di Fabio Ausenda
Via Canonica 72
20154 Milano, Italy
www.greenvol.com
E-mail: greenvol@iol.it

US & Canada distribution: Universe Publishing
A division of Rizzoli International Publications, Inc.
300 Park Avenue South,
New York, NY 10010

UK distribution: Vacation Work Publications
9 Park End Street,
Oxford OX1 1HJ, England

Printed in Dec. 2002 by: Consorzio Artigiano L.V.G. srl, Azzate (VA), Italy

ISBN: 88-900167-9-5
Library of Congress Control Number: 2002116391

AKNOWLEDGMENTS

The Editors wish to thank all the individuals and organisations who made this publication possible. In particular: Susan Watts for her assistance and dedication; Roel Cosijn from The Ecovolunteer Network, who encouraged the Editor to put together this guide; Anita Prosser of BTCV for her encouragement and assistance; and the Expedition Advisory Centre of the Royal Geographical Society. Special thanks goes to the Gland (Switzerland) office of the World Conservation Union (IUCN), Species Survival Commission and Social Policy Group, for considering this publication a valid instrument for helping conservation projects. The above organisations are listed in the guide.

WARNING!

PLEASE NOTE THAT THE INFORMATION HEREIN HAS BEEN OBTAINED FROM THE RELEVANT ORGANISATIONS OR OTHER PUBLIC SOURCES. ALL PROJECTS LISTED IN THIS GUIDE MAY BE CHANGED OR CANCELLED WITHOUT NOTICE AT ANY TIME. USERS SHOULD VERIFY CURRENT PROJECTS, DURATION, PERIOD, COST, LOCATION, ACCOMMODATION AND WORK PROGRAMME. ORGANISATIONS AND PROJECTS LISTED MAY CHANGE THEIR PROGRAMMES, OBJECTIVES, ADDRESS, TELEPHONE, FAX AND E-MAIL ADDRESS, OR MAY CEASE OPERATING WITHOUT NOTICE AT ANY TIME. THE EDITOR, PUBLISHER AND DISTRIBUTORS ACCEPT NO RESPONSIBILITY FOR INACCURACY OF INFORMATION GIVEN IN THIS PUBLICATION.

INDIVIDUALS WILL JOIN ANY OF THE PROJECTS OR ORGANISATIONS LISTED IN THIS PUBLICATION AT THEIR OWN RISK. THE EDITOR, PUBLISHER AND DISTRIBUTORS WILL NOT BE LIABLE FOR ANY LOSS OR DAMAGE THAT MAY OCCUR TO ANYONE JOINING ANY OF THE PROJECTS OR ORGANISATIONS LISTED IN THIS PUBLICATION.

HOW TO BE LISTED IN *Green Volunteers*

If you are an organisation or project based anywhere in the world and you would like to be listed in the next edition or on our website at www.greenvol.com at no cost to you, please contact *Green Volunteers* at the addresses on the previous page. Should you require any information on how to recruit and organise volunteers as a valuable instrument to support a nature conservation project *Green Volunteers* is willing to assist you.

TABLE OF CONTENTS

PREFACE

In recent years there has been a growing demand for volunteers for nature conservation projects in general and for wildlife related projects in particular. Volunteering provides wildlife and nature enthusiasts with an opportunity to become involved in world-wide conservation efforts. Students can gain experience allowing them to pursue a career in nature conservation as well as ideas for a thesis. Until recently, large organisations were mostly responsible for offering this kind of opportunity, but usually the financial contributions required limited the number of people who could afford them and become volunteers. However, there are many smaller nature conservation and wildlife protection projects with a constant shortage of funding which greatly need volunteers for research assistance and financial resources. Often these contributions by volunteers can maintain projects for years. The Gibbon Rehabilitation Project in Thailand, for example, has been running successfully for over 10 years exclusively on the contributions and help of international volunteers. Until now many of these projects throughout the world did not have a world-wide forum. With this guide these valuable projects have the opportunity to connect with prospective volunteers and vice versa.

The objective of *Green Volunteers* is to provide information to fill the communication gap between people who are willing to join interesting and valuable projects world-wide, and the projects in need of volunteers. For this reason, the Geneva-based World Conservation Union's Species Survival Commission (the body which publishes the "Red Lists" of endangered species) considers the *Green Volunteers* guide a useful instrument for supporting conservation projects throughout the world.

The Editors highly recommend the following introductory pages are read. These pages explain what conservation volunteering involves and will increase the volunteer's chances of being accepted to a project.

INTRODUCTION

Green Volunteers is a directory. There are 2 sections: one dedicated to organisations and one to specific projects.

Organisations play an important role in providing opportunities for volunteer work; listed are those offering projects on a wide range of species, habitats and geographic locations, at various costs to volunteers (from zero to a few ·thousand dollars.) Organisations are listed in alphabetical order. Should an organisation have an acronym, as many do, the organisation is listed according to the alphabetical order of the acronym. For example, BTCV, CVA, WWF, are listed according to the acronym's alphabetical order. For some of the larger organisations, or for those offering interesting projects to prospective volunteers, a few projects have been described in greater detail in the second section. These projects are listed at the end of the organisations' descriptions under the heading: Selected Projects. For most of the organisations no projects have been described in the second section due to limited space in this guide. Prospective volunteers are therefore encouraged to contact the organisations directly (or visit their websites), and inquire for further information about available projects.

Projects are found in the second section of this guide. Greater detail about the projects offered by the organisations is provided, and many more independent projects, which are not part of major organisations, are listed.

To be updated for the following years on new and previously published projects and to join our non-expiring free e-mail newsletter, readers must send an e-mail to: network@greenvol.com. Proof of purchase of this guide is required to receive a UserID and password, which allow you to access the *Green Volunteers* Network pages at www.greenvol.com where the updates are listed. Free annual updates of this guide will be available unless the Editor and Publisher cease operating but no such interruption of activities is anticipated.

MEANING OF ABBREVIATIONS

For each organisation and project the guide lists:

The **address** and the **telephone** and **fax** numbers with the international codes. Remember to change the local area code according to the country's telephone system. For example, to call The Monkey Sanctuary, (UK) phone number (listed as ++ 44 (1503) 262 532), people calling from the UK should not dial ++ 44 (the international code), but should add 0 (zero) before 1503 (the local area code). People calling from the Netherlands should add 00 before 44 to call the UK. Whereas people calling from the US should dial 011, then 44, the international access codes from the US to the UK. **E-mail** and World Wide Web (**www**) addresses are listed where available. If these references are not listed, a quick phone call to ask an organisation if they have recently activated an e-mail or www address will help you to communicate and get information much faster than through regular mail and will speed your selection of the right organisation for you.

Desc.: The main activity and objectives of the organisations or projects.

Spp.: The species or the group of species involved. The common name, and Latin name if necessary for clarification, is provided. For projects involving groups of species, families, classes or communities, these groupings are cited in more general terms such as marine mammals, tropical birds, African herbivores, etc. Abbreviations are occasionally used.

Hab.: Specific habitats or wider biogeographical areas an organisation is involved with, such as tropical seas and coasts, African savannah, Mediterranean islands, etc. Abbreviations are occasionally used.

Loc.: The countries, regions (such as Southeast Asia) or continents where an organisation conducts its projects.

Travel: A basic summary of travel directions. Organisations and projects will give full details to the volunteers once accepted.

Dur.: The duration of the volunteering time, either a set period or a minimum and maximum duration.

Per.: The period of the year when a volunteer can join a project such as year round, the summer, July to August, etc.

L. term: Long-term volunteering is a longer stay than the set volunteer duration. Some projects do not allow long-term volunteering, others do, but they typically continue charging the volunteers the same contribution (per week, for example) without recognizing any discount for the additional experience acquired by the volunteer. Other organisations or projects encourage long-term volunteering for this benefit. The Ecovolunteer Network is one organisation that encourages a longer permanence on some of the projects by considerably decreasing the cost to the volunteer the longer a volunteer stays. Some projects or organisations require professionally qualified labour and staff and accept graduate students for their thesis work.

Age: Minimum and maximum age for joining a project.

Qualif.: The qualifications and skills required of a volunteer who wants to join a project. Most of the time no special qualifications are needed, other than a strong motivation and enthusiasm. Adaptation to harsh climates, long walks, hot or cold temperatures, basic accommodation and very little comfort is almost always required. Where possible, the Editors have specified particularly extreme working or lodging conditions present at a given project. However, specific information is to be obtained from the organisation or project. Other typical requirements include a strong flexibility to work with other people, a willingness to accept very little privacy (very rarely volunteers will be able to lodge in a single or even double rooms) and the ability to adapt to different cultures. These requirements apply to almost all projects but are not always stated. A volunteer may offer special skills, such as photography, good computer literacy, mechanical skills, etc. Never expect, nor impose these skills onto a project—there may already be very qualified people performing these duties with the accuracy required by the project. For long-term volunteering, or for organisations or projects where little or no contribution is required, volunteers are often selected according to their qualifications or previous experience in related work. Contact the organisation directly for more information on the skills and qualifications required.

Work: The main activities performed by volunteers are listed for projects. Since most organisations manage several projects, the work performed by volunteers is not described in detail because it will vary with each project. Prospective volunteers can predict what kind of activities to expect from the description of an organisation and the projects it supports. Further details are given by the organisations directly.

Lang.: The languages that are required for a volunteer to work on a project. The importance of communicating with the project staff or with local or international researchers should not be overlooked. Prospective volunteers should never underestimate the importance of this aspect and never overestimate their ability to understand a foreign language in a working environment.

Accom.: (Not described within the organisation description.) The style of accommodation the volunteers will be lodged in. For most of the projects volunteers should be prepared for very basic accommodations such as bunk beds in research stations (rarely in houses) tents or hammocks. Bathroom facilities can also be very basic and hot showers, particularly in the tropics, can be quite rare. Chores such as housecleaning, cooking, washing dishes, etc., are often expected. Comfort and privacy is rare. The ability to do without these privileges must be considered for environmental volunteering.

Cost: Most of the projects require a contribution from the volunteers, which is often the major funding for a project. Projects are often conducted with the financial contribution and the work volunteers perform. The cost of projects may vary from a few hundred to a few thousands dollars US. The Editors have tried to list as many organisations as possible requiring little or no contributions. These organisations, however, are difficult to find; they are either small projects in developing countries that have no means for communication or until now did not perceive the importance of taking volunteers. It is fair, however, that even these small projects or organisations ask for a small contribution, especially in developing countries. Usually, the volunteer's contribution covers food and accommodation or there may be a common kitty for food costs. Very rarely will the cost include the international airfare to reach a project site.

Some projects have introduced a very useful 'progressively decreasing cost' policy, depending on the length of stay. The rationale is that the longer a volunteer stays with a project, the more useful he or she becomes because of the experience he or she gains. Long-term volunteers selected according to their skills are often reimbursed for their living expenses. This is typically the case for long-term volunteers with Government Agencies, such as the US National Park Service, the US Forest Service or The US Fish and Wildlife Service. Part of the volunteer contribution likely pays for the project costs: marketing, reservation staff, rent, telephone, mail, etc. Money going towards an agency or larger organisation or overhead should not be considered money diverted from the conservation objective. Larger organisations perform a basic role in a world-wide conservation effort by providing volunteers and funding to projects that alone would not have been able to reach these important resources. However, when overhead costs are in excess of a reasonable percentage (max. 20–25%) an organisation should try to become more efficient by reducing costs, in order to devote a higher percentage of a volunteer's contribution to actual projects. It is perfectly in the right of a volunteer to know how much of his or her contribution goes into a project, and what is the organisation's overhead.

Agents: The agents or organisations where a prospective volunteer can or should apply. Many organisations have branches in other countries that act as agents for projects. Other organisations use outside agents such as travel agencies to recruit volunteers. Many organisations do not have agents and require direct application.

Applic.: This section briefly describes application procedures that may be required such as filling out an application form, sending a deposit or initial contribution, or becoming a member of a specific organisation.

Selected Projects are listed for some organisations. If detailed description of projects are not provided, volunteers should contact the organisation directly in order to receive further information.

TIPS FOR CONTACTING
AN ORGANISATION OR PROJECT

1) **Have clear in mind what you want to do, the species or habitats you prefer, the geographical location, the duration of your volunteering period and the costs you can afford.** This will help you in selecting and reducing the number of organisations or projects you want to apply to. Select a list of both organisations and projects and divide them into your first and second priority. The first priority should include not only those organisations or projects that are of primary interest to you, but also those which are more remote and harder to contact.

2) **Use the fastest possible method to contact an organisation.** Remember that interesting projects or organisations also have many applicants, and they usually fill their available positions on a first come, first serve basis. Therefore, you want to be as fast as possible in letting them know that you are interested in taking a position with them. You may send via e-mail the *Green Volunteers* standard application form found at page 255. Should you not receive a reply within 3–5 days, be prepared to send reminders or telephone them to confirm their e-mail address. These addresses often change, particularly when an organisation finds a cheaper internet server.

3) **Inform as much as possible the organisation or project you would like to work for about yourself.** With your request for information, send a description of your skills and interests and possibly a CV. You can find at page 255 the *Green Volunteers* standard application form, modeled on the application forms of many organisations. This form may be sufficient for applying and it may help you to save time. The form (which is not an official application form but just a tool to help in the application process) is also available from the *Green Volunteers* **Network Pages** at www.greenvol.com (these webpages are accessible with your password, see page 6 for details). Always enclose a cover letter (preferably typed and not handwritten) and ask if the organisation accepts the *Green Volunteers* application form.

4) **Make an organisation's response easier.** Remember that organisations and projects often are short of funds. Therefore, help them by enclosing self-addressed stamped envelopes. If the organisation is located in a foreign country, enclose an international reply coupon. You

may also offer an organisation to fax you collect (give them an appointment, because in order to receive a fax collect you should first be able to answer vocally, accept the call, then switch on the fax mode). Better still, since a fax goes both ways regardless of who calls, you can offer the organisation to call them on their fax line, and have them fax back the information. Remember that you should arrange this over the phone. If you interact with a large organisation, well equipped for recruiting volunteers, they have all the means to contact you, particularly if they are in the more expensive range of projects. In general, the cheaper the project or organisation you want to volunteers for, the more you should try to help them by reducing their cost of contacting you. In the past few years, however, the diffusion of the Internet, also in developing countries, has considerably reduced communications costs.

5) **Do exactly what is required by an organisation for being accepted.** If they do not accept the *Green Volunteers* standard application form, fill in the proper application form, pay the required deposit or membership fee and comply with other requirements. Once accepted, don't miss an opportunity by not paying a deposit on time. Inquire about the fastest method to transfer funds: by international telegraph money order, credit card, money wire from bank to bank, etc.

6) **Contact many projects and organisations.** Select the projects well in advance. Properly plan your vacation or time off, find the best air fares and select the best research period. Get detailed information on what to expect: the type of work, accommodation, food, climate, clothing and equipment necessary, etc. Owing to a lack of space this information is not included in the *Green Volunteers* guide. This guide aims to give a general overview of a given project or organisation. Do not show up at a project location without having applied first and having been accepted and confirmed. Most projects have limited positions, lodging and personnel. Very rarely are they equipped to take on an unexpected volunteer. If you want to do so, because you were already travelling in a certain area, do not be disappointed if you are rejected.

IMPORTANT NOTE AND WARNING

The Editor and Publisher of *Green Volunteers* has decided, both in order to offer prospective volunteers the widest possible choice and most valid conservation instrument, to cite, whenever possible, small projects and organisations, particularly in developing countries, for the following reasons:

1) **Without** *Green Volunteers* **many small projects and organisations would not be able to receive volunteers** from developed nations. We think that we should help as best as we can this conservation potential, particularly if it comes directly from local organisations, without an input from large organisations from our side of the world.

2) **Prospective volunteers**, by purchasing this guide, **expect to find something different and unique** from what is normally offered by large organisations in developed countries.

3) **Often small projects require non-paying and long-term volunteers**, which is what many of *Green Volunteers* readers expect. These opportunities are also usually offered at extremely affordable costs to the volunteers, which is not the case of projects offered from large organisations, which are often expensive and don't allow long-term volunteering.

BEFORE JOINING PROJECTS AND ORGANISATIONS, PROSPECTIVE VOLUNTEERS SHOULD CAREFULLY READ THE FOLLOWING CONSIDERATIONS AND WARNINGS:

1) **Because of obvious cost reasons**, which would then reflect on the cover price, **the Editor and Publisher cannot personally visit every project** listed in this guide but have to trust what projects and organisations (or the websites or previous volunteers) declare.

2) **Small projects and organisations**, particularly in developing countries, mainly because of shortage of funding or qualified personnel or because of conflicts with local populations and/or local authorities, **often change their programmes or even interrupt their activities without informing the Editor and Publisher of** *Green Volunteers*.

3) **Before joining a project volunteers should verify the validity of what is declared** on the project website (if one exists) or in this guide.

4) **Prospective volunteers should exchange frequent e-mails**, or even fax or phone calls, **with project leaders** and ensure that communication is always prompt and clear. They should also confirm the project details, such as the living, working and safety conditions, prior to departure.

5) **Prospective volunteers to any project should ask names** and addresses **of previous volunteers and correspond with them** to further verify the conditions of the projects.

6) **Volunteers should never join a project by going directly to the location** without previous correspondence and verification of existing conditions.

7) **Prospective volunteers should read carefully the WARNING on the third page of this book.**

ORGANISATION LIST

À PAS DE LOUP 'VOLUNTEERS FOR NATURE'

18, allée des Promenades
26 220 Dieulefit   France
Tel.: ++33 (4) 75 46 80 18
Fax: ++33 (4) 75 46 80 18
E-mail: info@apasdeloup.org
www.apasdeloup.org

Desc.: À Pas de Loup is a conservation volunteering organisation founded in 1994. Its objectivs are to support local organisations in both developing and executing their schemes of nature conservation and to improve their local natural environment. During an assignment, volunteers are monitored by local staff to ensure quality results. Projects are in France, Europe and Africa. À Pas de Loup volunteers are required to pay only for transportation and living costs. Some projects are ornithological, such as the Bonelli Eagle Project, or of habitat restoration or reforestation, such as a project in Togo.

Hab.: Coastal Mediterranean or African savannah.

Loc.: France, Portugal or Togo (Africa).

Dur.: From 2 – 3 weeks.

Per.: In Europe in the summer, in Togo in February and August.

Age: Min. 18.

Qualif.: No qualifications required.

Work: Depends on the project, in general it is mostly manual, such as work in a tree nursery or planting trees in Togo, using traditional tools or cutting trees for recovering the Grouse habitats or building pigeon houses for the Bonelli eagle Project. Cultural activities and excursions are also planned.

Lang.: English, French, Portuguese.

Accom.: Always very simple; in a campsite, in local houses or in Togo in a school or in a village.

Cost: Volunteers must pay for travel and food (except for the Black Grouse Project) and must join the organisation (EUR 16).

Applic.: Send CV and letter of presentation and intentions.

Selected Project
Bonelli Eagle Project, Portugal

AFRICAN CONSERVATION EXPERIENCE

P.O. Box 9706
Solihull, West Mids. B91 3FF UK
Tel.: ++44 (1626) 879 700 – (870) 241 5816 (from the UK only)
Fax: ++44 (1626) 879 700
E-mail: info@conservationafrica.net
www.conservationafrica.net

Desc.: The organisation organises Educational Work Experiences with conservationists, game rangers and biologists. Applicants may attend an optional Open Day to gain first hand information on the Game Reserves and Conservation Projects.

Spp.: Large and small game, including mammals, reptiles, birds, marine and freshwater life, plants.

Hab.: Sub-tropical coasts, seas, mountains; southern African savannah, plains, bushveld; semi-desert, fresh water marshes, wetlands; coastal lowlands, mountain ranges.

Loc.: South Africa, Zimbabwe, Botswana, Mozambique.

Travel: All travel arrangements included in the package.

Dur.: 4 – 12 weeks.

Per.: Year round.

L. term: Only in exceptional circumstances and by special arrangement.

Age: Min. 18, no maximum. Reasonably fit and healthy.

Work: Varies with Reserves. May include relocation or collaring of rhinos and elephants; capturing, tagging, releasing and game counts; animal monitoring and habituation. Whale and dolphin, seal and seabird research projects. Use of horses on conservation programmes. Volunteers usually work as part of a team under the supervision of experienced co-ordinators.

Lang.: English.

Accom.: Shared house in staff accommodation.

Cost: Approx. GB£1,800–3,500 (EUR/US$2,700–5,300); inquire for details.

Applic.: Request Application Pack. An optional donation is requested.

Notes: Essential qualification required is enthusiasm for conservation and must be reasonably physically fit.

AFRICAN EXPERIENCE

18 Emerald Hill, 87 Ridge Road
New Germany, 3620, Kwa-Zulu, Natal South Africa
Tel.: ++27 (82) 433 2319
Fax: ++27 (31) 705 36 35
E-mail: louise@african-experience.co.za
www.african-experience.co.za

Desc.: An opportunity to experience a real African adventure in the beautiful setting of Southern Africa on "big five" game farms. The opportunities suit the individual needs of each volunteer.

Spp.: Various species of African Mammals.

Hab.: Bushveld and savannah.

Loc.: Various areas around South Africa, from the coastline to Kruger National Park.

Travel: Volunteers fly to the nearest local airport to the project.

Dur.: Varies from project to project; the main duration is 4 weeks.

Per.: Year round.

Age: Min.18.

Qualif.: No qualifications necessary, just a willingness to help and the desire to make a difference.

Work: The Wildlife volunteer work covers many broad spectrums that includes preparing the food and feeding the wild animals, hand rearing and bottle feeding the young animals (the lions and baboons in particular), cleaning the enclosures, general game farm management (alien plant eradication and bush clearing, etc.), working with the veterinarians to aid the sick, ill and injured animals. Some of the volunteers have the opportunity to spend time learning about various conservation related topics.

Lang.: A minimum knowledge of basic English is required.

Accom.: Varies from project to project, always clean and comfortable!

Cost: Prices start from US$200 per week, which includes food accommodation, transfers to and from the local airport.

Agents: Volunteers must contact African Experience directly.

Applic.: On-line application form.

AMERICAN BEAR ASSOCIATION

P.O. BOX 77, Orr, Minnesota 55771 USA
Tel.: ++1 (218) 757 0172
E-mail: bears@rangenet.com
www.americanbear.org

Desc.: This non-profit organisation is dedicated to protecting the welfare of the black bear, other wildlife and all natural resources through a better understanding. The Vince Shute Wildlife Sanctuary offers the opportunity for the public to view black bears in the hope to instill an appreciation and respect for the bears as well as the habitat that supports all wildlife.

Spp.: American black bear (*Ursus americanus*).

Hab.: Forest.

Loc.: Northwoods of Minnesota.

Per.: Summer.

L. term: Volunteers can stay for the entire summer with project leader's approval.

Qualif.: All volunteers must read the Volunteer Manual and complete a liability waiver. Jobs will be matched to the specific interests and skills of the volunteer. Students encouraged. New project proposals are welcome.

Work: Greeting and escorting visitors to and from the viewing platform, interpreting bear behaviour to visitors, providing security for the bears and other wildlife, picking up supplies, assisting in construction projects, conducting daily clean-up chores, cooking, completing routine maintenance projects, grounds-keeping, maintaining records on bear activity, etc.

Lang.: English.

Accom.: All services available in the town of Orr. Campgrounds and numerous resorts are at nearby Pelican Lake.

Cost: Volunteers are responsible for their food and lodging expenses.

Applic.: Contact the Association for more information.

AMERICAN LITTORAL SOCIETY

1478 Point Breeze Place
Far Rockaway, New York 11691 USA
Tel.: ++1 (718) 471 2166
Fax: ++1 (718) 471 0034
E-mail: donriepe@aol.com
www.alsnyc.org

Desc.: This organisation focuses its efforts on an annual beach clean-up that documents the debris collected. Goals are to raise awareness of marine pollution and to determine trends and sources of pollution.

Hab.: Coastal, shores of lakes, rivers, ponds.

Loc.: New York State.

Per.: September.

Age: Min. 6.

Qualif.: No particular skills needed.

Work.: Picking up litter off the beach and recording what is collected on data cards.

L. term: Not possible.

Lang.: English.

Agents: Ocean Conservancy, 1725 DeSales Street, NW, Suite 500, Washington, DC 20036.

Applic.: Call Beach Clean-up Coordinator Barbara Cohen at above number.

Notes: Northeast Chapter 29 West 9th Road, Broad Channel, New York 11693, tel.: ++1 (718) 318 9344, fax: ++1 (718) 318 9345.

APPALACHIAN TRAIL CONFERENCE

P.O. Box 10, Newport, Virginia 24128 USA
Tel.: ++1 (540) 544 7388
Fax: ++1 (540) 544 6880
E-mail: crews@appalachiantrail.org
www.appalachiantrail.org

Desc.: The Appalachian Trail is America's best-known long-distance trail. Each year over 400 volunteers help with trail construction and rehabilitation. Volunteers can enjoy great scenery, and are provided with food, lodging, tools, equipment, training, and the opportunity for lots of fun.

Hab.: Appalachian Mountain Range.

Loc.: Great Smoky Mountains National Park, Southwest Virginia, Pennsylvania, Maine, and Vermont, USA.

Travel: Detailed access directions to base camp are provided.

Dur.: From 1 to 6 weeks.

Per.: May through October.

L. term: Volunteers can work up to 6 weeks.

Age: Min. 18.

Qualif.: Enthusiasm, good health, physical vigour, and adaptability. Willingness to follow instructions and safety rules and to share equally in camp chores. Experience is not necessary.

Work: Trail work is hard, physical labour, with hand tools. The crews work 8-hour days, rain or shine, hot or cold, regardless of black flies, mosquitoes, and other insects.

Lang.: English.

Accom.: Rustic cabins at base camp and tents out in the field.

Cost: Only transportation to base camp. Most expenses are covered including shelter, food, transportation to and from work projects, tools, safety equipment, and group camping gear. Crew members need to bring work clothing, sturdy boots, and their own basic camping gear.

Applic.: Request an application from the Appalachian Trail Conference.

Notes: International applicants are responsible for necessary visas. Wether conditions can vary from very hot to below freezing.

ARCAS – Asociaciòn de Rescate y Conservaciòn de Vida Silvestre

21c Calle 9–44 'A' Zona 11 Mariscal, Guatemala, Guatemala
Tel./Fax: ++(502)476 6001
E-mail: arcaspeten@intelnet.net.gt – arcas@intelnet.net.gt
www.rds.org.gt/arcas/
www2.gol.com/users/chapa/cphomepage/arcasinfo.html

Desc.: ARCAS has 2 projects: a Wildlife Rescue and Rehabilitation Centre, established in 1990, in order to rescue, rehabilitate and release wild animals confiscated from traffickers. It has released 300–600 animals per year into the Mayan Biosphere Reserve (MBR). The project is also a focal point for environmental education and awareness-raising in the MBR through its Environmental Education and Interpretation Centre. The second project is a Sea Turtle Conservation Centre. Its goal is the conservation of the endangered sea turtles that come to beaches on the Pacific Coast to nest. The primary way to conserve the turtles is to collect and incubate as many eggs as possible. ARCAS has also a caiman and iguana breeding programme, mangrove reforestation and environmental education.

Spp.: The centre receives many different species from the MBR, which include: birds (parrots, scarlet macaws, toucans, aracaries), mammals (spider and howler monkeys, raccoons, coatimundis, pacas, margays, kinkajous, peccaries, bairds tapirs, jaguars) and reptiles (iguanas, turtles, crocodiles, caimans). The seaturtles are: Olive Ridley Sea Turtle, Leatherback Sea Turtle.

Hab.: Tropical forest, tropical beach, mangrove coastal wetland.

Loc.: The Wildlife Centre is near the city of Flores; the Seaturtle Conservation Project is on the Pacific Coast.

Travel: Airplane to Guatemala City, then bus to Flores or Monterrico, then by boat to the projects.

Dur.: For generic volunteers min. 1 week. For internships or research projects, min. 1 month.

Per.: Year round for the Wildlife Centre. From June to November, with a peak in August and September, for the Seaturtle Project.

Age: Min. 18.

L. term.: Volunteers can stay for as long as they want. Volunteers can also spend some time in each project.

Qualif.: No specific skills required for generic volunteers. Candidates for internships or research projects must be students or researchers in a conservation related field.

Work: Volunteers help cleaning cages and feeding and caring for the animals. Special projects may include: observing the animals in the rehabilitation area, building cages, animal releases, etc. Research and internship opportunities are in the area of wildlife veterinary medicine, rehabilitation, nutrition and environmental education. In the Seaturtle Project volunteers assist in patrolling beaches at night in search of nesting sea turtles, collection and burial of eggs in the hatcheries and collection of data. Volunteers can also take part in caiman breeding, mangrove reforestation, construction and upkeep of park facilities and environmental educational activities in area schools. Everyone is expected to help in house cleaning and dish washing.

Lang.: English, basic Spanish is highly desirable.

Accom.: Wildlife Rescue volunteers live in a house with toilet facilities and solar power. Sheets are provided, own sleeping bag useful in cooler months (Dec. – Feb.). Kitchen/dining (and socialising) room is in a separate facility. The Seaturtle Project provides comfortable housing withbeds, mosquito netting, toilets, kitchen facilities and12V solar power.

Cost: US$60–80/week for room and board in both projects. Volunteers must pay all travel expenses.

Agents: Contact ARCAS directly.

Applic.: A simple application for the regular volunteer programme. For the research and internship opportunities candidates must send a letter of reference from their university, a short essay explaining their personal motivation for participating in the project, a CV and 3 passport-size photographs.

Notes: ARCAS, as an under-funded non-profit volunteer organisation, may not be able to meet all expectations in terms of personal attention and work experience. Mail may also be sent to: Section 717, P.O. Box 52–7270 Miami, FL 33152–7270 USA.

ARCTUROS

Victor Hugo 3
546 25 Thessaloniki Greece
Tel.: ++30 (2310) 555 920
Fax: ++30 (2310) 553 932
E-mail: arcturos@arcturos.gr – volnat@the.forthnet.gr
www.arcturos.gr

Desc.: The management and conservation of wildlife and the natural environment focusing on the brown bear, a priority species, that encourages global management of the mountain forest ecosystems in northern Greece. Since 1993 ARCTUROS has operated the Bear Protection Centre at Nymphaion and Fanos in northern Greece, in an effort to solve the problem of captive and, especially, the 'dancing bears'. A project for the conservation of the wolf is also being carried out.

Spp.: Brown bear (*Ursus arctos*), wolf (*Canis lupus*).

Hab.: European temperate, deciduous and alpine forests.

Loc.: Mountains of Pindos and Rodopi (bear); central Greece (wolf).

Travel: Airplane to Thessaloniki, Greece.

Dur.: 2 weeks.

Per.: June to September.

L. term: With project leader's approval.

Age: Min. 18; most participants are between the ages of 18–30.

Qualif.: Biology or relevant background is strongly desired.

Work: Ranges from manual tasks to assistance in scientific research and participation in awareness-raising campaigns.

Lang.: English.

Accom.: Fully equipped house (cooker, fridge, washing machine) in Nymphaion. Field work in rented facilities or tents.

Cost: A food budget might be provided. Transportation not included.

Applic.: By April. Green Volunteers standard application form accepted.

Notes: ARCTUROS also coordinates the Greek Network Voluntary Service for the Natural Environment, which includes about 30 Greek NGOs and their voluntary service projects www.forthnet.gr/volunteersfornature (subject to change).

ASSOCIATION FOR THE CONSERVATION OF THE SOUTHERN RAINFORESTS

Inkanatura/Peru Verde
Calle Manuel Banon 461, San Isidro, Lima   Peru
Tel.: ++51 (1) 440 2022 – Fax: ++51 (1) 422 9225
E-mail: postmaster@peruverde.org – postmaster@inkanatura.com.pe
www.inkanatura.com – www.peruverde.org

Desc.: The association offers a 'resident naturalist guide' programme at 4 rainforest lodges, as well as a series of projects ranging from teaching English to local rainforest communities, wildlife observation and mapping fruiting trees and vines.

Spp.: Over 1,000 birds, 200 mammals and 1,200 insect species.

Hab.: Amazon rainforest (from cloud forest to lowland rainforest).

Loc.: Southeastern Peru.

Travel: Lodge reached by plane and then boat ride or by bus.

Dur.: Min. 3 months for resident naturalist guide volunteers.

Per.: Dry (April to October) or wet season (November to March).

L. term: Longer period of time at the discretion of the project leader.

Age: Min. 21, max. 65.

Qualif.: A background or strong interest in ecology/biology is essential.

Work: Numerous projects offered with different work times. Guiding guests of the lodges is the main task of resident naturalists.

Lang.: A working knowledge of Spanish is highly recommended.

Accom.: Bed with mosquito net on open sleeping platform. Bedding must be provided by the volunteer.

Cost: Only travel costs; food and accommodation provided.

Agents: Contact Peru erde directly, preferably by e-mail, but be ready to call or fax in case your e-mail get overlooked.

Applic.: Applications for resident naturalist guide volunteers should be received by December for dry season and by July for wet season.

Notes: Prospective volunteers should be aware that work will probably be in hot and humid conditions not experienced before and that lodges are in very remote areas. Please note that during 2003 Inkanatura/PeruVerde for re-organisation reasons will not take volunteers. Please inquire for 2004.

ASVO – Asociacion de Voluntarios para el Servicio en las Areas Protegidas

c/o Programa de Voluntariado – Servicio de Parques Nacionales
P.O. Box 11384–1000/10104–1000 San José Costa Rica
Tel.: ++ (506) 257 0922 (ext.–182–135)/256 8467
Fax: ++ (506) 233 4989
E-mail: asvo89@racsa.co.cr – info@asvocr.com www.asvocr.com

Desc.: ASVO is the Costa Rican organisation responsible for volunteer programmes in their National Parks and Reserves. Volunteers are needed for research, construction and maintenance work. Tourist assistance and interpretation are also important activities where volunteers are needed. Volunteers can also participate in seaturtle conservation programmes on the Atlantic or Pacific Coasts. Biology or Ecology students can participate into special projects, such as "reintroduction of monkeys" in a given area.

Spp.: Primates, tropical birds and mammals, sea turtles.

Hab.: Tropical coast, rainforest, cloud forest.

Loc.: Parks and Reserves in Costa Rica.

Dur.: Min. 30 days, 2 months for special projects.

Per.: Year round.

L. term: Inquire with organisation.

Age: Min. 18.

Qualif.: Volunteers should be in good physical condition and able to tolerate the tropical climate. A flexible and enthusiastic attitude is essential. Two reference letters signed by Costa Rica residents or by organisations in the home country are required. Special qualifications are necessary for some research projects.

Lang.: Spanish. Inquire for English.

Cost: Food and accommodation in Parks and Reserves is approx. US$12/day. Travel costs are paid by the volunteer.

Applic.: Contact ASVO for application form.

Notes: Personal health and repatriation insurance is strongly recommended.

BIOSPHERE EXPEDITIONS

Sprat's Water, near Carlton Colville,
The Broads National Park, Suffolk NR33 8BP UK
Tel.: ++44 (1502) 583 085
Fax: ++44 (1502) 587 414
E-mail: info@biosphere-expeditions.org
www.biosphere-expeditions.org

Desc.: Worldwide wildlife conservation expeditions. The projects are not tours, photographic safaris or excursions, but genuine expeditions with real conservation content. Adventure, remote locations, different cultures and people are part and parcel of these expeditions, but also the knowledge that you will have played an active role in conserving part of our planet's biosphere.

Spp.: Snow leopards, wolves, bears, primates, rainforest birds, etc.

Hab.: Rainforest, desert, savannah, tropical coasts, seas, etc.

Loc.: Worldwide.

Travel: Volunteers are met at the airport and taken to the project area.

Dur.: Min. 2 weeks up to 3 months.

Per.: Year round.

L. term: Volunteers can join an expedition for several months.

Age: No age restrictions. Minors with parents' consent.

Qualif.: No specific skills required, only a reasonable level of fitness.

Work: Expect to work (e.g., surveying, tracking, identification) for several hours a day, often independently. All necessary training is given and a Biosphere Expedition leader is always present.

Lang.: English. German is also spoken.

Accom.: Basic, in huts or tents depending on the climate and location.

Cost: Variable and depending on project. Expedition contributions start from GB£ 900 (EUR/US$ 1,400) for 2 weeks, for longer periods discounts are available.

Agents: In Germany tel. ++ 49 (931) 407 0107, fax. (931) 407 0577.

Applic.: Contact organisation for more details and application forms.

BRATHAY EXPLORATION GROUP

Brathay Hall
Ambleside, Cumbria LA22 0HP   UK
Tel./Fax: ++44 (15394) 33 942
E-mail: admin@brathayexploration.org.uk
　　　brathay.exploration@virgin.net
www.brathayexploration.org.uk

Desc.:	The Brathay Exploration Group, a non-profit organisation founded in 1947, runs 10–15 expeditions each year in remote areas all over the world. Projects concern field sciences from glaciology to ornithology. They are lead by former experienced volunteers.
Hab.:	Mountain, tropical rainforest, desert.
Loc.:	Europe, Malaysia, Africa, Mongolia, North America, New Zealand.
Dur.:	2–4 weeks.
Per.:	July to August.
L. term:	Inquire with organisation.
Age:	Min.15, max. 25.
Qualif.:	No special qualification or prior field experience is required, but self-motivation and a sense of humour are needed.
Lang.:	English.
Cost:	GB£200–700 (approx.EUR/US$300–1,000) for European expeditions, GB£1,400–2,750 (approx. EUR/US$2,000–4,000) for worldwide expeditions; grants are available (ask for bursary grant application form).
Applic.:	Ask for application form and medical questionnaire, to be sent in with a deposit.
Notes:	Each expedition can be joined by 20 or less volunteers. Members of the Brathay Exploration Group join a club with benefits such as the use of a mountain hut, an information magazine, discounts. The Brathay Exploration Group also offers courses in Mountain First Aid and Leader Training. Further information is available from the above address.

BTCV

36 St. Mary's Street Wallingford
Oxfordshire, OX10 0EU   UK
Tel.: ++44 (1491) 821 600
Fax: ++44 (1491) 839 646
E-mail: information@btcv.org
www.btcv.org.uk

Desc.: BTCV was founded in 1959 under the name Conservation Corps and is now the largest practical conservation organisation in the UK. BTCV provides information and advice on urban and rural projects, organises conservation holidays, weekend and weekday projects and supports around 2,500 community groups.

Spp.: Wolves, sea turtles, vultures, otters.

Hab.: Wetlands, woodlands, tropical forests, boreal forests, Mediterranean islands, coastal sites.

Loc.: UK, several countries in Europe, North America, Australia, Iceland, Japan.

Dur.: 1 day to 3 weeks.

Per.: Year round.

L. term: Volunteer Officer positions available (min. 3 months).

Age: Under 18 with parental consent for UK projects; min. 18 for international projects.

Qualif.: Some international expeditions require experienced volunteers.

Work: Restoring paths and dry stone walls or doing drainage work in the UK. International projects can involve revegetation, construction, woodland and wetland management or wolf research.

Lang.: English. Other languages encountered with various projects.

Cost: From GB£45 (approx. EUR/US$70) for UK projects; GB£200–1,000 (approx. EUR/US$300–1,500) for overseas expeditions.

Applic.: Deposit of GB£30–50 required (approx. EUR/US$45–75).

Notes: Conservation Holidays Brochure Available on request.

Selected projects:

Black Vulture Protection, Bulgaria
Living and Working Within a Sustainable Village, Hungary
Skaftafell National Park, Iceland
Wolf Tracking, Slovakia

BTCV Scotland

Balallan House , 24 Allan Park
Stirling FK8 2QG   Scotland UK
Tel.: ++44 (1786) 479 697 – Fax: ++44 (1786) 465 359
E-mail: scotland@btcv.org.uk –   stirlng@btcv.org.uk
www.btcv.org

Desc.: BTCV Scotland is the Scottish division of BTCV and it is involved in practical conservation work to improve the quality of Scotland's environment. Each year more than 7,000 volunteers join its activities, which include tree planting, restoration, rebuilding and footpath repair. BTCV Scotland offers various programmes for long-term volunteering. It also offers training courses, special projects, recycling activities.

Hab.: Urban areas, forests, lakes.

Loc.: Scotland.

Dur.: 7–10 days.

Per.: March to December.

L. term: Inquire with organisation.

Age: Min. 16, max. 70.

Qualif.: No specific qualifications required; some projects involve hard work.

Lang.: English.

Cost: Varies with project.

Agents: Contact BTCV Scotland directly.

Applic.: Call or write to BTCV Scotland to obtain the application form.

CARAPAX – European Center for Conservation of Chelonians

International RANA Foundation
C.P. 34 – Località Le Venelle
58024 Massa Marittima (GR) Italy
Tel.: ++39 (0566) 940 083 – Fax: ++39 (0566) 902 387
E-mail: volunteers@carapax.org – carapax@cometanet.it
www.carapax.org

Desc.: The Carapax Center was established in 1989 by the International RANA Foundation (Reptiles, Amphibians in Nature) the European Union and the Tuscany Region. The Carapax Center conducts research and works towards the recovery and reintroduction of tortoises. Carapax reintroduces animals saved from captivity (private donations to the centre) and from illegal sale (confiscated by the authorities) back to nature. Once set free in natural reserves, the tortoises are marked and followed using radio-tracking techniques or by local environmental organisations or responsible authorities. For 8 years volunteers have worked at the Carapax Center to provide general care of the animals. Volunteers also help experts in their scientific research in the field.

Spp.: Priorities are the Mediterranean tortoises and fresh water turtles or terrapins. *Testudo hermanni hermanni, T. hermanni boetgheri, T. marginata, T. graeca.*

Loc.: Central Italy, in the Tuscany region, 18 km from the west coast.

Travel: Airplane to Rome, train to Grosseto and Follonica, then bus to Massa Marittima where Carapax staff will pick up volunteers.

Dur.: Min. 2 weeks.

Per.: Mid-April to mid-October.

Age: Min. 18.

Qualif.: Experience is not required; motivation and interest is important.

Work: Management of infrastructure (upkeep, build or repair); care of animals (feed, sometimes help with veterinary care, scrupulously respecting hygiene standards); provide information to the public (receive and guide visitors); scientific research inside and outside the centre (depending on individual knowledge of the programmes linked to universities).

The activities take place mainly in the spring and September, the most active period for tortoises. Participation in the repatriation of tortoises (Italy, Greece, Tunisia, Morocco, France) is generally reserved for volunteers who have already taken part in field projects, are able to recognise species and are familiar with the marking system. Basic training is given to volunteers on their first day.

Lang.: English, Italian, German, French, Dutch.

Accom.: The centre can accommodate about 20 people. Accommodation is in wooden chalets (1 room; 6 beds) with electricity. There are 4 outdoor showers and 2 toilets (1 for women and 1 for men). There is an open-air kitchen protected by a large roof.

Cost: Travel expenses are not reimbursed by the centre and volunteers pay a daily participation fee of EUR13 (approx. GB£8.50 or US$13) for accommodation and food. This must be paid at least 2 weeks prior to arrival at the centre.

Applic.: Contact Carapax directly for an application form.

Notes: Volunteers must carry health and accident insurance.

CEDAM INTERNATIONAL

One Fox Road
Croton-on-Hudson, NY 10520 USA
Tel.: ++1 (914) 271 5365
Fax: ++1 (914) 271 4723
E-mail: cedamint@aol.com
www.cedam.org

Desc.: Cedam International is a non-profit organisation dedicated to conservation, environmental education, marine research, archaeology and fundraising. The main objective of the organisation is to promote research in marine sciences through programmes conducted by expert divers, photographers and biologists.

Spp.: Marine species.

Hab.: Tropical seas.

Loc.: Mexico, Seychelles, Galapagos, Kenya, Australia, Belize, Indonesia and other locations worldwide.

Dur.: 7–10 days.

Per.: Year round.

Age: Min. 18.

Qualif.: Scuba qualifications are welcome but not essential; skills in underwater photography/video, cartography and other subjects can be very helpful. Enthusiasm and ability to work in a team are required.

Lang.: English.

Cost: US$1,500–4,000.

Applic.: Contact Cedam for information.

CENTRE FOR ALTERNATIVE TECHNOLOGY

Machynlleth, Powys
SY20 9AZ Wales   UK
Tel.: ++44 (1654) 705 950
Fax: ++ 44 (1654) 702 782
E-mail: info@cat.org.uk
www.cat.org.uk

Desc.: The Centre for Alternative Technology, open to the public since 1975, has working displays of wind, water and solar power, low energy buildings, organic farming and alternative sewage systems. It offers residential courses on topics such as water power, bird watching, organic gardening and rustic furniture making. The Centre also hosts an information service and a bookshop (with mail-order service). The Centre receives 80,000 visitors per year.

Loc.: Wales, Great Britain.

Dur.: 1–2 weeks.

Per.: Specified weeks between March and September inclusive.

L. term: A limited number of long-term volunteers work in specific departments such as engineering, building, gardening and information for up to 6 months. Accommodation and food are provided but not pay. Prospective long-term volunteers must stay for a 'trial' week as short-term volunteers, stating in advance what kind of work they want to do.

Age.: Min. 18.

Qualif.: Particular skills are not needed for short-term volunteers. Certain skills and previous experience may be criteria for the selection of long-term volunteers, as places are limited.

Lang.: English.

Cost: Volunteers contribute GB£7 (EUR/ US$10.50) waged or GB£4 (EUR/US$6.50) low-waged or no wage per weekday and GB£7 (EUR/US$10.50) per weekend day towards the cost of room and board. Accommodation and food are provided.

Agents: Contact the Centre directly.

Applic.: Application forms for the short-term volunteer programme are published in January. Early booking is necessary. Contact the Centre for details on the long-term volunteer programme.

CHANTIERS DE JEUNES PROVENCE CÔTE D'AZUR

La Maison des Chantiers La Ferme Giaume
7 Avenue Pierre de Coubertin
06150 Cannes la Bocca France
Tel.: ++33 (4) 93 478969 – Fax: ++33 (4) 93 481201
E-mail: cjpca@club-internet.fr
www.cjpca.fr.st

Desc.: This organisation offers programmes for teenagers who want to experience community life, work for heritage protection, and spend an unusual summer holiday.

Loc.: St. Marguerite Island, Cannes, in the Region of Provence, France, ans in the region of Piedmont, Italy.

Dur.: 2 weeks.

Per.: Summer, but also year round during school holidays.

Age: Min. 13, max. 17.

Qualif.: No qualifications necessary.

Lang.: French.

Cost: Approx. EUR 350 (approx. GB£ 220).

Agents: Contact the organisation directly.

Work: Different for each project, from simple construction to trail maintenance.

Applic.: Call or e-mail the organisation to receive an application form.

COORDINATING COMMITTEE FOR INTERNATIONAL VOLUNTEERS

1 rue Miollis
75015 Paris France
Tel.: ++33 (1) 4568 4936 – Fax: ++33 (1) 4273 0521
E-mail: ccivs@unesco.org
www.unesco.org/ccivs/

Desc.: The Coordinating Committee for International Voluntary Service (CCIVS) is an international non-governmental organisation that plays a coordinating role in the sphere of voluntary service. CCIVS has 250 members and branches in over 100 countries. The aims of the CCIVS are to fight against the dangers of war, social and racial discrimination, underdevelopment, illiteracy and the consequences of neo-colonialism; to promote international understanding, friendship and solidarity as pre-conditions to firm and lasting peace on earth; to enable social and national development and to establish a just international economic and social order. Volunteers from different countries live and work together on a common project to benefit the local population working in the fields of agriculture, archeology, construction and re-construction, disaster relief work, protection of the natural environment and health and welfare.

Dur.: Usually 3–4 weeks.

L. term: CCIVS member organisations also organise long-term projects for medium (1–6 months) or long-term (1–3 years) volunteers.

Agents: Contact CCIVS for further information.

Notes: CCIVS produces several publications on volunteer service. Contact CCIVS for the list of publications and ordering.

CORAL CAY CONSERVATION (CCC)

The Tower, 13th Floor
125 High Street, Colliers Wood
London SW19 2JG   UK
Tel.: ++44 (870) 750 0668 – Fax: ++44 (870) 750 0667
E-mail: info@coralcay.org
www.coralcay.org

Desc.: CCC sends teams of volunteers to survey some of the world's most endangered coral reefs and tropical forests in partnership with governments, NGO's, local communities and education groups. Since 1986, CCC volunteers have been responsible for the establishment of World Heritage Sites, marine reserves and wildlife sanctuaries. CCC offers its volunteers the opportunity to combine marine and terrestrial scientific research with international travel and cultural exploration.

Spp.: Terrestrial and marine organisms.

Hab.: Tropical coasts and rainforests.

Loc.: Philippines, Honduras, Fiji and Malaysia.

Dur.: Min. 2 weeks.

Per.: Year round.

L. term: Inquire with organisation.

Age: Min. 16.

Qualif.: CCC offers: 1 Scuba Training wk, 2 Skills Development and Conservation wks. PADI Open Water divers are trained up to Advanced Open Water (AOW) and PADI AOW divers (BSAC Sports/Club/Sports, CMAS, SAA- recognised equivalents) are accepted directly onto the Skills development week.

Work: Training in marine and/or terrestrial ecology and survey techniques and assist in local community training programmes.

Lang.: English.

Accom.: Basic on-site accommodation provided.

Cost: GB£350–2,200 (approx. EUR/US$550–3,200), including food, accommodation, equipment and training. Flights not included.

Applic.: Download or call or write CCC to obtain application form.

Notes: Monthly presentations are organised throughout the UK. Contact Volunteer Recruitment (acs@coralcay.org) to book a place.

COTRAVAUX

11 Rue de Clichy
75009 Paris
France
Tel.: ++33 (1) 4874 7920
Fax: ++33 (1) 4874 1401

Desc.: Cotravaux coordinates 12 French workcamps. Its role is to promote voluntary work and community projects concerning environmental protection, monument restoration and social projects. The organisation offers many workcamps in different regions of France. Many of the organisations members of Cotravaux work with foreign partners.

Loc.: France.

Dur.: 2–3 weeks.

Per.: Year round; most projects run between June and October.

L. term: Certain projects offer 4–12 month volunteering.

Age.: Min. 18.

Qualif.: No specific skills needed.

Lang.: A few projects require French.

Cost: Volunteers must pay for their own transportation to the camps. Room and board provided (some camps require a daily contribution).

Agents: Some partner organisations (inquire with Cotravaux).

Applic.: Contact Cotravaux by fax or mail to obtain the list of partner workcamps in France or other specific countries.

Notes: A list of Cotravaux member organisations can be obtained by the website of Jeunesse et Réconstruction, one of the largest French volunteering organisations. Their website is www.volontariat.org, while the list of Cotravaux members is at the bottom of the page www.volontariat.org/cotravaux.htm; no links are provided but any search engine can help.

CTS – Centro Turistico Studentesco e Giovanile

Via A. Vesalio 6
00161 Roma Italy
Tel.: ++39 (06) 4411 1473/4
Fax: ++39 (06) 4411 1401
E-mail: ambiente@cts.it
www.cts.it/ambiente/

Desc.: Founded in1974, CTS is now the largest youth association in Italy. Its Environmental Department organises research activities, ecotourism and environmental education programmes, training courses and workshops. It also publishes books and produces videos on environmental subjects. Projects concern endangered species, animal behaviour, habitat protection, and wildlife management.

Spp.: Bears, dolphins, whales, sea turtles, wolves, chamois.

Hab.: Alpine, Mediterranean Sea and coast, temperate forest, lagoons.

Loc.: Italian Alps, Appennines, Mediterranean coasts and islands, often inside protected areas.

Dur.: Depends on the project; average period is 6–15 days.

Per.: Year round.

L. term: Inquire with organisation.

Age: Min.18. Younger members with parental and CTS consent.

Qualif.: Physically fit, flexible, cooperative. Able to swim for marine projects.

Cost: EUR250–700 (approx. GB£170–450), excluding food and transportation.

Lang.: Italian, English.

Agents: CTS offices are throughout Italy and in London, Paris, Madrid, Barcelona and New York.

Applic.: Membership is required to join the expeditions (EUR 28).

Notes: CTS cooperates with organisations such as the Ecovolunteer Network (see organisation list).

Selected Projects:
Bottlenose Dolphin Project, Italy
Loggerhead Sea Turtles in Linosa, Italy

CVA – Conservation Volunteers Australia

National Head Office
P.O. Box 423, Ballarat 3353
Victoria Australia
Tel.: ++61 (3) 5333 1483 – Fax: ++61 (3) 5333 2166
E-mail: info@conservationvolunteers.com.au
www.conservationvolunteers.com.au

Desc.:	Founded in 1982, CVA (formerly ATCV) is a non-profit organisation dedicated to practical conservation. CVA's activities concern environmental topics such as water salinity, soil erosion, biodiversity and endangered species. Volunteers are primarily between the ages of 16–25/30. Each team working in a project is provided with a vehicle (usually a minibus or 4WD with trailer), first-aid equipment, hand tools and cooking equipment. CVA projects offer a unique opportunity to see parts of Australia, off the regular track, as well as to make international friendships through team activities.
Spp.:	Turtles, penguins, birds, local vegetation.
Hab.:	Rivers, coasts, dryland, swamps.
Loc.:	Various locations in Australia.
Dur.:	4 – 6 weeks.
Per.:	Year round.
L. term:	Inquire with organisation.
Age:	Min. 16.
Qualif.:	Experience and qualifications related to the environment are welcome but not essential.
Lang.:	English.
Cost:	Min. AUS$790–920 (approx. EUR/US$450–525) for 4 – 6 weeks, including food, accommodation and project-related transportation within Australia.
Applic.:	Call, write or e-mail CVA National Head Office for information. Applications are accepted on-line.

CVG – Conservation Volunteers Greece

Omirou 15,
GR–14562 Kifissia, Athens   Greece
Tel.: ++30 (1) 623 1120
Fax: ++30 (1) 801 1489
E-mail: cvgpeep@otenet.gr
www.cvgpeep.gr

Desc.: Summer work camps in Greece. These projects usually take place in remote areas of Greece in co-operation with Forestry Departments, Local Authorities, Cultural Associations, etc. Intercultural exchanges and conservation work allow young people to contribute to a hosting community. CVG is also involved in European Voluntary Service (EVS) projects.

Spp.: Various: birds of prey, forest flora and fauna.

Hab.: Mediterranean ecosystems, forests and wetlands.

Loc.: Greece, usually remote areas.

Travel: Contact the organisations for specific projects.

Dur.: 2–3 weeks; fixed dates are provided for every project.

Per.: Summer.

Age: Min. 18.

Work: Nature conservation (forest-fire protection, tree-planting, footpath maintenance, construction and placement of signs), cultural heritage (restoration of traditional buildings, ancient cobbled-stone footpaths and help in archaeological digs) or social benefit (restoration of school buildings, construction of playgrounds). Work is 5 – 6 hours/day, 6 days/week.

Lang.: English.

Accom.: Facilities are modest. Hosting is usually in schools and community or youth centres. Volunteers should bring along a sleeping bag and sleeping mat. Household chores involved.

Cost: Approx. EUR120 (approx. GB£80).

Agents: The Alliance of European Voluntary Service Organisations (www.alliance-network.org).

Applic.: A Volunteer Exchange Form to apply is provided by Alliance partner organisations or CVG web site.

EARTHWATCH INSTITUTE

3 Clock Tower Place – Suite 100, Box 75
Maynard, MA 01754   USA
Tel.: ++1 (978) 461 0081 – (800) 776 0188 (toll free in US/Canada)
Fax: ++1 (978) 461 2332
E-mail: info@earthwatch.org
www.earthwatch.org

Desc.: Earthwatch is an international charity that supports around 130 scientific field research projects in 45 countries. All projects are open to paying volunteers who work alongside leading scientists as field assistants for 3 days to 3 weeks. Volunteers work as part of a team of people from all corners of the world with one thing in common – a commitment to doing something to protect the environment. From tracking crocodiles in the Okavango Delta, to studying dynamic glaciers in Iceland or to observing dolphin behaviour in New Zealand, Earthwatch has a wide range of projects around the globe that vary greatly in terms of levels of physical activity, field conditions and tasks. Volunteers can also get a taste of the Earthwatch experience during the 'Discovery Weekends'.

Spp.: Wolves, chimpanzees, mountain lions, dolphins, birds, snakes, rhinos, crocodiles, echidnas and many others.

Hab.: Rainforest, desert, savannah, tropical coasts, temperate coasts, tropical seas, temperate seas, arctic, antarctic, sub-arctic, alpine.

Loc.: Many countries in North America, South America, Europe, Africa, Asia, Australia, Antarctica.

Dur.: 3 days to 3 weeks.

Per.: Year round.

L. term: Inquire with organisation.

Age: Min. 16.

Qualif.: No specific qualifications. No restrictions on age, education or expertise. Particular skills welcome.

Lang.: English.

Cost: US$650–3,695, including accommodation and food. Earthwatch Europe offers programmes starting from GB£80.

Agents: **Earthwatch Europe**, 267 Banbury Rd. Oxford OX2 7HT UK, tel. ++44 (1865) 318 831, fax ++44 (1865) 311 383, e-mail: info@uk.earthwatch.org, www.earthwatch.org/europe

Earthwatch Australia, 126 Bank Street, South Melbourne Vic. 3205, tel. ++61 (3) 9682 6828, fax ++61 (3) 9686 3652 e-mail: earth@earthwatch.org

EarthwatchJapan, Sanbancho TY Plaza 5F Sanbancho 24–25, Chiyoda-ku, Tokyo 102–0075 Japan, tel.++81 (3) 35113 360, fax ++81 (3) 35113 360, e-mail: info@earthwatch-japan.gr.jp, www.earthwatch-japan.gr.jp

Applic.: Write to or call the nearest office for programmes and application material. Membership (US$35) required.

Notes: Contributions to Earthwatch are tax-deductible for US citizens; grants are available for students, teachers and artists applying for expeditions in the US, Australia and Europe. In Europe, a fellowship programme provides fully funded places and partial awards for teachers and students.

Selected projects:
Black Rhino, Kenya
Cheetah Conservation Fund, Namibia
Costa Rican Sea Turtles, Costa Rica
Ecology of Common Dolphins in Alboran Sea, Spain
The Golden Eagles of Mull, Scotland
Wild Dolphin Societies, USA

THE ECOVOLUNTEER NETWORK

Central Office
Meyersweg 29   7553 AX Hengelo The Netherlands
Tel.: ++31 (74) 250 8250
Fax: ++31 (74) 250 6572
E-mail: info@ecovolunteer.org
www.ecovolunteer.org

Desc.: About 35 projects offer hands-on experience in wildlife conservation and research, assisting in fieldwork, monitoring research and in wildlife rescue and rehabilitation centres. Volunteers work with local conservationists, researchers and rangers and are expected to adapt to local culture and food. Minimum 75% of the price is forwarded to projects.

Spp.: Gibbons, macaques, elephants, rhinos, fruitbats, tiger, jaguar, lion, Asiatic black bear, Malayan bear, Przewalski horse, European wolf, dolphins, whales, monk seal, sea turtles, macaw/ara, scarlet ibis, Siberian crane.

Hab.: Ranging from subarctic to tropical rainforest.

Loc.: Worldwide.

Dur.: Min. 1, 2, 3 or 4 weeks, depending on projects.

Per.: Some projects are seasonal, others are year round.

L. term: Possible with many projects, especially for academic research.

Age: Most projects min. 18; some projects min. 20.

Qualif.: Variable. Physically fit and able to work independently.

Lang.: English.

Cost: Variable Starting from EUR/US$450 (approx. GB£300). See Ecovolunteer website .

Agents: Belgium: www.ecovolunteer.be
Brazil: http:// br.ecovoluntarios.org
Britain:www.ecovolunteer.org.uk
France: http:// fr.ecovolunteer.be
Germany: www.oekovolontaer.de or www.ecovolunteer.de
Hungary: www.vadonprogram.co.hu
Netherlands: www.ecovolunteer.nl or www.ecovrijwilliger.nl
Spain: http:// es.ecovoluntarios.org

Applic.: Mail or fax the application form on www.ecovolunteer.org or the Green Volunteers application form to the nearest agency or ask the agency for an appropriate form in the preferred language.

Notes: For projects and new agencies that would like to be included in the Ecovolunteer Network, contact the Ecovolunteer Program, attn.: Roel Cosijn, at the central office.

Selected Projects:
El Amargal Tropical Rainforest Research, Colombia
Beluga Research Project, White Sea, Russia
Bieszczady Wolf Project, Poland
Carpathian Large Carnivore Project, Romania
Gibbon Rehabilitation Project, Thailand
Griffon Vulture Conservation Project, Croatia
Humpback Research Project, Abrolhos, Brazil
Monk Seal Project, Turkey
Przewalski Horse Reintroduction Project, Mongolia
Rhino Rescue Project, Swaziland
River Otter Project, Brazil
Whale and Dolphin Project, La Gomera, Spain
Wolf and Brown Bear Research, Russia

EUROPARC DEUTSCHLAND

Bundesgeschaftsstelle
Marienstrasse 31
D–10117 Berlin Germany
Tel.: ++49 (30) 2887 8820 – Fax: ++49 (30) 288 7882–16
E-mail: info@europarc-deutschland.de
www.europarc-deutschland.de

Desc.: The German section of the EUROPARC was founded in 1991 to support existing protected areas in Germany. Europarc Deutschland works towards the promotion of environmental education as well as a system's plan of protected areas in Germany so the natural heritage can be preserved for future generations. Each year, there are about 60 volunteer placements in protected areas, most of them National Parks, through the project "Praktikum fuer Umwelt", supported by the Commerzbank. The project is addressed to students who would like to contribute their knowledge and skills to the Parks.

Hab.: Temperate forest, coastal habitats, lakes, etc.

Loc.: Germany.

Dur.: 3–6 months.

Per.: April to October.

L. term: Up to 6 months.

Age: Min. 18.

Qualif.: Education, geography and biology backgrounds are advantageous. Sometimes field experience and a valid driver license are required.

Work: Environmental education, public relations.

Lang.: German.

Accom.: Provided.

Cost: No contributions, most of the positions are paid.

Applic.: Deadline January. Request brochure with positions listed between October and December; form has to be returned together with a CV.

Notes: Volunteers will be invited to a 4-day workshop in April. Mandatory work visa requirements for non-EU residents.

EXPEDITION ADVISORY CENTRE

Royal Geographic Society, with The Institute of British Geographers
1 Kensington Gore
London   SW7 2AR   UK
Tel.: ++44 (20) 7591 3030 – Fax: ++44 (20) 7591 3031
E-mail: eac@rgs.org
www.rgs.org/eac

Desc.: The Expedition Advisory Centre (EAC), founded by the Royal Geographical Society and the Young Explorer's Trust, is primarily concerned with advising those who are planning their own expeditions, with an emphasis on field research projects overseas. The Centre provides information on all aspects of expedition planning and organises the annual Expedition Planning Seminar each November. A wide variety of expedition publications and pamphlets are available including a booklet *Joining an Expedition*, listing 50 organisations that regularly arrange expeditions from environmental research and conservation work to community projects and adventurous training. Guidelines are also given on fund-raising. The Bulletin of Expedition Vacancies lists specific expeditions recruiting members. Those who have a particular skill to offer (either scientific or medical) can be included on a special register of personnel available for overseas projects (send a stamped, self-addressed envelope to the Centre to receive the appropriate form). The Centre is open from10am–5pm, Monday to Friday. Write for information or ask for an appointment.

Notes: The Centre only provides information and cannot place individuals on any planned expedition.

FONDO PER LA TERRA – EARTH FUND

Via C. Battisti 58 bis
20143 Castiglione Olona (VA) Italy
Tel.: ++39 (0331) 858 051
Fax: ++39 (0331) 857 899
E-mail: info@fondoperlaterra.org
www.fondoperlaterra.org

Desc.: The goal of the organisation is to contribute to the conservation of the world natural resources. It operates in 3 primary areas: management and support of applied research projects; training of new professionals in the conservation field; information and fund-raising campaigns in Europe. Currently, the Fund is involved in projects in Africa, Asia and South America. Activities range from an environmental education programme in schools in Zanzibar, to research in rhino genetics and vocalisation, to sustainable development work in Brazil and India. Other volunteering opportunities currently offered are on lions in Tanzania and giant otters in Brazil.

Spp.: African lion, Amazon giant otter.

Hab.: African savannah, Amazon rainforest.

Loc.: Taranigre National Park, Tanzania, Xixuau Ecological Reserve, north of Manaus, Brazil.

Travel: Fly to Arusha (Tanzania), or Manuas (Brazil), then jeep or boat.

Dur.: 14-day shifts.

Per.: June to January.

L. term: Volunteers can stay for more than 1 term.

Age.: Min. 18, max. 70.

Qualif.: Photography skills are useful.

Work: In Tanzania, photo-ID of individuals, distribution analysis, playback experiments. In Brazil, boat surveys of otter colonies and black caymans (the main predator), also at night.

Lang.: Italian (or Spanish or Portuguese), English.

Accom.: In tents, sleeping bags required.

Cost: Approx. US$1,000 including food and accommodation.

Applic.: Request an application form.

Notes: See website for new projects and exact dates and costs.

FRONTIER

50–52 Rivington Street
London EC2A 3QP UK
Tel.: ++44 (20) 7613 2422
Fax: ++44 (20) 7613 2992
E–mail: info@frontier.ac.uk
www.frontier.ac.uk

Desc.: Frontier expeditions are conservation and research projects conducted in partnership with host-country institutions, focusing on environmental issues. Current projects focus on biodiversity surveys and habitat mapping of coral reefs and mangrove areas in Madagascar and Tanzania; savannah grasslands and tropical forests in Tanzania; arid forests in Madagascar; and rainforests in Vietnam. Full training is provided, leading to a BTEC qualification in Tropical Habitat Conservation or Expedition Management (biodiversity research).

Hab.: Rainforests, tropical forests, savannah, coral reefs.

Loc.: Tanzania, Madagascar, Vietnam.

Dur.: 4, 10 or 20 weeks.

Per.: Year round.

L. term: Inquire with organisation.

Age: Min. 17.

Qualif.: To be selected for an expedition, applicants must be enthusiastic and have a commitment to conservation issues in developing countries.

Work: Data collection, surveys, collecting supplies from local villages.

Lang.: English.

Cost: Cost start from GB£1,850 (approx. EUR/US$2,700), excluding flights and visa; contact Frontier for details.

Applic.: Contact Frontier for an application form.

GLOBAL SERVICE CORPS

Earth Island Institute
300 Broadway, Suite 28
San Francisco, California 94133–3312 USA
Tel.: ++1 (415) 788 3666 ext.128 – Fax: ++1 (415) 788 7324
E-mail: gsc@earthisland.org
www.globalservicecorps.org

Desc.: Global Service Corps provides opportunities for adult volunteers to live and work on projects in developing nations. Volunteers do village-based community work in Africa and Southeast Asia.

Loc.: Tanzania, Thailand.

Dur.: Short term projects 3–4 weeks; long term 2 months or more.

Per.: Year round.

L. term: Most long-term volunteers participate on a short-term GSC trip and continue afterwards in their placement. The short-term project provides a good orientation to the country, area, organisations and people. Long-term volunteers pay a monthly fee that covers room, board and supervision.

Age: Min. 18.

Qualif.: No specific skills needed.

Work: In Tanzania, volunteers help in implementing an organic farming project and in training local communities. In Thailand, the work focuses on developing an environmental education programme.

Lang.: English.

Cost: For Thailand 3-week project cost approx. US$1,900 up to US$3,300 for 10 weeks. Tanzania (4–10 weeks) project cost range from approx. US$2,000 to US$3,250. Project fee covers all in-country expenses, except personal items. Items covered include scheduled pick-up from and delivery to the airport, room and board, transportation throughout the trip, sightseeing activities, entrance fees and costs of project materials.

Applic.: Contact organisation for an application form. A CV and a 2–3 paragraph statement must be included with application. A deposit of US$300 must be included with the application form.

GREENFORCE – Careers in Conservation

11–15 Betterton St. Covent Garden
London WC2H 9BP UK
Tel.: ++44 (20) 7470 8888 – (0870) 770 2646 (within the UK)
Fax: ++44 (20) 7470 8889 – (0870) 770 2647 (within the UK)
E-mail: greenforce@btinternet.com
www.greenforce.org

Desc.: Greenforce carries out projects to assist developing countries with wildlife resources management. Work includes biodiversity inventory, population estimates and distribution mapping. Results are used for management planning for protected areas. With the co-operation of local experts and students, these long term projects, both terrestrial and marine, fulfil the needs of local management authorities.

Spp : Large and small mammals, reptiles and amphibians, birds, selected invertebrates, coral communities.

Hab.: African savannah, Amazon rainforest, tropical islands.

Loc.: Africa, Asia, Southeast Asia, South Pacific, Bahamas.

Dur.: Volunteers join for 10-week periods.

Per.: Year round.

L. term: Traineeships are available, after 2 years MS funding available.

Age: Min. 18.

Qualif.: No scientific knowledge required; full training (including diving training for marine projects) is provided.

Work: Preparation and identification of specimens, mapping and radiotracking of wildlife resources.

Lang.: English.

Accom.: Traditional thatch huts, depending on location. Sleeping bags, mosquito nets and mats required.

Cost: GB£ 2,200 (approx. EUR/US$3,300). The fee includes food and accommodation, visa, local transportation and training. International flight not included.

Applic.: A free training weekend in the UK is optional.

Notes: Non-British applicants may arrive 3 days before the rest of the team for briefing. Distance learning kits are supplied.

HELLENIC ORNITHOLOGICAL SOCIETY

Vas. Irakleiou 24
GR – 106 82 Athens Greece
Tel.: ++30 (1) 822 8704/822 7937
Fax: ++30 (1) 822 8704
E-mail: birdlife-gr@ath.forthnet.gr
www.ornithologiki.gr   (click on English version)

Desc.: Protecting bird fauna of Greece.

Spp.: All endangered species of Greek bird fauna.

Hab.: All habitats of Greece (forests, lagoons, rivers, sealife).

Loc.: Greece.

Travel: Bus, train or plane to the project area.

Dur.: Min. 3 weeks for foreign volunteers; 2 weeks for Greek volunteers.

Per.: May to October (mostly the summer period); some projects year round.

L.term: With project leaders approval.

Age: Min. 18.

Qualif.: Able to work sometimes in difficult conditions, to do manual work, and to be punctual. Able to live and work with people from different countries and cultures and to cooperate with the local communities. Experience in similar projects or studies in biology, environment, ornithology are more than welcome.

Work: Work in the field (constructing & monitoring nests, counting birds, feeding, monitoring of the habitats, etc.) and in public awareness.

Lang.: English, French, German.

Accom.: Provided by HOS either in organized campsites or in rooms rented for the project (tents, sleeping bags, sheets, towels, sanitary articles, etc. are required).

Cost: A EUR30 (approx. GB£20) membership fee is required. Travel, food and other personal expenses are covered by the volunteer. Expenses needed for work during the project are covered by the HOS.

Applic.: Application form can be found on the HOS website and sent by post, fax or e-mail from March to August.

i to i
9 Blenheim Terrace
Leeds LS2 9HZ UK
Tel.: ++44 (870) 333 2332
Fax: ++44 (113) 242 2171
E-mail: travel@i-to-i.com
www.i-to-i.com

Desc.: i to i is a volunteer travel & TEFL training organisation, specialising in meaningful conservation work-placements for dedicated travellers of any age. i-to-i's projects, known as i-Ventures, provide inspirational learning opportunities – both for the volunteer and their host community, and their projects aim to preserve the environment, tradition and culture of areas that really need support. i-Ventures include rainforest projects in South America, ecotourism in Sri Lanka, safari-park conservation in South Africa, elephant conservation in Thailand and Sri Lanka and also marine biology in the Caribbean. Every year, i-to-i train over 3000 volunteers.

Hab.: Lowland rainforest, mountains, coastal areas, veldt.

Loc.: Costa Rica, Honduras, Ecuador, Bolivia, South Africa, Sri Lanka, Thailand, Australia, and Ireland.

Dur.: 2 weeks – 3 months.

Per.: Year round.

Age: Min 17.

Work: Costa Rica: tagging and monitoring leather back turtles, living and working on an experimental lowland rainforest farm. Working with Bri Bri Indians on agriculture methods. Australia: beach reclamation, weed control and tracking echidnas.

Lang.: English.

Accom.: Tents, huts or with local families.

Cost: Min GB£750 (approx. EUR/US$1150); max GB£2,795 (approx. EUR/US$4,300). Deposit £195 (approx.EUR/US$300). Travel not Included.

Applic.: Request by phone a brochure and application form or look on www.i-to-i.com.

INTERNATIONAL OTTER SURVIVAL FUND

Skye Environmental Centre
Broadford, Isle of Skye
Scotland, IV49 9AQ   UK
Tel./Fax: ++44 (1471) 822 487
E-mail: iosf@otter.org
www.otter.org

Desc.: IOSF works to conserve otters by safeguarding areas of good habitat and supporting people working in research and rehabilitation worldwide. The Fund's mission is to protect 13 species of otter worldwide.

Spp.: Eurasian otter (*Lutra lutra*).

Hab.: Subarctic tundra, boreal forest.

Loc.: Islands of Skye and Coll, Scotland.

Dur.: 1 week.

Per.: April to October.

L. term: Inquire with organisation.

Age: Min. 19, max. 65.

Qualif.: No specific skills needed.

Lang.: English.

Cost: GB£ 240–495 depending on the project (approx. EUR/US$360–750).

Applic.: Call or write IOSF for application form.

Notes: IOSF supports several otter conservation projects overseas (for example in Belarus or Vietnam) where occasionally volunteers are needed. Inquire with IOSF for details.

INVOLVEMENT VOLUNTEERS ASSOCIATION INC.

P.O. Box 218, Port Melbourne
Victoria 3207 Australia
Tel.: ++61 (3) 9646 9392
Fax: ++61 (3) 9646 5504
E-mail: ivworldwide@volunteering.org.au
www.volunteering.org.au

Desc.: Involvement Volunteers Association Inc. (IVI) is a non-profit, NGO; providing Networked International Volunteering Programmes to individuals in 1 or more countries for a maximum of 12 months.

Loc.: Australia, Asia and the Pacific, Europe, Africa, USA and Latin America.

Dur.: 2 – 12 weeks.

Per.: Year round.

Age: Min.18.

Qualif.: Suitable qualifications appreciated but not necessary.

Lang.: English, Spanish in Latin America.

Cost: AUS$242 (approx. US$140–GB£90) to apply. Participation costs depend on the project and the country.

Applic.: Contact the organisation directly.

IUCN – The World Conservation Union

28, rue Mauvernay
1196 Gland Switzerland
Tel.: ++41 (22) 999 0001
Fax: ++41 (22) 999 0002
E-mail: mail@iucn.org
www.iucn.org

Desc.: Founded in 1948, IUCN – The World Conservation Union brings together more than 950 governmental and non-governmental members and 10,000 technical and scientific experts in its 6 Commissions. IUCN's mission is to influence, encourage and assist societies throughout the world to conserve the integrity and diversity of nature and ensure that any use of natural resources is equitable and ecologically sustainable.

Loc.: Refer to www.iucn.org – About IUCN – Offices.

Dur.: Min. 3 months to 1 year.

Per.: Inquire to the appropriate IUCN Regional/Country Office in the preferred location.

L. term: Long-term assignments are preferred.

Age: Min. 21.

Qualif.: Vary according to specific assignments.

Work: Assist in collecting information, desk research and report writing. Organise and facilitate meetings and workshops. Develop project proposals and communication materials. Maintain databases and web-pages.

Lang.: English, French, Spanish.

Cost: Conditions vary according to location and assignment.

Agents: Refer to www.iucn.org - About IUCN – Vacancies – Offices and Members – Directory. Contact the IUCN Regional/Country Office and/or IUCN members in the preferred location.

Applic.: Send CV and information on availability of time to preferred IUCN Regional/Country Office in the preferred location.

LEGAMBIENTE

Via Salaria 403 – 00199 Rome Italy
Tel.: ++39 (06) 862 681 – Volunteer office: ++39 (06) 8626 8324
For SCUBA activities: ++39 (06) 8626 8400
Fax: ++39 (06) 8626 8319
E-mail: legambiente.vol@tiscali.it
www.legambiente.com/canale8/campi/

Desc.: Founded in 1980, Legambiente is a non-profit organisation involved primarily with public awareness and environmental campaigning activities. Volunteer opportunities include work camps and events such as the 'Clean up the World' day. Current projects include restoration and protection camps in small islands near Sicily, underwater archaeology and ecology camps in Sicily, ecological research in the Italian Alps, archeological study in southern Italy and many others.

Spp.: Various species.

Hab.: Mediterranean seas, islands and coasts, temperate forest, lagoons, Alps.

Loc.: National Parks and Reserves, Mediterranean islands, Italian Alps, Germany, Brazil, Japan, France, Wales, Czech Republic, Mexico, Belarus, Turkey, Spain, Denmark, Poland, Belgium.

Dur.: 10–20 days.

Per.: Year round.

L. term: EU citizens can join the EVS (European Voluntary Service) programme from 3 months to 1 year. See Notes below.

Age: Min.18. Special programmes available for those under 18.

Qualif.: No specific qualifications are required.

Lang.: Italian, English.

Cost: Min. EUR150, max. EUR350 (approx.GB£100–240).

Applic.: Contact the Volunteer office of Legambiente for further information and application forms.

Notes: Legambiente is entitled to offer the EVS programme open to young EU citizens. The programme covers all the expenses of the volunteers for training in languages or in professional skills. For more information contact Paolo Madonni Tel.:++39 (06) 8626 8324, e-mail: legambiente.madonni@tiscali.it

LIPU – Lega Italiana Protezione Uccelli

(Italian League for the Protection of Birds)
Via Trento 49 – 43100 Parma Italy
Tel.: ++39 (0521) 273 043/273 563
Fax: ++39 (0521) 273419
E-mail: info@lipu.it
www.lipu.it

Desc.: LIPU, founded in 1965, is the Italian representative of BirdLife International. The aim of the organisation is the protection of nature and in particular of birds. It supports bird rescue centres, research programmes for the conservation of endangered species, awareness campaigns and environmental education programmes.

Spp.: Birds.

Hab.: Mediterranean coasts and islands, temperate forest, Alps.

Loc.: Various locations in Italy.

Dur.: 7–10 days.

Per.: June to October.

L. term: Inquire with organisation.

Age: Inquire with organisation.

Qualif.: Previous experience and qualifications are not required. Some camps need expert ornithologists.

Work: Birdwatching, counts, ringing, data collection, fire prevention, trail maintenance and restoration.

Lang.: Italian, English.

Cost: Min. EUR300, max. EUR700 (GB£200–450).

Applic.: Contact LIPU for information on international application.

MINGAN ISLAND CETACEAN RESEARCH EXPEDITIONS

Mingan Island Cetacean Study, Inc.
378 Rue Bord de la Mer
Longue-Pointe-de-Mingan, Québec, GOG 1VO Canada
Tel./Fax: ++1 (418) 949 2845
E-mail: mics@globetrotter.net
www.rorqual.com

Desc.: Volunteers join a team of marine biologists conducting cetacean research in Northeastern Quebec (Canada), and in Baja California (Mexico). In the projects, participants spend most of their time on the water; there is no working facility on land.

Spp.: Blue, fin, humpback and minke whales.

Hab.: Gulf of the St. Lawrence River, Sea of Cortez.

Loc.: Northeast Quebec; Gaspé Peninsula and Estuary, Quebec. During winter in Loreto, Baja California, for blue whale studies.

Travel: Airplane to Sept-Iles. For Loreto fly to LA and then to Loreto.

Dur.: 7–14-day sessions.

Per.: June to October in Quebec; February to March in Loreto.

L. term: Possible to stay up to 1 month.

Age: Min. 16.

Qualif.: Be prepared to spend long periods on the water—sometimes up to 12 hours. Recommended a good physical form.

Work: Help collect field data: take notes, observe researchers do biopsies and some photographic work. Assist with organizing daily logistics such as gas, food and boat preparation.

Lang.: English, French, German. Spanish useful in Mexico.

Accom.: B&B, inn or hotel.

Cost: CAD$1,690 (approx. US$1,150) in Gaspé and Longue Pointe; including transportation, accommodation, food and a 7-day session with the biologists. US$1,375 in Loreto; including all activities on the water, hotel and meals; does not include air transportation and transfers to and from the airport. A Richard Sears blue whale expedition costs CAD$1,850 (approx. US$1,250); all-inclusive package excluding air transportation.

Applic.: Request from the organisation registration and medical forms.

THE NATIONAL TRUST

Volunteering Office
33 Sheep Street, Cirencester, Glos GL7 1RQ UK
Tel.: ++44 (870) 429 2428
Fax: ++44 (1285) 657 935 – (870) 429 2427
E-mail: working.holidays@ntrust.org.uk
www.nationaltrust.org.uk/volunteering/

Desc.: The National Trust offers 400 working holidays in outdoor conservation, woodland management, heritage, restoration and other countryside maintenance.

Loc.: England, Wales, Northern Ireland.

Dur.: 1–2 weeks.

Per.: Year round.

L. term: Inquire with the organisation. Many opportunities are listed on the website.

Age: Min. 17 or 18 depending on the project.

Qualif.: No specific skills required. Some projects need botanists, archaeologists or builders.

Lang.: English.

Cost: GB£54–65/week (approx. EUR/US$80–95). Food and accommodation are included.

Agents: Contact the organisation directly.

Applic: On-line application form or to receive an application form call ++44 (870) 429 2429.

Notes: The National Trust has special programmes for young people and for volunteers over 35.

NZTCV – The New Zealand Trust for Conservation Volunteers

Three Streams,
343 SH17, RD3 Albany
Auckland New Zealand
Tel.: ++64 (9) 415 9336 – Fax: ++64 (9) 415 9336
E-mail: conservol@clear.net.nz
www.conservationvolunteers.org.nz

Desc.: NZTCV is a member of the International Conservation Volunteers Alliance. Projects offer opportunities to visit scenic locations in both the North and South Islands of New Zealand. NZTCV allows overseas visitors to share New Zealand's unique environment and culture. Patrons: Dr. David Bellamy, Stephen King, Sir Paul Reeves & Lady Beverley Reeves.

Spp.: Various species of New Zealand's flora and fauna.

Hab.: Coasts, dryland, National Parks and Reserves, forests, wetlands, natural bush.

Loc.: Throughout New Zealand

Dur.: 2 – 3 weeks (varies).

Per.: Year round.

L. term: Inquire with organisation.

Age: Min. 18.

Qualif.: Experience and qualifications related to the environment are welcome but not essential.

Work: Species monitoring, general maintenance, planting, island revegetation, forest restoration.

Lang.: English.

Cost: Air travel to and from New Zealand. Free accommodation offered with some projects. Food costs for duration of stay and cost of transportation to and from project location are paid by the volunteer. See website for more information.

Applic.: Applications are accepted on-line or write to the address above for information.

OCEANIC SOCIETY EXPEDITIONS

Fort Mason Center, Building E
San Francisco, CA 94123   USA
Tel.: ++1 (415) 441 1106 – (800) 326 7491 (toll free in US/Canada)
Fax: ++1 (415) 474 3395
E-mail: info@oceanic-society.org
www.oceanic-society.org

Desc.: Founded in 1972, Oceanic Society Expeditions (OSE) is a non-profit organisation that conducts research to protect aquatic environments and promote environmental education. OSE organises over 30 projects classified as 'Natural History Expeditions' (NHE) and 'Research Expeditions' (RE); the latter are designed to accomplish specific scientific objectives. For these projects volunteers work with field biologists, collecting data and logging information.

Spp.: Dolphins, manatees, corals, monk seals, seabirds.

Hab.: Tropical seas, temperate seas, rainforest.

Loc.: Midway, Palmyra, Japan, Baja California, Caribbean, Belize, Bahamas and various locations in Central, South and North America.

Dur.: 4 – 10 days for NHE; 1 week for RE.

Per.: Year round.

L.term: Inquire with organisation.

Age: Min. 18. Anyone under 18 must be accompanied by a guardian.

Qualif.: Enthusiasm and willingness to take directions are necessary. Some projects may require scuba certification.

Lang.: English.

Cost: Approx. US$1,000–3,000 for NHE, US$1,000–2,000 for RE.

Applic.: Request application form to be returned with a deposit of US$300/person/trip.

Notes: OSE also raises contributions through adopt-a-dolphin and adopt-a-whale programmes.

Selected Projects:
Bottlenose Dolphin Project, Belize
Manatee Research Project, Belize

ONEWORLD VOLUNTEERS

2458 River Road
Guilford, Vermont 05301 USA
Tel.: ++1 (802) 257 0152
Fax: ++1 (802) 257 2784
E-mail: explore@volunteertravel.com – info@oneworldvolunteer.org
www.volunteertravel.com – www.oneworldvolunteer.org

Desc.: Oneworld volunteer is a non-profit organisation that arranges individual volunteer placements working with a variety of conservation and environmental organisations and wildlife rehabilitation centres.

Spp.: Sea turtles, primates marine mammals, birds, flying foxes (fruit bats), and domestic animals.

Hab.: Rainforests, marine environments, island ecosystems, farms.

Loc.: Costa Rica, Mexico, Puerto Rico, New Zealand, Australia, Belize, Ecuador, Guatemala, Nepal.

Travel: Contact the organisation.

Dur.: 1 month to 1 year or more.

Per.: Year round.

L. term: Placement durations are flexible and vary from site to site.

Age: Min. 18.

Qualif.: Volunteers must be mature, flexible and independent.

Work: Variable depending on project.

Lang · English, Spanish.

Accom.: In shared housing, dorms or with host families.

Cost: A placement fee of about US$775–975 is required regardless of the duration of the project. Transportation, room and board are not included at most sites.

Applic.: Request application form and submit with CV and reference letters. A non-refundable registration fee of US$35 must be enclosed to the application form.

OPERATION CROSSROADS AFRICA, Inc.

P.O.Box 5570
New York, NY 10027 USA
Tel.: ++1 (212) 289 1949
Fax: ++1 (212) 289 2526
E-mail: oca@igc.apc.org – oca@igc.org
www.oca.igc.org/web/index.html

Desc.: This organisation offers many opportunities for concerned persons with interest in areas such as ecology and environment, traditional medicine, archaeology, reforestation, wildlife, agriculture/farming and teaching.

Loc.: Botswana, Gambia, Ghana, Eritrea, Ivory Coast, Kenya, Senegal, South Africa, Tanzania, Uganda, Zimbabwe.

Dur.: 6–7 week programme.

Per.: Mid-June to mid-August.

Cost: US$3,500, including all expenses (not personal) and airfare from New York. Crossroads assists volunteers in raising funds for their travel and living expenses.

Applic.: On-line applications are available for Volunteers/Interns and Project Directors/Group Leaders. Volunteer information available by e-mail. For Project information, brochure/update, send a request to oca@igc.org. Project Directors/Group Leader applicants must be at least 25 years old with appropriate expertise. To receive the leader packet, send an e-mail message to oca@igc.org, plus include LEADER in the subject field.

Note: Students generally arrange to receive academic credit, typically 7–15 units.

OPERATION WALLACEA

Roughton Moor
Woodhall Spa, Lincolnshire LN10 6YQ   UK
Tel.: ++44 (1526) 354 204
Fax: ++44 (1526) 354 683
E-mail: info@opwall.com
www.opwall.com

Desc.: Operation Wallacea (OW) is a not for profit scientific conservation project. The project, started in summer 1995, consists of a scientific survey of the marine habitats of the Tukanbesi islands and has expanded to include the rainforest areas of Buton Island, in Southeast Sulawesi, Indonesia. OW is also starting another project in Cuba, in both marine and rainforest habitats. OW recruits volunteers who want to contribute towards worthwhile conservation projects in the above areas.

Spp.: Marine and rainforest, encompassing corals, fish, marine mammals, birds, small mammals, macaques, snakes lizards and frogs, Educational and anthropological projects.

Hab.: Coral reefs, primary rainforest.

Loc.: Southeast Sulawesi, Indonesia and Cuba.

Travel: Airplane to Singapore, then internal flight to Sulawesi. Airplane to Havana, Cuba.

Dur.: 2, 4, 6 or 8 weeks.

Per.: June to October, Indonesia; June to August ,Cuba.

L. term: Inquire with organisation.

Age: Min. 16.

Qualif.: Enthusiasm and a positive attitude towards the environment are the only qualifications necessary, as full training for diving, jungle survival and field skills are given.

Work: Volunteers work alongside scientists to complete surveys of the endemic species. Both flora and fauna in the marine and rainforest habitats are surveyed.

Lang.: English.

Accom.: The marine volunteers are based in traditional wooden bungalows, while the rainforest volunteers are based in village houses and will live amongst the local community, or in base camps in the rainforest.

Cost: Marine surveys: GB£875 (approx. EUR/US$1,300) for 2 weeks, GB£1,700 (EUR/US$2,550) for 4 weeks, GB£2,300 (EUR/US$3,450) for 6 weeks and GB£2,700 (EUR/US$3,950) for 8 weeks, these prices include all food and accommodation and internal transfers between sites. Prices do not include flights and insurance.

Applic.: Prospective volunteers need only to contact the UK office; those living in Great Britain have the opportunity to attend some University presentations.

Notes: Diving equipment may be hired on site for a nominal sum. Dive tanks and weights are provided free of charge.

RALEIGH INTERNATIONAL

Raleigh House
27 Parsons Green Lane
London, SW6 4HZ   UK
Tel.: ++44 (20) 7371 8585 – Fax: ++44 (20) 7371 5116
E-mail: info@raleigh.org.uk
www.raleighinternational.org

Desc.: Raleigh International, formerly known as Operation Raleigh, organises 10-week expeditions in the UK and overseas for young people. Projects may include, but are not limited to, scientific research, surveys, community work, building schools or bridges and helping doctors in remote villages.

Hab.: Various.

Loc.: Namibia, Chile, Costa Rica, Nicaragua, Borneo, Ghana.

Dur.: 10 weeks.

Per.: Year round.

L. term: Each expedition lasts 10 weeks. Volunteers (known as Venturers) may continue their involvement with Raleigh at home after the expedition. Volunteers may also continue travelling independently.

Age: Min. 17, max. 25.

Qualif.: Volunteers must be physically fit, able to swim 200 metres and speak basic English. If able to do so, prospective Venturers attend an introduction weekend that includes physical and mental challenges.

Accom.: Tents. Living conditions during the expeditions are very basic.

Cost: Approx. GB£ 3,500 (EUR/US$5,200) including airfare from the UK. Venturers raise funds for the expedition through sponsorship. With support from Raleigh head office, 1,000 young people succeed to take a place on an expedition every year.

Agents: Contact Raleigh International directly.

Applic.: Send a self-addressed, stamped envelope to receive the information package and application form.

RSPB – THE ROYAL SOCIETY FOR THE PROTECTION OF BIRDS

The Lodge, Sandy
Bedfordshire SG19 2DL   UK
Tel.: ++44 (1767) 680 551
Fax: ++44 (1767) 692 365
www.rspb.org/helprspb/volunteering/

Desc.:   RSPB Residential Voluntary Warden Scheme operates in 32 reserves in England, Scotland and Wales, providing an opportunity for those interested in ornithology and conservation to gain practical experience of the day-to-day running of a RSPB reserve.

Spp.:   Birds.

Hab.:   Woodland, swamps, ponds, lakes, moorland, coastal lagoons.

Loc.:   England, Scotland, Wales.

Dur.:   Min. 1 week (Saturday to Saturday); max. 1 month.

Per.:   Year round.

L. term: Negotiable by arrangement.

Age: Min.16 (18 for international volunteers and in some reserves).

Qualif.:   Good physical health.

Work: Duties vary and may include: management, tourist assistance, reception work, survey/research assistance, car park duties, grass cutting, bird counts, animal population monitoring. Duties allocated according to volunteer knowledge and experience.

Lang.:   English.

Accom.:   Chalets, cottages, houses, cabins, caravans or bungalows. May have to share a room with at least 1 other person of same sex. Bedding is provided (except sleeping bag). Cooking facilities available (volunteers must provide and cook their own food).

Cost: Free accommodation. Food and travel expenses not included.

Applic.:   The web address above features an on-line brochure and an application form.

Selected Project:

Operation Osprey, Scotland

SANCCOB – The Southern African National Foundation for the Conservation of Coastal Birds

P.O. Box: 1111 6   Bloubergrant, 7443 Cape Town South Africa
Tel.: ++27 (21) 557 61 55
Fax: ++27 (21) 557 88 04
E-mail: info@sanccob.co.za
www.sanccob.co.za

Desc.: Sanccob rehabilitates sea birds, mostly from oil pollution, some injured or ill. The species most affected is the African penguin, a bird only found along the southern African coast and classified as 'vulnerable.' The main problem is oil pollution. The South African route is a popular ship-faring route and is very polluted.

Spp: African (jackass) penguin (*Spheniscus demersus*), Cape gannet, Cape, crowned and whitebreasted cormorants, kelp and hartlaub gulls, petrel, tern, albatross.

Hab.: Coastal.

Loc.: 20 km north of Cape Town, South Africa.

Travel: Airplane to Cape Town.

Dur.: Min. 3 weeks.

Per.: May to October is busy but oil spills can happen any time.

L. term: Possible, with project leaders approval.

Age: Min. 16.

Qualif.: Willingness to work hard with wild, difficult birds.

Work: Keeping the centre clean, scrubbing pools and pens daily (cleaning after 30–200 birds), feeding and stabilizing birds, washing birds, and assisting veterinary staff.

Lang.: English.

Accom.: Bed & Breakfast or contact the organisation for other possibilities.

Cost: Volunteers are responsible for food, transport and accommodation costs, approx. US$30–40/day.

Agents: Contact the organisation directly.

Applic.: Fill out application form from the web page.

Notes: Winters can be cold and wet in Cape Town. Old clothes to work in should be brought.

SAN GORGONIO WILDERNESS ASSOCIATION (SGWA)

Volunteer Ranger Program
34701 Mill Creek Road
Mentone, California 92359   USA
Tel./Fax: ++1 (909) 794 1123
E-mail: info@sgwa.org
www.sgwa.org

Desc.: This volunteer programme is open to naturalists, information specialists and persons willing to help with maintenance work, recreation and forest patrolling in the San Gorgonio Wilderness, not far from Los Angeles.

Loc.: The San Gorgonio Wilderness is located on the San Bernardino National Forest, approx. 75 miles east of Los Angeles.

Dur.: Min. 2 days, max. 3 months.

Per.: May to September, primarily on weekends and holidays.

L. term: Inquire with organisation.

Age: Min. 18. Persons under 18 may participate with a guardian.

Qualif.: Volunteers must be able to perform the type of service chosen, be experienced in hiking, backpacking, horseback riding or mountain biking on mountain trails (should the service require it) and have their own equipment. Volunteers are trained.

Work: Naturalists give nature walks and/or present programmes. Information Specialists provide permits, maps and other information to forest visitors. Trail Crew improve trails throughout the National Forest. Recreation Maintenance Crew improve recreation facilities. Forest Patrol day hike, backpack or ride horses or mountain bikes along trails and dirt roads throughout the forest to assist visitors, protect the forest and perform minor trail and camp maintenance.

Lang.: English.

Cost: Volunteers must purchase part (approx. US$30) of Forest Service uniform.

Applic.: Contact SGWA for further information and application form.

SCA – Student Conservation Association, Inc.

P.O. Box 550
Charlestown, New Hampshire 03603 USA
Tel.: ++1 (603) 543 1700
Fax: ++1 (603) 543 1828
E-mail: internships@thesca.org
www.thesca.org

Desc.: SCA is an educational organisation operating volunteer and internship programmes in conservation and natural resource management. The Conservation Internship Programs (CIP) are for anyone 18 or older to serve alongside seasonal staff for public and private natural resource management agencies. The Conservation Crew Program (CCP) allows high school students aged 15–19 to join summer conservation projects.

Loc.: USA: opportunities exist in all 50 states

Dur.: Usually 12–52 weeks for CIP; 3–5 weeks for CCP.

Per.: CIP are available year round, CCP from June to August only.

L.term: Max. 12 months, depending upon project.

Age: Min. 18 for CIP, no upper age limit; 15–19 for CCP.

Qualif.: Good health, enthusiasm, flexibility, fluent English.

Work: Interns work with widlife, in back country patrol, trail building, hydrology and engineering, visitor services and interpretation, environmental education with youth, research, public outreach, and in museum curator positions to name a few.

Lang.: English.

Cost: No cost: CIP Interns receive paid travel (within the US), free housing and related expenses, weekly living allowance of US$50 and free accident insurance. CCP volunteers receive free room and board and equipment but no travel.

Applic.: An application must be submitted with a medical form and at least 2 references. Request by mail or phone or download from SCA's website. Applicants can apply directly on-line. No deadline for CIP; deadline for CCP is March 1, or until all positions are filled. Application fee of US$10–40.

Notes: Listings of positions on website. Searchable database updated weekly; applications can also be filled out on website directly.

SCI – Service Civil International

International Secretariat
St–Jacobsmarkt 82, B–2000 Antwerpen Belgium
Tel.: ++32 (3) 226 5727
Fax: ++32 (3) 232 0344
E-mail: sciint@sciint.org (general)
www.sciint.org (to find all the national contacts)

Desc.: SCI is a voluntary NGO founded in 1920 that aims to promote international understanding and peace. It provides volunteers for projects in communities that cannot afford labour. Every year more than 20,000 volunteers of all nationalities work in over 100 camps.

Loc.: Western and Eastern Europe, United States, Australia.

Dur.: 2–3 weeks.

Per.: Year round, mainly June to September.

L. term: People with workcamp experience can join projects for 3–6 months; short-term volunteers need approval of host in order to stay longer.

Age: Min. 18 for Europe; min. 16 for the United States.

Qualif.: Ability to work as part of a team and live simply.

Lang.: English. For other languages, inquire with local SCI office.

Cost: Volunteers must provide transportation; contributions are US$65 in the United States, EUR120 in Europe, EUR250 in Eastern Europe. Accommodation, food and insurance are provided.

Agents: Local SCI offices listed in the above website. SCI has many branches in the world and cooperates with many organisations: contact the nearest office for information.

Applic.: Standard application; no need to be a member.

Notes: Smallest projects could be for 6 volunteers and largest for 20 volunteers. Usually only 2 volunteers from the same country can join the same project in order to form international teams.

SCI Germany: www.sci-d.de
SCI-IVS USA: www.sci-ivs.org
IVS UK: www.ivsgbn.demon.co.uk
IVP Australia: www.ivp.org.au

SOUSSON FOUNDATION

3600 Ridge Road
Templeton, California 93465 USA
Tel.: ++1 (805) 434 0299
Fax: ++1 (805) 434 3444
E-mail: info@sousson.org
www.sousson.org

Desc.: The Sousson Foundation recruits volunteers to work on projects in National Parks in California and Hawaii, such as Yosemite, Sequoia, Channel Islands and Hawaii Volcanoes National Park. Projects vary from revegetation and tree planting to species preservation.

Hab.: Rainforest, high sierra.

Loc.: California and Hawaii, USA.

Dur.: 6–8 day excursions.

Per.: May to October.

L. term: The Foundation will help volunteers make arrangements to stay after the 8–day period.

Age: Min. 18 (12–17 with parents' permission).

Qualif.: No particular skills needed, photography welcome.

Lang.: English.

Cost: Adults fees start from US$595, including food and camping arrangements. Volunteers must provide for their own transportation. A portion of the adults' contribution goes to supporting the 6–day Youth Expeditions. Youth and students fees are about US$170.

Agents: Contact the Sousson Foundation directly.

Applic.: Ask for an application form.

Notes: Half of the excursion is work and half is devoted to recreation and education. Further information available from the Foundation.

TETHYS RESEARCH INSTITUTE

c/o Civic Aquarium
Viale G.B. Gadio 2
20121 Milano Italy
Tel.: ++39 (02)7200 1947 – Fax: ++39 (02)7200 1946
E-mail: tethys@tethys.org
www.tethys.org

Desc.: This private non-profit organisation is dedicated to the study and protection of marine habitats, focusing on Mediterranean cetaceans. Founded in 1989, TRI is formed by a team of researchers conducting research with the help of volunteers.

Spp.: Cetaceans.

Hab.: Mediterranean Sea.

Loc.: Mediterranean (France, Greece, Italy).

Dur.: 1–2 weeks.

Per.: April to October.

L. term: Biology students or researchers may assist TRI biologists for the duration of projects with the leader's approval.

Age: Min.18. Minors may be accepted if accompanied by an adult.

Qualif.: Volunteers must be enthusiastic and flexible; ability to swim is necessary. Photography, video and computer skills are helpful.

Work: Assist the researchers with observations, photo-ID, data entry, operation of hydrophones and recording instruments. Share household duties (shopping, cleaning, cooking).

Lang.: English, Italian, Spanish.

Accom.: Aboard the 19–metre ketch *Gemini Lab* for research cruises. In house along the coast for dolphin project in Greece.

Cost: Approx. EUR/US$ 600–900/week (approx. GB£400–600). Food, insurance and travel to and from project not included.

Applic.: Contact TRI for information and application forms.

Selected projects:

Ionian Dolphin Project, Greece
Mediterranean Fin Whale Program, Ligurian Sea

TREKFORCE EXPEDITIONS
Community & Conservation Projects
34 Buckingham Palace Road, London SW1W 0RE UK
Tel.: ++44 (20) 7878 2275
Fax: ++44 (20) 7878 2276
E-mail: info@trekforce.org.uk
www.trekforce.org.uk

Desc.: Trekforce is a registered UK charity that raises funds to support conservation and scientific projects in the rainforests of Central and South America, and East Malaysia. Expeditions offer the opportunity to make a valuable contribution to conservation. All projects are organised by project partners in host countries, and work is also supported by local governments. Projects include construction work, flora and fauna surveys, archaeological surveys and work in national parks, nature reserves and rainforests. Recent projects include working with the Royal Society of South East Asia on a large biodiversity experiment in Sabah, upgrading the infrastructure at several National Parks in Belize and building research centres and visitor centres in nature reserves

Hab.: Rainforest.

Loc.: Central and South America (Belize, Guyana), Borneo.

Dur.: 2 – 5 months.

Per.: Year round.

L. term: Many 'trekkers' return for more than 1 expedition at discounted rates.

Age: Min. 17.

Qualif.: No specific skills needed.

Lang.: English. Longer programmes involve learning local languages.

Accom.: Hammocks under mosquito nets and waterproof shelters.

Cost: Between GB£2,500 and GB£3,700 (approx. EUR/US$3,800–5,500) depending on expedition length.

Applic.: Call for, or find on-line, the application form.

Notes: Prospective volunteers join introduction days in London where they are offered help and advice on fund-raising and can discuss project work and meet ex-volunteers.

UNITED NATIONS VOLUNTEERS (UNV)

P.O. Box 260–11,
D–53153 Bonn Germany
Tel.: ++49 (228) 815 2000
Fax: ++49 (228) 815 2001
E-mail: information@unvolunteers.org
www.unv.org

Desc.: The United Nations Volunteers programme is open to specialists in various fields. Since 1971 over 30,000 volunteers have joined the programme in about 140 countries (particularly in developing ones), co-operating with local organisations and communities for teaching or offering their professional skills. UNV programmes include: education, environment, peace operations and democracy, humanitarian relief and rehabilitation, technical co-operation and refugee assistance. Today, some 10% of the serving UNVs work with environmental or conservation issues in specific areas such as plant protection, forestry conservation, sanitation/waste disposal, energy engineering, meteorology, coastal erosion, preservation of cultural heritage and tourism. UN Volunteers have been assigned to projects on pandas in a reserve in China or on global warming policy planning in the Maldives.

Loc.: Developing countries throughout the world such as India, Brazil, Mali and Burkina Faso (for the environmental programme).

Dur.: Assignments usually last 2 years. Shorter assignments may be authorized.

Per.: Year round.

L. term: Some assignments can be extended beyond the 2-year period.

Age: Min. 21, but UNV volunteers are usually older than 35, as a professional working experience is necessary.

Qualif.: Volunteers must be professionals or technicians with at least 2 years of experience. Teachers, medical doctors, nurses, mechanical or electrical engineers, geologists, automotive mechanics, librarians, midwives, etc.

Work: Varies depending on programme and location.

Lang.: English, French, Spanish, Arabic, Portuguese. Language ability of selected volunteers will be tested.

Accom.: Simple accommodation provided for volunteer and dependent relatives (spouse and up to 2 children under 21 years of age). Furniture and utilities are normally provided. If these arrangements cannot be made, the paid rent will be reimbursed.

Cost: UNV volunteers receive a monthly living allowance that ranges from US$600–1,400 for single specialists and from US$800–1,900 for specialists with direct dependents. Upon completion of an assignment, a resettlement allowance will also be paid. Life, health and permanent disability insurance is provided free of charge. Return travel to duty station is also provided (includes direct dependents).

Applic.: Write or call for the PHS (Personal History Statement) form (either in French or English), which must be completed and sent in together with 2 photos and reference forms completed by both professional and personal referees. If the PHS is approved by UNV headquarters, the application is added to the roster of candidates. If a volunteer is selected for a particular post, the PHS is submitted for clearance by a UN agency and for approval by the Government requesting the services of a UNV specialist. Submission and selection of candidates may take several months. Candidates who are accepted must begin the assignment within 8 weeks of being notified of final selection.

UNIVERSITY RESEARCH EXPEDITIONS PROGRAM (UREP)

University of California
One Shields Avenue, Davis, California 95616 USA
Tel.: ++1 (530)757 3529 – Fax: ++1 (530) 757 3537
E-mail: urep@ucdavis.edu
www.urep.ucdavis.edu

Desc.:	Founded in 1976, UREP offers a wide range of opportunities to participate in field research around the world, including wildlife, archaeology, earth sciences, environmental and conservation studies.
Spp.:	Birds, frogs, manatees, monkeys, foxes.
Hab.:	Rainforest, alpine, desert, lagoons, tropical seas, grasslands, savannah.
Loc.:	Various locations in North, Central and South America, Africa, Europe, Polynesia.
Dur.:	Usually 2 weeks.
Per.:	March to September.
L. term:	Inquire with organisation.
Age:	Inquire with organisation.
Qualif.:	No special academic or prior field experience is required. Curiosity, flexibility and co-operation are essential. Wilderness experience, skills in observation, drawing, photography, diving can be helpful. A physical examination may be required for certain expeditions.
Lang.:	English.
Cost:	Min. US$700, max. US$1,800 including food and accommodation.
Applic.:	Send application form with US$200 deposit.
Notes:	An information catalogue can be obtained by sending US$5 for postage to the above address. Special programmes are available for teachers; scholarships are available for teachers and students. In the first semester of 2003 UREP is taking a pause to evaluate the programme after 25 years and revitalize it for the future.

U.S. DEPARTMENT OF AGRICULTURE – Forest Service
Volunteering in the National Forests
P.O. Box 96090, Washington, DC 20090 – 6090 USA
or
Sidney R. Yates Federal Building
201, 14 Street, SW at Independence Ave., SW Washington, DC
www.fs.fed.us   (then search for 'volunteers')

- Region 1–Northern Region, Federal Bldg., P.O. Box 7669, Missoula, Montana 59807, tel. ++1 (406) 329 3675
- Region 2–Rocky Mountain, P.O. Box 25127, Lakewood, Colorado 80255, tel. ++1 (303) 275 5350
- Region 3–Southwestern, 333 Broadway, SE, Albuquerque, New Mexico 87102, tel. ++1 (505) 842 3292
- Region 4–Intermountain, Federal Bldg. 324, 25th St., Ogden, Utah 84401, tel. ++1 (801) 625 5412
- Region 5–Pacific Southwest, 1323 Club Drive, Vallejo, California 94592, tel. ++1 (707) 562 8737
- Region 6–Pacific Northwest, 333 SW First Avenue, P.O. Box 3623 Portland, Oregon 97208–3623, tel. ++1 (503) 808 2180
- Region 8–Southern, 1720 Peachtree Rd., NW, Atlanta, Georgia 30309, tel. ++1 (404) 347 4191
- Region 9–Eastern, 310 W. Wisconsin Ave., Suite 580, Milwaukee, Wisconsin 53203, tel. ++1 (414) 297 3600
- Region 10–Alaska, Federal Office Bldg., P.O. Box 21628 Juneau, Alaska 99802–1628, tel. ++1 (907) 586 8806
- Pacific Northwest Research Station, 333 SW 1st Avenue, P.O. Box 3890, Portland, Oregon 9208–3890, tel. ++1 (503) 808 2592
- North Central Research Station, 1992 Folwell Avenue, St. Paul Minnesota 55108, tel. ++1 (651) 649 5285
- Rocky Mountain Research Station, 240 W. Prospect Road, Fort Collins, Colorado 80526–2098, tel. ++1 (970) 498 1100
- Northeastern Area State and Private Forestry, 11 Campus Drive, Newtown Square, Pennsylvania 19073, tel. ++1 (610) 557 4200
- International Institute of Tropical Forestry, P.O. Box 25000, UPR Experimental Station, Rio Piedras, Puerto Rico 00928, tel. ++1 (787) 766 6302

Desc.: The Forest Service manages and protects the National Forest System and cooperates with private forest and woodland owners, State and local government agencies and private organisations. It performs research for improving the quality of the forest and forest products. Volunteer service is needed in US National Forests because the Forest Service has a limited budget. The programme goal is to provide fulfilling work experience to volunteers while accomplishing necessary tasks.

Spp.: Various in the United States.

Hab.: Various in the United States.

Loc.: National Forests throughout the United States.

Dur.: Inquire with the National Forest of choice.

Per.: Inquire with the National Forest of choice.

L. term: Inquire with the National Forest of choice.

Age: No age limit. Those under 18 must have the written consent of a parent or guardian.

Qualif.: No specific skills required. Volunteers must be in good health to allow them to perform their duties without risk to themselves or others. A medical examination may be required for some tasks. Persons with disabilities are encouraged to volunteer.

Work: Maintaining and hosting campgrounds, working at visitor centres and ranger stations, planting trees, presenting environmental education programmes, building and repairing structures, taking photographs. Training provided if necessary.

Lang.: English.

Accom.: Housing may be available. Inquire with National Forest of choice.

Cost: Some expenses such as transportation, lodging, subsistence and uniforms may be reimbursed on a case-by-case basis.

Applic.: Write or call the volunteer coordinator of the region of interest. See list in the previous page or from the directory on the website: www.fs.fed.us/intro/directory/orgdir.shtml (or search for 'directory').

U.S. FISH AND WILDLIFE SERVICE

Alaska Regional Office
Division of Refuges, 1011 E. Tudor Rd.
Anchorage, Alaska 99503   USA
Tel.: ++1 (907) 786 3391 – Fax: ++1 (907) 786 3976
E-mail: bill-kirk@fws.gov
www.r7.fws.gov

Desc.: The U.S. Fish and Wildlife Service mission is to conserve, protect and enhance fish, wildlife and their habitats for the continuing benefit of the American people. Primary responsibilities are for migratory birds, endangered species, freshwater and anadromous fisheries. The Service has 7 regional offices, headquarters in Washington, D.C. and many field units; wildlife refuges, fish hatcheries and research labs.

Spp.: Migratory birds, fish.

Hab.: Arctic and sub-Arctic coastal areas, deciduous and coniferous forests, taiga, tundra.

Loc.: Alaska, USA.

Dur.: From a few days to several months.

Per.: Year round, primarily April to September.

Age: Min. 18.

Qualif.: Experience with the life sciences is preferable. Some positions require teaching, public speaking or other specialized skills.

Lang.: English.

Cost: Volunteers must pay their way to the United States. Assistance is available at times for travel within the US, for US applicants. Travel, food and lodging are usually covered while on duty .

Applic.: Contact the Alaska Coordinator (only for Alaska positions), Dr. William L. Kirk, and request an application form.

Notes: Non-US citizens must plan well ahead and secure a proper visa or entry papers to enter the US and work as a volunteer. For positions outside Alaska prospective volunteers should contact the national USFWS website (www.fws.gov or http://volunteers.fws.gov), and should not contact the Alaska office; it will slow their application process. The USFWS does not work with whales and dolphins.

U.S. NATIONAL PARK SERVICE

VIP (Volunteers-In-Parks) Program
National Capital Region
1100 Ohio Dr., SW, Washington, DC 20242 USA
Tel.: ++1 (202) 619 7222
www.nps.gov/volunteer/

Desc.: The U.S. National Park Service is officially entrusted with preserving more than 350 national parks in the US Through the VIP (Volunteers-In-Parks) Program, anyone can help conserving the parks' natural and historical resources.

Spp.: Various of North America.

Hab.: Various of North America.

Loc.: National parks throughout the United States.

Dur.: Inquire with the park or the field area of choice.

Per.: Inquire with the park or the field area of choice.

L. term: Inquire with the park of choice.

Age: Min. 18. Persons under 18 years of age must have permission of their parents or guardian or be accompanied by adults in a family or group.

Qualif.: Various skills and talents desired. Reasonably good health is expected. A medical examination may be required for some jobs. Disabled individuals are encouraged to volunteer.

Work: Providing information at a visitor centre, accessioning artifacts into a park's archaeological or historic collection, conducting surveys of plant and animal species in the park or doing construction and repair work on hiking trails. Accepted volunteers receive appropriate training and orientation at the beginning of the service.

Lang.: English.

Accom.: Some of the larger parks may provide free housing for VIPs. Arrangements made between the volunteer and the park.

Cost: Some parks reimburse volunteers for some expenses, such as local travel costs, meals and uniforms. Volunteers must cover the cost of travel to and from the park.

Agents: **Alaska Area Region**, 2525 Gambell St., Room 107, Anchorage, Alaska 99503–2892, tel. ++1 (907) 257 2580.

Intermountain Region, 12795 West Alameda Parkway, Denver, Colorado 80225–0287, tel. ++1 (303) 969 2500.

Midwest Region, 1709 Jackson St., Omaha, Nebraska 68102, tel. ++1 (402) 221 3471.

Northeast Region, U.S. Customs House, 200 Chestnut St. Fifth Floor, Philadelphia, Pennsylvania 19106, tel. ++1 (215) 597 7013.

Pacific West Region, One Jackson Center, 1111 Jackson Street, Suite 700, Oakland, California 94607, tel. ++1 (510) 817 1300.

Southeast Region, 100 Alabama St., SW, 1924 Bldg. Atlanta, Georgia 30303, tel. ++1 (404) 562 3100.

Applic.: The website lists hundred of opportunities (click on opportunities) and gives detailed application contacts for each position. Addresses of parks can be obtained from the Regional offices listed above. Ask for a VIP application form. Prospective volunteers can apply to more than 1 park. Selection for summer positions are usually made between February and April.

Notes: Non–US citizens must obtain a work permit or a special student visa to be accepted as park volunteers. The US Immigration and Naturalisation Service considers the reimbursement to cover out-of-pocket expenses and the free housing offered by the parks as a form of payment for work: since it is illegal for a person travelling under a regular tourist visa in the US to work for pay, the INS can send these persons back to their country without allowing them to enter the US When applying for the VIP programme, be prepared to face the long procedure to obtain the correct permit or visa. There are also insurance requirements for all international volunteers.

VOLUNTEER FOR NATURE

Federation of Ontario Naturalists & Nature Conservancy of Canada
355 Lesmill Road
Don Mills, Ontario M3B 2W8 Canada
Tel: ++1 (416) 444 8419 ext. 222
Fax:++1 (416) 444 9866
E-mail:vfn@ontarionature.org – www.ontarionature.org

Desc.: Together, the Federation of Ontario Naturalists (FON) and the Nature Conservancy of Canada (NCC) are creating new conservation volunteering opportunities in Ontario through their Volunteer for Nature (VfN). VfN's goal is to provide people with opportunities to work as part of a team outdoors, to learn new skills and participate in hands-on conservation projects throughout Ontario's spectacular natural areas.There are 2 types of VfN events. NCC hosts 1-day events called Nature Conservation Days.The FON hosts Ontario Nature Volunteers expeditions, which are 3 – 16 day working vacations.

Hab.: Habitats protected through Volunteer for Nature include limestone alvar, oak savannah, tall grass prairie, Great Lakes shoreline, Carolinian forest and northern boreal forest.

Loc.: Ontario, Canada.

Dur.: Min. 1 day, max. 16 days.

Per.: April to October.

Age: Min.16 for Nature Conservation Days; min.19 to join Ontario Nature Volunteers.

Qualif.: No specific qualifications required. Must be reasonably fit.

Lang.: English.

Cost: Nature Conservation Days are free. Ontario Nature Volunteers expeditions have a fee to cover direct expenses, including food and the transit of leaders and tools to the work sites.

Accom.: Accommodations range from basic camping to dormitory style to Park staff houses, lodges, field study centres or bed and breakfasts. All volunteers are responsible for contributing to cooking and general duties at the accommodation.

Applic.: For registration contact Steve Robinson at address above.

Notes: See website for full Volunteer for Nature Schedule of Events.

VOLUNTEERS FOR OUTDOOR COLORADO (VOC)

600 South Marion Parkway
Denver, Colorado 80209–2597   USA
Tel.: ++1 (303) 715 1010
Fax: ++1 (303) 715 1212
E-mail: voc@voc.org
www.voc.org

Desc.: This non-profit organisation, founded in 1984, promotes and fosters citizen and visitor responsibility for Colorado's public lands. VOC organises 1-day to week-long conservation and trail construction projects and provides volunteers and training to land management agencies, other non-profits and user groups. The VOC Network serves as a resource opportunity to state, federal and local agencies: with more than 900 volunteer positions in botany, construction, environmental education, recreation, research, wildlife, visitor information and trail work.

Hab.: Urban gardens and parks, streams, lakes, mountains.

Loc.: Urban and natural areas, National Parks, National Forests, State Parks, mountains of Colorado, USA.

Dur.: 1 day to 4 months.

Per.: Year round.

L. term: For projects listed in the VOC Network.

Age: Min. 9 for VOC projects; under16 must be accompanied by an adult. Min. age for Network positions varies with agency.

Qualif.: Skilled carpenters desired. Network qualifications vary.

Lang.: English.

Cost: No cost, people may receive room and board.

Applic.: Request application form.

Notes: VOC volunteers can later attend Crew Leader Training, which involves classes, a field weekend and apprenticeship. Contact VOC for a catalogue of other volunteer opportunities. The VOC website has an excellent list of links to other volunteering organisations in the US and in Colorado.

THE WILDERNESS TRUST

The Oast House
Hankham, Near Pevensey, East Sussex BN24 5AP UK
Tel.: ++44 (1323) 461 730
Fax: ++44 (1323) 761 913
E-mail: info@wilderness-trust.org
www.wilderness-trust.org

Desc.: The Wilderness Trust promotes self-financed educational journeys and camps into wilderness areas. Programmes focus on conservation, self discovery and teaching wilderness skills for groups of young people and adults. Groups size is from 6 to 8 people.

Loc.: Junior (13–16) trail programmes are available in Wales. Young programmes (16–18 plus) and adult programmes are available in South Africa, Canada and Wales.

Dur.: Min. 7 days, max. 30 days. Junior Programmes 3 – 5 days. Adult Programmes 7, 14 and up to 30 days.

Qualif.: No specific qualifications required. Must be reasonably fit.

Lang.: English.

Cost: Junior Programme from GB£50 (approx. EUR 80). For all other programmes details are available upon request but costs will depend on length of journey, time of year and context.

Accom.: Normally in the open or in remote bush camps for journeys in Africa and Canada. Basic indoor bunk accommodation is provided in Wales.

Notes: Details of programme itineraries and costs available upon request.

WWF – Italy

Ecotourism and Education Division
Via Orseolo 12
20144 Milano Italy
Tel.: ++39 (02) 831 33245 – Fax: ++39 (02) 831 33222
E-mail: turismo@wwf.it
www.wwf.it

Desc.: WWF Italy is the largest national environmental association, managing 100 wildlife refuges. Volunteers are recruited for field study projects, restoration activities and fire prevention workcamps.
Spp.: Birds, wolves, sea turtles, whales, dolphins, bears.
Hab.: Temperate and tropical seas, alpine, wetlands, lakes.
Loc.: Brazil, France, Greece, Ireland, Italy, Scotland.
Dur.: Min. 5 days; max. 2 weeks.
Per.: Summer. Every year programmes are posted on the webpage in March.
L. term: Inquire with organisation.
Age: Min. 18.
Qualif.: Previous experience and specific qualifications are not required.
Lang.: Italian, English.
Cost: Starting from EUR 200 (approx.GB£130), insurance, food and accommodation included.
Agents: WWF has offices in many countries. International volunteers can apply to WWF International, 1196 Gland, Switzerland.
Applic.: Request an application form. Volunteers must be WWF members to participate.
Notes: Contact your national WWF office for information on workcamps in your country or on international volunteering opportunities. For a complete list of national offices see www.wwf.org.

YCI – Youth Challenge International

20 Maud Street, Suite 305
Toronto, Ontario M5V 2M5 Canada
Tel.: ++1 (416) 504 3370
Fax: ++1 (416) 504 3376
E-mail: generalinfo@yci.org
www.yci.org

Desc.: Youth Challenge International combines community development, health promotion and environmental work in adventurous projects carried out by teams of volunteers aged 18–30. Volunteers are accepted from across the world and represent different backgrounds. Conditions are basic and work schedules are demanding. Experienced staff teams ensures projects are dynamic and results oriented. Self-discovery, personal growth and community development are key elements.

Spp.: Rainforest and riverine fauna.

Hab.: Rainforest.

Loc.: Cuba, Nicaragua, Costa Rica, Guyana and Vanuatu.

Dur.: 5-, 6- and 10-weeks projects.

L. term: Placements for field staff are for 4–6 months at a time. Upon review, volunteers can work for another placement period.

Age: Min. 18, max. 30.

Qualif.: No specific qualifications are needed.

Lang.: English.

Cost: Cost range from CDN$2,700 to CDN $3,500 (US$1,700–2,200) plus airfare. Volunteers must pay for inoculations and personal equipment.

Agents: Partner organisations are present in Guyana (Youth Challenge Guyana), Costa Rica (Reto Juevenil) and Australia (Youth Challenge Australia).

Applic.: Participants and field staff can apply at any time; applications can be submitted on-line.

Notes: Due to insurance limitations YCI is unable to accept applications from US citizens.

PROJECT LIST

ACORUS RESTORATION NATIVE PLANT NURSERY

R.R. 1 Walsingham, Ontario, NOE 1XO Canada
Tel.: ++1 (519) 586 2603
E-mail: info@ecologyart.com
www.ecologyart.com

Desc.: Acorus Restoration is a Native Plant Nursery on a 95-acre former tobacco farm, which is in the process of being restored.
Spp.: Southern Ontario native vegetation.
Hab.: Carolinian landscape, sandy soils near Long Point World Biosphere Reserve on Lake Erie.
Loc.: Southwestern Ontario, Canada.
Travel: 2 hours southwest of Toronto, Ontario.
Dur.: Min. 2 months.
Per.: March to November.
Age: Min. 18.
Qualif.: Ability to work long hours and to endure heat or cold, insects, occasional heavy lifting.
Work: Volunteers will participate in all duties in the nursery: from seeding, seed cleaning and collecting to planting and greenhouse maintenance.
Lang.: English. French can be mustered by coordinators.
Accom.: Bunkhouse with cooking facilities and shower.
Cost: No fees. Volunteers must provide own transportation and some food. A small weekly stipend is also provided.
L.term: Not at the present time.
Agents: Contact the project directly with the information provided above.
Applic.: Apply via e-mail, telephone or mail.
Notes: See website for basic information and contact the project for further questions.

ADRIATIC DOLPHIN PROJECT

Blue World – Plavi Svjet
Zad Bone 11 – 51551 Veli Losinj   Croatia
Tel./Fax: ++385 (51) 236 406
E-mail: adp@blue-world.org
www.adp.hr or www.blue-world.org

Desc: Founded 1987 by the Tethys Research Institute (see Organisation list) this project has been an ongoing study of the ecology of the bottlenose dolphin inhabiting the Cres and Losinj waters (Croatia, northern Adriatic Sea). These dolphins are now among the most intensively studied in the Mediterranean Sea. The size of this community has been estimated at around 100–150 individuals. The majority of these have been identified and are regularly resighted and followed in their daily movements. The standard research procedure includes photo-ID and behavioural sampling. Information on dolphin habitat use, association patterns and reproductive rate are also obtained.

Spp.: Bottlenose dolphin (*Tursiops truncatus*). Other marine species occasionally observed include: marine turtles, blue sharks, tuna, cormorants, seagulls, terns and other marine birds.

Hab.: Coastal waters.

Loc: Cres–Losinj archipelago, northern Adriatic Sea (Croatia).

Travel: The island of Losinj can be easily reached by bus, via Rijeka, from Trieste (Italy), Zagreb (Croatia) and Ljubljana (Slovenia), or (during the summer) by ferry from Venice or hydrofoil from Trieste (Italy); all these cities have major train and flight connections.

Dur.: 12 days. Up to 5 volunteers can participate in each shift.

Per.: May to September.

L. term: Extra days beyond the initial 12 can be arranged.

Age: Min.18.

Qualif.: Interest in the research and positive motivation is required. Volunteers must be physically fit and able to endure long hours, possibly in hot sun or in harsh sea conditions on a small boat.

the team cooperates in data handling and analysis. Slide projections and lectures are organised and volunteers are also free to visit the island and enjoy its sights.

Work: Behavioural observations and photo-ID of the dolphins from the inflatable boat. With good weather researchers and volunteers conduct boat surveys. With bad weather volunteers stay at the base, entering and analysing data and matching the catalogued slides. Lectures on the dolphin biology are also carried out by the researchers.

Lang.: English. Italian and German are also spoken by researchers.

Accom.: Shared rooms in a house in Veli Losinj. Volunteers take part in cooking and housekeeping.

Cost: Min. EUR/US$600, max. EUR/US$700 (approx. GB£ 400– 470), depending on the season. Volunteers must confirm that they have personal insurance. The contributions of volunteers are used to defray part of the research costs and food. Fees do not include travel expenses. All tourists coming to Losinj are required to pay the local touristic fee (about EUR/US$1/ day for the duration of the programme).

Applic.: Write, e-mail, phone or refer to the website for further information. A downloadable application form is available on the website. Given the limited availability of places and the high number of applications, early booking is suggested.

Notes: From 2–3 researchers reside at the field station with the volunteers. Safety gear for on the boat is provided. Volunteers must be aware that they are participating in scientific research rather than a vacation programme.

AFRICAN CONSERVATION TRUST, South Africa

P.O.Box 310, 3652 Linkhills South Africa
Tel.: ++27 (31) 201 6180
Fax: ++27 (31) 201 6180
E-mail: info@projectafrica.com
www.projectafrica.com

Desc.: The African Conservation Trust in collaboration with the University of Malawi and University of Natal has initiated a project to quantify and map the distribution of the hippo population in Lake Malawi.

Spp.: Hippopotamus (*Hippopotamus amphibius*).

Hab.: Fresh water tropical lake.

Loc.: Lake Malawi, Malawi.

Travel: Flight to Lilongwe, where volunteers are met.

Dur.: From 2 weeks up to 1 year.

Per.: Year round, this is a permanent project.

L. term: Will accept long term volunteers.

Age: Min. 18.

Qualif.: Volunteers must have good physical health, a very flexible attitude, be able to swim and to withstand long working hours on a boat and in a remote environment.

Work: Travel by boat and road, mapping hippo distribution with GPS, ecological study of larger pods, protective mechanisms, local education and training. Working closely with local communities.

Lang.: English.

Accom.: Volunteers must provide their own tents.

Cost: Varies according to length of stay: 2 weeks GB£400 (approx. EUR/US$600), 3rd week GB£100 (approx. EUR/US$150), and every week thereafter GB£50 (approx. EUR/US$75). For example: 3 months cost GB£ 950 (approx. EUR/US$1,425).

Applic.: Request application form.

Notes: The trust has other projects in Malawi: a reforestation project, an environmental education project and a research base construction project.

EL AMARGAL TROPICAL RAINFOREST RESEARCH

Fundacion Inguede, Colombia
The Ecovolunteer Network
Meyersweg 29   7553 AX Hengelo The Netherlands
Tel.: ++31 (74) 250 8250 – Fax: ++31 (74) 250 6572
E-mail: info@ecovolunteer.org
www.ecovolunteer.org

Desc.: The project focuses on the preservation of the tropical rainforest. It organises educational programmes in support of the local communities by developing small-scaled economic activities for a sustainable use of forest products.

Spp.: Tropical plants and animals.

Hab.: Tropical rainforest.

Loc.: Northwestern Colombia.

Travel: Airplane to Nuqui, Colombia. Book and coordinate travel with The Ecovolunteer Network or national agent. Volunteers will be picked up at the airstrip and taken to El Amargal by boat (approx. 1-hour trip). If the tide and weather conditions do not allow to sail the same day, volunteers must spend the night in the village at their own expense. There are no roads connecting this part of the coast to the rest of Colombia: the only way to reach the area is by air from Medellin or by boat from the southern port Buenaventura to Nuqui.

Dur.: Min. 3 weeks.

Per.: Year round.

L. term: Volunteers can stay as long as they want.

Age: Min. 18.

Qualif.: Volunteers must have good physical health, a very flexible attitude, be able to swim and walk long distances. People who are very impatient or who cannot work under stress may experience some problems during this programme. The humidity of the working area is at a constant high level.

Work: Volunteers assist researchers with field work: measure and mark trees, climb trees with special equipment to collect botanical samples, observe flowering and fruiting tree species, collect plants and mushrooms for botanical research, record birdsongs. Volunteers also assist with designing and constructing a footpath through the jungle, help with opening up certain inaccessible areas in the forest (e.g., build small bridges, remove fallen trees, etc.), help with the construction of infrastructure (house and lab), collect material (palm leaves, rocks) for construction work and transport supplies for the station.

Lang.: English, Spanish.

Accom.: Volunteers stay at the Station with the Colombian manager and the temporary Colombian researchers. The Station is lighted with oil-lamps—there is no electricity or radio equipment.

Cost: US$1,200 for the first 3 weeks and US$265 for each additional week. Not included: travel to and from Colombia, transfers, airport taxes and excess luggage charges, visa, personal expenses, travel and cancellation insurance (all participants should carry both), excursions.

Agents: Local agents of The Ecovolunteer Network: see website.

Applic.: The Ecovolunteer Network (see Organisation list).

Notes: The station is located in a remote area: volunteers should not have romantic expectations about the life there, which can be very primitive and sometimes difficult. Volunteers must be able to appreciate this situation and be tolerant.

ARFA – ASOCIACION DE RESCATE DE FAUNA

Calle La Vista, Edif. La Vista, Apto. 11–B, Colinas de Los Caobos,
Caracas 1050   Venezuela
Tel.: ++58 (212) 782 4182
Fax: ++58 (212) 793 4421
E-mail: valio1@cantv.net
www.geocities.com/arfavenezuela/index.html

Desc.: ARFA is an NGO devoted to the conservation of wildlife in Venezuela, through educational programmes and its centre where animals of the central plains are rescued and rehabilitated.

Spp.: Capuchin monkey (*cebus olivacea*), howler monkey (*allouata sealicus*), aquatic turtles and terrapins, parrots, macaw (*Ara spp.*). Occasionaly deer (*Manzama americana*), ant eating bear (*Myrmecophaga tridactila*), iguana, alligator, some birds of prey and many other bird species from the area.

Hab.: Plains or flatlands, 'llanos' (similar to savannah), rainforest.

Loc.: Flatlands of the Edo.Cojedes, between the towns of Las Vegas and Tirado, Central Venezuela.

Travel: Airplane to Caracas , car or bus from Caracas to project area. Transportation from Caracas to project area will be provided.

Dur.: Min. 1 month.

Per.: Year round.

L. term: There is no limit of time for long-term stays.

Age: Min. 20.

Qualif.: High school diploma, veterinary or biology studies helpful but not necessary and good physical condition.

Work: Feeding the animals, facility maintenance, assistance with the ecological educational programmes, wildlife record keeping and observation, assistance on wildlife rehabilitation.

Lang.: Spanish, but staff also understands English.

Accom.: Private room in a house with indoor bathroom and shower.

Cost: Room, accommodation and simple meals are provided.

Applic.: Via e-mail with the subject heading: 'Volunteer program'. In the text, include CV, letter of intentions and possible dates.

Notes: Web page has other volunteers' experiences. Health insurance and vaccinations (yellow fever, tetanus and rabies) mandatory.

AYUTTHAYA ELEPHANT CAMP, Thailand

Ayutthaya Elephant Palace & Royal Kraal and Elephant Care
Assembly – Pathon Rd., Ayutthaya Historical Park
Phranakornsri Ayutthaya province, 13000 Thailand
Tel.: ++66 (35) 211 001/321982 – Fax: ++66 (35) 211 001
E-mail: elephant@ksc.th.com – ayutthaya_elephant@hotmail.com
www.saveelephant.com

Desc.:	Asian elephants are endangered species. The Ayutthaya Elephant Palace & Royal and Elephant Care Assembly is striving to help the elephants survive into the future in a sustainable way. The importance of the elephant in Thai Culture and the unique life-time relationship that the Mahout creates with the elephant are other important aspects that the project tries to preserve.
Spp.:	Asian elephant (*Elephus maximus*).
Hab.:	Tropical rainforest.
Loc.:	Ayutthaya Elephant Palace & Royal Kraal World Heritage Site in Ayutthaya province.
Travel:	1 hour drive north from Bangkok International Airport.
Dur.:	Min. 3 weeks, max. 3 months (2 volunteers at a time).
Per.:	Year round.
L.term:	Only after initial period and approval by project manager.
Age:	Min. 18 in good physical health.
Qualif.:	No particular skills needed. Veterinarians are especially welcome as are specialists in animal science or other relevant fields.
Work:	Volunteers must take initial training with the elephants and an examination to receive a certificate before working with the elephants. Volunteers learn also about Thai rural culture.
Lang.:	English.
Accom.:	Bunkhouse and communal facilities.
Cost:	US$750/month (includes accommodation); inquire for details.
Applic.:	Send e-mail to request an application form.
Notes:	Health insurance is needed. The Project has 2 satellite projects: the Kanchanaburi Elephant Camp in Kanchanaburi province and the Koh Chang Elephant Camp in Trad province.

BELUGA RESEARCH PROJECT, Russia

The Ecovolunteer Network
Meyersweg 29   7553 AX Hengelo The Netherlands
Tel.: ++31 (74) 250 8250
Fax: ++31 (74) 250 6572
E-mail: info@ecovolunteer.org
www.ecovolunteer.org

Desc.: Each year in July and August a large group of belugas assemble near the coast of the Solovetsky archipelago in the southern White Sea. This project, conducted by scientists from the Shirshov Oceanological Institute of the Russian Academy for Sciences, examines the behaviour and communication of these belugas, which gather in this area to socialize.

Spp.: Beluga (*Delphinapterus leucas*).

Hab.: Subarctic marine and coast.

Loc.: Solovetski Islands, Archangelsk District, White Sea Russia.

Travel: Airplane to Solovetski via Archangelsk; meeting at the airport.

Dur.: Min. 2 weeks.

Per.: June, July, August.

L. term: Not possible.

Age.: Min. 18.

Qualif.: No particular skills needed, good health.

Work: Volunteers and researchers observe belugas, inform visitors of the beluga project, build a new observation post, keep the encampment in repair or improve the camp. Volunteers also prepare food, gather timber in the forest or by beach combing, cut wood, fetch groceries from the village, fish and gather mushrooms.

Lang.: English.

Accom.: Camping in tents.

Cost: Approx. US$725 for 2 weeks, approx. US$ 50 for every extra day.

Agents: Local agents of The Ecovolunteer Network: see website.

Applic.: The Ecovolunteer Network (see Organisation list).

BIESZCZADY WOLF PROJECT, Poland

The Ecovolunteer Network
Meyersweg 29   7553 AX Hengelo The Netherlands
Tel.: ++31 (74) 250 8250
Fax: ++31 (74) 250 6572
E-mail: info@ecovolunteer.org
www.ecovolunteer.org

Desc.: Started in 1988 by W. Smietana, an associated biologist of the Polish Academy of Science, the project aims to improve protection of wolves in Poland and raise public awareness to abolish hunting. Researchers collect faeces and prey leftovers, observe prey, apply transmitters and track wolves and red deer.

Spp.: Wolf (*Canis lupus*), brown bear, lynx, red deer, moose.

Hab.: Boreal forest.

Loc.: Bieszczady National Park (BNP), 300 km south of Krakow.

Travel: Airplane or train to Krakow.

Dur.: Min. 1 week from Monday to Sunday.

Per.: January to November.

L. term: Volunteer can stay for more than 1 week.

Age: Min. 18.

Qualif.: Good physical health and able to walk 15 km/day (in snow in winter). Those with hearing impairments or severe weight problems might have difficulty with this programme.

Work: Assist the researchers with the work described above. Training on research methods, slide-shows and lectures are scheduled.

Lang.: English.

Accom.: Simple National Park Huts or Agrotourist Farms with shared rooms and communal facilities.

Cost: Approx. EUR 585 for 1 week, EUR 350 for each extra week, for accommodation, meals, Park work permit and transfers between the park and Krakow. Insurance not included.

Agents: National agencies of the Ecovolunteer Network.

Applic.: The Ecovolunteer Network www.ecovolunteer.org.

Notes: Woody and marshy terrain requires strong walking shoes and waterproof and windproof clothing. Expect low morning temperatures in autumn (-5°C to +5°C) and winter (to -30°C).

BIMINI LEMON SHARK PROJECT, Bahamas

Bimini Biological Field Station
c/o RSMAS University of Miami
9300 SW 99 Street, Miami, Florida 33176 – 2050 USA
Tel./Fax: ++1 (305) 274 0628
E-mail: sgruber@rsmas.miami.edu
www.miami.edu/sharklab/

Desc.:	Study of the feeding, predator-prey relations, growth, survival, movements and community relations of the lemon shark using field techniques and computer modelling/simulations. Disciplines of systems ecology, bioenergetics, life history studies, population genetics, ethology and sensory biology involved.
Spp.:	Lemon shark, (*Negaprion brevirostris*) and its prey organisms, primarily mojarra fish, (*Gerres spp.*).
Hab.:	Coastal reefs, mangrove forest, seagrass meadows.
Loc.:	Bimini Bahamas, 85 km east of Miami across the Florida straits.
Travel:	Flight to Fort Lauderdale International Airport; taxi to Fort Lauderdale Executive Airport for Bimini Island Air charter.
Dur.:	Min. 1 month.
Per.:	Year round.
L. term:	With project leader's approval.
Age:	Min.22, max. 35.
Qualif.:	Students or graduates with a biology background are given priority, preferably with an interest in graduate school. Also necessary: good boating skills, swimming and computer literacy.
Work:	Field research on boats in shallow water all hours of the day; cooking, household and mechanical maintenance, etc.
Lang.:	English.
Accom.:	Wood frame, air-conditioned house with 4 person bunk beds in small dorm-type rooms.
Cost:	Room and board approx. US$525/month. Transportation not included. Return flight to Bimini approx. US$220.
Applic.:	Contact Dr. Samuel H. Gruber or Marie Gruber.

BIRDS OF TORTUGUERO, Costa Rica

Caribbean Conservation Corporation
4424 NW 13th Street, Suite A–1
Gainesville, Florida 32609   USA
Tel.: ++1 (352) 373 6441 Fax: ++1 (352) 375 2449
E-mail: resprog@cccturtle.org
www.cccturtle.org

Desc.: Tortuguero is the most important site in Costa Rica for resident and migratory neotropical birds. Caribbean Conservation Corporation (CCC) is working to gather information on the status of the bird populations and the number of species residing or migrating here (up to 300).

Spp.: Resident and migratory neotropical birds.

Hab.: Tropical coast.

Loc.: Tortuguero, Costa Rica.

Travel: Airplane to San José, where participants are met.

Dur.: 1, 2 or 3 weeks.

Per.: March to June and August to November.

L. term: Volunteers can stay longer than 2 weeks with prior approval.

Age: Min. 18.

Qualif.: Volunteers must be in good physical condition, able to live in a rustic setting and tolerant of harsh weather.

Work: Assist researchers in mist netting, point counts, identification and transects.

Lang.: English.

Accom.: Dormitory style with shared baths in research station.

Cost: US$1,210 for 1 week; US$1,650 for 2 weeks; US$1,975 for 3 weeks. Cost includes 2 nights in San José, transfers to Tortuguero, all room and board at CCC station in Tortuguero.

Agents: Contact the organisation directly.

Applic.: On-line application form to be submitted with a US$200 deposit.

BLACK HOWLER MONKEY PROJECT, Argentina

Refugio del Caraya
Paraje Tiu Mayu, La Cumbre, CP: 5178, Cordoba Argentina
Tel.: ++54 (351) 457 6364 – Tel./Fax: ++54 (351) 4713852
E-mail: marianacarrascosa@yahoo.com.ar
      refugiodelcaraya@yahoo.com.ar

Desc: The centre works to rescue and rehabilitate ex-pet monkeys. The monkeys are re-educated and released in the forest, their original environment . The centre conducts also environmental education programmes.

Spp.: Black howler monkey (*Alouatta caraya*).

Hab.: Mountain forest.

Loc.: La Cumbre, Cordoba, Argentina.

Travel: Airplane to Buenos Aires, then bus to La Cumbre, by taxi, horse or foot to the centre.

Dur.: There are no limits of duration.

Per.: Year round.

L. term: Volunteers can stay as long as they want.

Age: Min. 18.

Qualif.: Ability to work with cold, snowy, rainy or hot days, and with other animals like pumas, or farm animals, in a very rustic environment. Free-ranging animals observations are often done on horseback. Horses are also used to go to the nearby town (11 km).

Work: Feeding the monkeys, cleaning the cages of the monkeys in rehabilitation, care of the orphans, observation and study of the free-ranging groups. Volunteers have the possibility of working on weekends in the local zoo with an NGO called Guardazoo.

Lang.: Spanish, English.

Accom.: A bedroom separated from the main house with bathroom.

Cost: Approx. US$ 250-300/month for room and board.

Applic.: By fax or e-mail.

BLACK RHINO, Kenya

Earthwatch Institute
3 Clock Tower Place – Suite 100, Box 75
Maynard, MA 01754   USA
Tel.: ++1 (978) 461 0081 – (800) 776 0188 (toll free in US/Canada)
Fax: ++1 (978) 461 2332
E-mail: info@earthwatch.org – www.earthwatch.org

Desc.: The number of Black Rhinos in Kenya has declined from an estimated 20,000 in 1970 to about 500 today. The principal reason for this decline is unrelenting poaching—the rhino is sought for the medicinal and decorative use of its prestigious horn. This project is in the enclosed 100 km^2 Sweetwaters Black Rhino Reserve, which has an healthy and well protected rhino population. But new concerns have arisen: competition with other large herbivores, predation of calves by hyenas and lions and an excessive concentration of rhinos. Only an accurate study of these factors can help preserving the balance of the ecosysitem.

Spp.: Black rhino (*Diceros bicornis*), zebra, impala, kudu, lion, leopard, hyena, wild dog, giraffe, elephant, wildebeest, buffalo.

Hab.: Savannah with acacias.

Loc.: Sweetwaters Black Rhino Reserve, Nanyuki, Kenya.

Travel: Airplane to Nairobi then bus to Nanyuki.

Dur.: 12 days.

Per.: January, February, August, September.

L. term: No long-term volunteer opportunities available.

Age: Min. 16.

Qualif.: No special skills required.

Work: Volunteers observe rhinos and other large mammals and gather data on vegetation and feeding preferences of the competing species. Acacia trees damage is also assessed.

Lang.: English.

Accom.: Confortable single rooms in the Reserve Research Centre.

Cost: US$ 2,245 (GB£1,585).

Agents: Earthwatch Institute (see Organisation list).

Applic.: A deposit of GB£200 (US$250) will be required.

BLACK SHEEP INN, Ecuador

Andres Hammerman & Michelle Kirby
P.O. Box 05-01-240 Latacunga, Cotopaxi Ecuador
Tel.:   ++ 593 (3) 814 587
Fax: ++ 593 (3) 814 588 (call ahead)
E-mail: info@blacksheepinn.com
www.blacksheepinn.com

Desc.: A small Ecological Lodge in the Ecuadorian Sierra. It grows its organic vegetables, uses composting toilets, gray water systems and a recycling programme. Volunteers learn how low impact sustainable tourism works. A small reforestation programme is also carried out with native tree species. Lodge managers also help the local community and in conservation work in the Iliniza Ecological Reserve.

Spp.: The Reserve has over 172 species of birds; it also hosts the endangered Andean spectacled bear (*tremarctos ornatus*).

Hab.: High Andean Sierra and Andean Cloud Forest.

Loc.: Western Cordillera of Central Ecaudor, Cotopaxi.

Travel: Flight to Quito, then bus to Chugchilan and to the Inn.

Dur.: Min. 1 month.

Per.: Year round.

L. term: Long term welcome after initial period.

Age: Min. 25, no max.

Qualif.: Volunteers must be fit and physically active. No allergies, to animals: dogs, llamas, sheep, chickens and ducks. Useful skills are: small business administration, farm work, trip leading, hotel service, computer skills and construction.

Work: Volunteers help in the lodge and in taking care of guests needs (hiking and travel information, etc.) general maintenance, gardening, cooking and cleaning, animal care and participating in all the hikes, horseback rides and excursions.

Lang.: English is essential, Spanish helpful.

Accom.: Comfortable private room at the Inn with full bedding.

Cost: First week of trial period volunteers pay US$7.50/day for room and board. After trial week, room and board are usually free.

Applic.: Send e-mail or visit website for more information.

BLACK VULTURE PROTECTION, Bulgaria

BTCV
36 St. Mary's Street Wallingford
Oxfordshire OX10 OEU   UK
Tel.: ++44 (1491) 821 600
Fax: ++44 (1491) 839 646
E-mail: information@btcv.org – www.btcv.org

Desc.: The project is carried out with the local organisation "Green Balkan" in a rural and predominantly forested area boasting the second largest number of birds of prey in Europe.

Spp.: Black (cinereous) vulture.

Hab.: Forested area.

Loc.: Eastern Rhodope Mountains (rural and predominantly forested area), Bulgaria.

Travel: Airplane to Sofia (meeting point at the Airport).

Dur.: 2 weeks.

Per.: August.

L. term: Contact organisation for details.

Age: Min. 18.

Qualif.: No specific skills required.

Work: Construct fences and feeding platforms to protect the birds from predators. Build artificial nest sites and feed and monitor the vultures.

Lang.: English.

Accom.: Camping.

Cost: GB£610 (approx. EUR/US$930) (excluding flight).

Agents: BTCV at www.btcv.org.

Applic.: BTCV (see Organisation list).

BOHOROK ENVIRONMENTAL CENTRE

P.O. Box 1472, Medan 20001
Sumatera Utara Indonesia
Tel./Fax: ++62 (61) 570 150/545 061
E-mail: lawang@indosat.net.id – mail@paneco.ch
www.sumatraorangutan.com
www.paneco.ch

Desc.: The Centre originates from a programme started in 1995 to help control the environmental impact of tourism on the Orangutan Rehabilitation Station of Bohorok. The Centre has input in the town planning process and in environmental management programmes (such as water pollution control/ waste water treatment). Other goals include environmental education in general and development of eco-friendly tourism.

Spp.: Orangutan.

Hab.: Tropical rainforest.

Loc.: Bukit Lawang, Bohorok, Langkat, North Sumatra, Indonesia.

Travel: Airplane to Medan, then bus to Bukit Lawang.

Dur.: Min. 2, max. 4 months.

Per.: Year round.

L. term: Inquire with the organisation.

Age: Min. 20.

Qualif.: Specific skills are required depending on the topic. Teamwork capacities and interest in Indonesian culture are important.

Work: Development of the Centre: environmental education (school programme), ecotourism, environmental management (waste, water bio-filtration). Work at the Orangutan Rehabilitation Station will only be possible later in the future.

Lang.: English. Bahasa Indonesian would be helpful.

Accom.: Simple local accommodation. Free housing food not included.

Cost: US$500 for students, US$1,000 for persons with regular income, travel and insurance are covered by the volunteer.

Agents: PanEco Foundation, Ms. Cornelia Jenny, Chileweg 5, CH– 8415 Berg am Irchel, Switzerland, tel.: ++41 (52) 318 2323, fax: ++41 (52) 318 1906, e-mail: mail@paneco.ch

Applic.: Send e-mail to PanEco Foundation.

BONELLI EAGLE PROJECT, Portugal

À Pas de Loup 'Volunteers for Nature'
18, allée des Promenades
26 220 Dieulefit   France
Tel.: ++33 (4) 7546 8018 – Fax: ++33 (4) 7546 8018
E-mail: info@apasdeloup.org
www.apasdeloup.org

Desc.: The Douro and Côa valleys have one of Iberian most important populations of cliff nesting birds (15 breeding pairs of black stork, 300 pairs of griffon vultures, 100 pairs of Egyptian vulture, 20 pairs of golden eagle, 16 pairs of Bonelli's eagle, 15 pairs of peregrine falcon, etc.). In particular Bonelli's eagle is threatened by disturbance, hunting and lack of food as a result of the of decline of rabbits caused by diseases and lack of traditional agriculture and also because of the abandonment of traditional pigeon houses. The project's objectives are: 1) recovering pigeon houses to increase preys for the eagle; 2) decreasing hunting pressure with the creation of non-hunting areas; 3) promoting traditional cereal agriculture practices. Educational activities with students and hunters also exist.

Spp.: Bonelli Eagle (*Hieraaetus fasciatus*).

Hab.: Mediterranean landscape.

Loc.: North east of Portugal, natural international Park of Douro.

Travel: By train until Vilar Formoso.

Dur.: 2 weeks.

Per.: July and August.

L. term: Inquire with the organisation.

Age: Min. 18.

Qualif.: No qualifications required.

Work: Recovering pigeon houses: mainly a manual work. Moments for leisure and cultural/ornithological visits will be organised.

Lang.: English or Portuguese.

Accom.: Camping or in a house.

Cost: Volunteers pay for their food and travel and must join the organisation (16 EUR).

Applic: Send CV and a letter of intentions.

BOTTLENOSE DOLPHIN PROJECT, Belize

Oceanic Society Expeditions
Fort Mason Center, Building E
San Francisco, California 94123 USA
Tel.: ++ 1 (415) 441 1106 – 1 (800) 326 7491 (Toll free in USA)
Fax: ++ 1 (415) 474 3395
englund@ocanicsociety.org – www.oceanic-society.org

Desc.: The Oceanic Society has been studying the behavioural ecology of free-ranging bottlenose dolphins in Belize since 1992 at its Blackbird Caye research station in the pristine waters of coral reef-ringed Turneffe Atoll. This is the first long-term study of dolphins in such a diverse ecosystem. The objective is to examine foraging patterns and social behaviour, as well as continue long-term baseline monitoring of dolphin distribution. Participants work directly with researchers in small teams, from small boats inside the atoll. There will also be some free time for snorkeling and birdwatching.

Spp.: Bottlenose dolphin (*Tursiops truncatus*).

Hab.: Tropical coastal waters.

Loc.: Turneffe Atoll, Belize, Central America.

Travel: Airplane to Belize City.

Dur.: 8 days.

Per.: Year-round.

L. term: Inquire with organisation.

Age: Min. 18.

Qualif.: Volunteers must be able to swim.

Work: Assist researchers with fieldwork such as collecting environmental data, searching for dolphins, recording behaviour, and identifying dolphins individually through natural markings.

Lang.: English.

Accom.: Beachfront cabanas with porches, double rooms with private bath.

Cost: US$1,490, excluding flight.

Applic.: Request application form to be returned with a deposit of US$300.

BOTTLENOSE DOLPHIN PROJECT, Italy

CTS – Centro Turistico Studentesco e Giovanile
Via A. Vesalio 6, 00161 Rome Italy
Tel.: ++39 (06) 44111473/4
Fax: ++39 (06) 44111401
E-mail: ambiente@cts.it
www.cts.it

Desc.: The goals of this research project are to study and protect the bottlenose dolphin in Italy. Research activities include: mapping the distribution of bottlenose dolphins in Italy; determining health status of these dolphins; examining the impact of tourism and fishing activities; and outlining a strategic plan.

Spp.: Bottlenose dolphin (*Tursiops truncatus*).

Hab.: Coastal sea waters.

Loc.: Italian islands of Sardinia. Lampedusa (a little island the southern coast of Sicily).

Travel: The island of Sardinia is easily reached by boat from Civitavecchia (Rome) and Livorno and by plane from all the principal Italian cities. Direct flights to Lampedusa leave from Rome, Milan and Palermo.

Dur.: 7–10 days.

Per.: June to September.

L. term: Inquire with the organisation.

Age: Min. 18 (16 if authorised by a parent).

Qualif.: No particular skills are needed except being able to swim.

Work: Volunteers will undergo a short training period before being involved in data gathering on the behaviour of this marine mammal.

Lang.: Italian, Spanish or English.

Accom: In tents or guestrooms.

Cost: EUR250–700 (approx. GB£160–450) excluding food and transportation.

Agents: CTS regional offices in Italy (see Organisation list).

Applic.: Request application form. Membership to CTS required.

CANO PALMA BIOLOGICAL STATION, Costa Rica

Tortuguero Costa Rica SJO 1882 Tel.: ++(506) 381 4116
COTERC, Canadian Organization for Tropical Education
 and Rainforest Conservation
P.O. Box 335, Pickering, Ontario L1V 2R6, Canada
Tel.:++1 (905) 831 8809 – Fax: ++1 (905) 831 4203
E-mail: coterc@interhop.net – info@coterc.org   www.coterc.org

Desc.: The station serves as a facility for visiting biologists and student groups interested in studying various aspects of neotropical lowland forest biology. The station also supports a volunteer programme.

Spp.: Over 300 bird species, 120 mammal species, 100 reptile and amphibians.

Hab.: Lowland Atlantic tropical wet forest.

Loc.: 9 km north of the village of Tortuguero and Tortuguero National Park, in northeastern Costa Rica.

Travel: Tortuguero is accessible only by bus then boat, or by small airplane from San José. There are no roads nearby. Contact station staff for travel details 2–3 days prior to arrival.

Dur.: Min. 2 weeks.

Per.: Year round.

L. term: Applicants with useful skills will be taken into consideration.

Age: Min. 18.

Qualif.: Volunteers should be enthusiastic, self-starting, in good physical condition and able to fit in with remote field station conditions.

Work.: Participation in the station's activities, including grounds and equipment maintenance, helping out in the kitchen, etc. Assisting visiting researchers.

Lang.: English, Spanish.

Cost: US$100 or colone equivalent per week, in cash. No travellers cheques or personal cheques. Tortuguero has no banks.

Accom.: A 4-bedroom dormitory with bunks capable of sleeping 20 persons. Bedding is provided, but volunteers should bring mosquito nets. Conditions are basic but clean and comfortable.

Applic.: Contact COTERC in Canada.

CAPE TRIBULATION TROPICAL RESEARCH STATION

PMB 5, Cape Tribulation
Qld. 4873
Australia
Tel.: ++61 (7) 4098 00 63 – Fax: ++61 (7) 4098 0147
E-mail: austrop@austrop.org.au
www.austrop.org.au

Desc.: This small field research station (listed as a World Heritage site) is open to all researchers interested in working in the area. It is an independent research facility funded through the Australian Tropical Research Foundation. Station staff conduct research on a wide range of issues, from radio-tracking bats to researching alternative technology.

Spp.: About 12 microbats and 5 mega bats; figs: at least 12 species; angiosperm plant species, many rare and locally endemic. Captive colony of 9 flying foxes (*Pteropus* spp.) at the Station.

Hab.: Rainforest and tropical coastal communities.

Loc.: Australia (far north Queensland).

Travel: Contact the station for travel details.

Dur.: Usually volunteers are accepted for 2 weeks initially.

Per.: Year round.

L. term: Encouraged; duration is negotiable after the first stay.

Age: Over 23 preferred.

Qualif.: Any skills; carpenters, botanists, computer programmers, etc. Researchers must provide a proposed research summary.

Work: From routine maintenance to assisting with research projects.

Lang.: English.

Accom.: The station has bunkhouse accommodation and 2 air-con labs.

Cost: US$15/day for food and accommodation. Researchers and assistants pay more depending on the external funding available. Rates are negotioable for overseas volunteers.

Applic.: Applications should be sent via e-mail (be prepared to send reminders) to the Station director. Also send a brief CV with photo and a statement of research interests. Faxes can only be received during working hours (recognise time differences).

Notes: The climate and conditions can be difficult in this remote area.

CARETTA RESEARCH PROJECT

Savannah Science Museum
P.O.Box 9841
Savannah, Georgia 31412 USA
Tel.: ++ 1 (912) 447 8655 – Fax: ++1 (912) 447 8656
E-mail: wassawCRP@aol.com
www.carettaresearchproject.org

Desc.: Since 1973, the Savannah Science Museum, in co-operation with the U.S. Fish and Wildlife Service and the Wassaw Island Trust has been conducting a research and conservation programme on the endangered loggerhead sea turtle. The program's purpose is to learn more about population levels, trends, and nesting habits of loggerheads. It also hopes to enhance the survival of eggs and hatchlings and to involve the public in this effort.

Spp.: Loggerhead sea turtle (*Caretta caretta*).

Hab.: Coastal barrier island.

Loc.: Wassaw Island, about 10 miles south of Savannah.

Travel: Bus or airplane to Savannah, then boat to Wassaw. The island is accessible only by boat.

Dur.: 1 week.

Per.: May to September.

L. term: Inquire with organisation.

Age: Min. 15.

Qualif.: No previous experience required.

Work: Volunteers patrol the beaches in search of female turtles, tag and measure the animals, record data, monitor the nests and escort hatchlings to the sea.

Lang.: English.

Accom.: Rustic cabins (dormitory style).

Cost: US$550/week. The registration fee is tax-deductible and includes lodging, meals, leadership/instruction and transportation to and from the island.

Applic.: Full payment must accompany the application (refund is granted if cancellation takes place at least 60 days prior to departure).

Notes: Academic credit may be available.

CARPATHIAN LARGE CARNIVORE PROJECT

Str. Dr. Ioan Senchea 162,
2223 Zarnesti   Romania
Tel.: ++40 (94) 532 798
Fax: ++40 (68) 223 081
E-mail: info@clcp.ro
www.clcp.ro – www.ecovolunteer.org

Desc.: Directed by Christoph Promberger of the Munich Wildlife Society, this project studies wolves and bears through radio-tracking in order to understand their daily movements and habits. Analysis of the impact of human activities (e.g. hunting) on the survival of the species is also part of the research.

Spp.: Wolf (*Canis lupus*), brown bear (*Ursus arctos*), lynx (*Lynx lynx*).

Hab.: Mixed temperate forest.

Loc.: Brasov area, 180 km from Bucarest, Romania.

Travel: Airplane or train to Bucarest, then train to Brasov.

Dur.: 2–4 weeks.

Per.: Year round.

L. term.: Long-term positions are available, at no cost, to biology/ecolgy students who meet specific requirements. See website for details.

Age: Min. 18, max 65.

Qualif.: No particular qualifications required. Volunteers must be physically fit, flexible and able to work throughout the night.

Work: Participants will use radio-tracking techniques, collect biological samples, follow wolves' tracks in the snow (winter). Caring of captive wolves is also included in the activities.

Lang.: English. German and Rumanian welcome.

Accom.: Mountain log cabin and renovated farm house.

Cost: EUR 1,040 for 2 weeks, each extra week EUR 520, including food and accommodation. Volunteers must provide their own transportation to Brasov.

Agents: In Germany: One World Reisen mit Sinnen (www.reisen mitsinnen.de); in Switzerland: Gaea Tours (www.gaea.ch); in all other countries: The Ecovolunteer Network (see Organisation list).

Applic.: Request further information and application form.

Notes: The programme is not taking volunteers in 2003, it will in 2004.

CENTRAL COAST CETACEAN PROJECT

Coastal Ecosystems Research Foundation
Allison Harbour, P.O. Box 124
Port Hardy, British Columbia, V0N 2P0 Canada
Tel.: ++1 (604) 202 9350 – Fax: ++1 (815) 327 0183
E-mail: info@cerf.bc.ca
www.cerf.bc.ca

Desc: The Coastal Ecosystem Research Foundation conducts research from shore stations and a 38-foot converted fishing boat on the distribution, abundance and movements of a group of summer resident grey whales and their environment. Projects include: population census, home-range determination, micro-habitat use, social behaviour on the feeding grounds and toxicology. Graduate student research currently includes work on the migration of grey whales between feeding and breeding grounds and a study of the underwater behaviour of the whales in relation to the bottom topography and distribution of their prey. Studies on other marine mammal species include abundance, distribution and association patterns of humpback whales, Pacific white-sided dolphins, harbour seals and killer whales. In some years, depending on funding and staffing, research is also conducted on the biodiversity of the intertidal, subtidal and coastal forest ecosystems.

Spp.: Marine mammals: grey whales (*Eschrichtius robustus*), killer whales (*Orcinus orca*), humpback whales (*Megaptera novaeangliae*), Pacific white-sided dolphins (*Lagenorhynchus obliquidens*).

Hab.: Northern Pacific coastal waters, temperate rainforest coast.

Loc.: Central coast of British Columbia, Canada (along the mainland shore, between Port Hardy and Bella Bella).

Travel: Port Hardy can be reached by road or by air. Participants will be met in Port Hard for the day-long boat trip to CERF's research base at Duncanby Landing, Rivers Inlet.

Dur.: 6 days (Sunday to Friday).

Per.: June to September.

L. term: Possible with approval. Subject mostly to space and funding.

Age: Min. 15.

Qualif.: No particular skills required. Volunteers must be willing to spend long hours at shore stations or on boats. Previous experience with boat handling and photography is an asset, but not necessary.

Work: Volunteers are incorporated into the research team for the duration of their stay, and will participate in all of the research, including: boat handling (training provided), photo-ID (taking photos of the animals and identifying individuals by pigmentation patterns), data collection (behaviour, distribution, theodolite tracking from shore, micro-habitat use, and movements). Short talks are given every morning on research methods and evening lectures provide a background for the work.

Lang.: English, French, German. Spanish on some trips.

Accom.: Double rooms (bunks) with shared facilities at Duncanby Landing. Single rooms available at additional price. Once a week overnight aboard ship.

Cost: Adults: CAD$1,395 (approx. US$900); students: CAD$1,275 (approx. US$850). All food and accommodation provided. Participants must provide their own transportation to Port Hardy. The organisation can arrange details at time of booking.

Applic.: Deposit of CAD$250 (approx. US$170) is due at time of booking, balance is due 60 days before trip date.

Notes: Max. group size is 10.

CERCOPAN Forest Based Research and Education Centre

CERCOPAN, Forest Monkey Rehabilitation and Conservation
4 Ishie Lane, Housing Estate
P.O. Box 826, Calabar, Cross River State Nigeria
Tel.:/Fax: ++234 (87) 234 670 – Mob.: ++234 (803) 717 6920
E-mail: cercopan@compuserve.com
www.cercopan.org

Desc.: CERCOPAN's current centre in Calabar, Cross River State was established in 1995 and presently cares for over 80 primates of 7 forest species. Environmental education is a primary focus of the centre. Basic veterinary facilities and equipment are in place, including blow darting and capture equipment, surgical and emergency equipment and a basic laboratory. A forest site with open-topped electric fence enclosures for rehabilitation work is being developed, a research and rural education centre and a community forest protection programme is in place. The Centre has an excellent relationship with the local community (8 km from the forest).

Spp.: Red-capped mangabey (*Cercopithecus torquatus*) and forest guenons (*Cercopithecus sclateri*, *C. mona*, *C. nictitans*, *C. erythrotis*, *C. preuss*, *C. pogonias*).

Hab.: Tropical rainforest.

Loc.: Southeast Nigeria (close to Cameroon border).

Travel: Flight to Lagos; internal flight Lagos-Calabar.

Dur.: Short-term volunteers: min. 2 weeks; max. 3 months. Long term: min. 1 year, preference given to those who would consider extending to 2 years, possibility for small stipend after 1 year (holiday time between years).

Per.: Any time of year. Rainy season is June to September.

L. term: Min. 1 year with permission.

Age: Short-term volunteers min. 19; long-term volunteers min. 25.

Qualif.: Short-term (paying) volunteers should have a skill to offer: photography, field experience in ecology or primatology, engineering or building skills, biological surveying. Long-term volunteers are desired with any of the following qualifications: veterinary skills, preferably with some experience of wildlife;

116

engineering (roads, primitive bridges) or building skills; environmental education and/or community development/ communication skills (in developing countries, preferably in Africa); general biological research (ecology, animal behaviour, botany).

Work: Varies with skills and needs of the project. Assist in maintaining and improving bush roads and bridges, building enclosures and other structures (water supply, etc.); assist with ongoing surveys, animal behaviour studies; fundraising, caring for incoming orphans in quarantine, buying supplies, etc. Long-term volunteers will develop the project using their area of expertise and supervise and train local staff (ability to transfer skills is very important); assist with general administrative and management tasks and animal husbandry at certain times; respond in medical emergencies and animal escapes.

Lang.: English.

Accom.: At forest site: bush sheds with tent/mosquito net, minimum solar power for evening lighting, fridge, outdoor showers and toilets. In Calabar: shared house, shared cooking responsibilities, maybe shared room, electricity and running water (but often limited).

Cost: Short-term volunteers: room and board (approx. US$100/week). Long-term volunteers: room and board provided. International travel, medical insurance and visa are the responsibility of the volunteer.

Agents: Prospective volunteers may also contact the UK based trustee: Bob Baxter, 13 Prestbury Crescent, Banstead, Surrey ++44 (7771) 873 178, e-mail: bob@bbaxter81.fsnet.co.uk.

Applic.: Send letter of interest, whether long or short term, outline travel experience, state age and when available. Send C.V. with referees with telephone no. Referees may be contacted as required. Applicants in the UK may apply to the above trustee address. E-mail is the preferred method of application.

Notes: Nigeria can be a very difficult and frustrating country to work in and has had problems associated with the oil industry. Cross River State remains unaffected by the difficulties of the oil producing areas, and is well known as one of the best places to live in the south.

CETACEAN RESEARCH & RESCUE UNIT (CRRU)

P.O. Box 11307,
Banff AB45 3WB, Scotland UK
Tel: ++44 (1261) 851 696
E-mail: volunteer@crru.org.uk
www.crru.org.uk

Desc: The CRRU is a small non-profit research organisation dedicated to the understanding, welfare, conservation and protection of cetaceans (whales, dolphins and porpoises) in Scottish waters through scientific investigation, environmental education and the provision of professional veterinary assistance to sick, stranded and injured individuals.

Spp.: Primarily the bottlenose dolphin (*Tursiops truncatus*) and minke whale (*Balaenoptera acutorostrata*).

Hab.: Marine, coastal.

Loc.: Moray Firth, Northeastern Scotland.

Travel: By plane, bus or train to Aberdeen, then bus to Banff.

Dur: Min. 2 weeks, max. 2 months.

Per.: May to October.

L. term: Possible for outstanding volunteers.

Age: Min. 18.

Qualif.: Commitment to wildlife conservation and positive attitude towards living and working in a small group of enthusiastic people from different backgrounds and cultures is essential.

Work: Counting animals, recording behaviour, determining geographical positions and taking photographs under scientific supervision from a 5.6 m inflatable boat. On shore, identifying animals, cataloguing slides, and inputting data into the computers (full training provided). Opportunities to train in marine mammal rescue techniques will also be available.

Lang.: English

Accom.: Researchers and volunteers will be accommodated together in 1 of 2 furnished houses.

Cost: GB£700 (approx.EUR/US$1,150) for 2 weeks including food.

Applic.: By e-mail or post.

CHARLES DARWIN FOUNDATION, Galapagos

Volunteer Programme
Charles Darwin Foundation
P.O. Box 17–01–3891
Quito   Ecuador
E-mail: vol@fcdarwin.org.ec
www.darwinfoundation.org.

Desc.: In 1971 the Charles Darwin Foundation (CDF) began the National and International Volunteer Programme. Its purpose is to collaborate with the training of university and undergraduate students, who focus their careers in biology and conservation science and those who want to improve their skills through field experience in the Galapagos Islands.

Spp.: Terrestrial and marine flora and fauna of the Galapagos.

Hab.: Various marine and terrestrial habitats of the Galapagos.

Loc.: Galapagos Islands, Ecuador. Stations on 4 different Islands.

Travel: Flight to Quito or Guayaquil, then Puerto Ayora, Galapagos.

Dur.: Min. 6 months.

Per.: Year round.

L. term: Duration is set by the project: 6 months minimum.

Age: Min. 20.

Qualif.: Qualifications vary according to position available. Volunteers must be at least a second year undergraduate.

Work: The CDF has 4 different areas of investigation : vertebrate ecology monitoring , invertebrate research , botany and marine investigation and conservation. Non-scientific areas include communication, participation, education and institutional development. Volunteers can participate in any of these areas.

Lang.: English and Spanish. Fluency not essential.

Accom.: Dormitory in the Station or apartment or hotel in town.

Cost: International volunteers cover all their expenses: a 50% discount is awarded on the flight Continent/Galapagos. Food approx. US$8–10/day. Room approx. US$10/day.

Applic.: Application form to be downloaded and sent with specified documentation via regular mail at least 2 months in advance.

Notes: For information of available openings see website.

CHEETAH CONSERVATION FUND, Namibia

P.O. Box 1380
Ojai, California 93024 USA
Tel.: ++1 (805) 640 0390
Fax: ++1 (805) 640 0230
E-mail: info@cheetah.org
www.cheetah.org

Desc.: CCF sponsors scientific research and education programmes in areas such as cheetah population biology, ecology, health and reproduction and human impacts; and works with stakeholders.

Spp.: Cheetah.

Hab.: Semi-arid, bush-encroached savannah.

Loc.: Central Namibia, Southwest Africa.

Travel: Flight to Windhoek International Airport; shuttle bus or taxis to Windhoek city centre. Transport from Windhoek to Otjiwarongo (3 hours) can be arranged prior to arrival.

Dur.: 2 – 4 weeks.

Per.: Year round.

L. term: Depending on the needs of CCF, the volunteers qualifications and commitment and on the CCF Director's approval.

Age: Min. 20.

Qualif.: No particular skills required.

Work: Cheetah collecting, feeding and care; habitat monitoring of game and vegetation; assisting with data input, mapping, radio tracking; assisting with goat, sheep and livestock guarding dog healthcare and education programmes.

Lang.: English.

Accom.: Two-person thatched huts with beds: detached latrine block. All bedding is provided.

Cost: US$3,000 for 2 weeks, US$5,000 for 4 weeks, US$ 35 processing fee.

Agents: Earthwatch Institute (see Organisation list).

Applic.: Contact the organisation at the above address.

EL CHOCOYERO – EL BRUJO CO-MANAGEMENT PROJECT

Centro de Acción y Apoyo al Desarrollo Rural (CENADE)
Del cine Altamira 3 cuadras al este # 423 Managua, Nicaragua
Tel.: ++ (505) 278 3711
Fax: ++ (505) 270 6074
E-mail: cnd@ibw.com.ni – www.ibw.com.ni/~cnd/
(to obtain the ~ sign press Alt+126 on the numeric keyboard)

Desc.: The project involves 2 main objectives: participation of all local actors in the decision-making process in the management of the protected area, which results in the creation of a co-management committee; and to establish microprojects to offer services to tourists, which should be managed by the communities while training them in the management of a micro-business and in the management of their land. As a complimentary activity there will be the creation of a database of the area's biodiversity and the constant monitoring of the area's resources through aerial photographs.

Spp.: 70 species of birds; 28 mammals; 10 reptiles.

Hab.: Tropical dry and wet forests.

Loc.: El Chocoyero – el Brujo Reserve, Nicaragua.

Travel: The reserve is 45 minutes by car from the capital Managua.

Dur.: Min. 8 months.

Per.: July to February.

L. term: A longer term is negotiable with the consent of the organisation.

Age: Min. 20, no maximum but must be in good physical health.

Qualif.: Experience in community work or marketing; knowledge of economic activities in protected areas, some neotropical taxonomic group or watershed management are helpful.

Work.: Support the creation of community group to manage many projects to serve the tourists while using in a sustainable way the local natural resources.

Lang.: Spanish or English with Spanish.

Accom.: In a house of the community or in the warden's lodgings with bed, electricity, potable water, kitchen and bathroom.

Cost: No cost, excluding flight and land transportation.

Applic.: Contact the organisation directly.

COSTA RICAN SEA TURTLES

Earthwatch Institute
3 Clock Tower Place – Suite 100, Box 75
Maynard, MA 01754   USA
Tel.: ++1 (978) 461 0081 – 1(800) 776 0188 (toll free in US/Canada)
Fax: ++1 (978) 461 2332
E-mail: info@earthwatch.org   –   www.earthwatch.org

Desc.: Leatherback sea turtles are the largest and oldest living reptiles. For over 20 million years, these sometimes 1,000 kg ancients have inhabited waters from New Zealand to the Arctic Circle. Volunteers are needed to study the leatherbacks and will have the opportunity to witness and assist the moonlit nesting period.

Spp.: Leatherback sea turtles (*Dermochelys coriacea*).

Hab.: Tropical beach/shallow sea water.

Loc.: La Baulas Guanacaste National Park, Northwest Costa Rica.

Travel: Airplane to San José, then to Tamarindo.

Dur.: 10 days, approx.

Per.: October to February.

L. term: No long-term volunteer opportunities available.

Age: Min. 16.

Qualif.: No particular skills required.

Work: Volunteers count and tag nesting turtles, record measurements, nest position, number of eggs laid and nest temperatures, and help attach satellite transmitters to turtle shells for long-distance migration tracking.

Lang.: English.

Accom.: Share confortable A/C rooms in a nearby hotel annex.

Cost: US$1,745 (GB£1,195).

Agents: Earthwatch Institute (see Organisation list).

Applic.: A deposit of US$250 (GB£200) will be required.

Notes: Work is carried out at night and ends early in the morning. Days are free for sleep, relaxing on the beach and horse riding.

DOLPHIN RESEARCH CENTER

58901 Overseas Highway
Grassy Key, Florida 33050–6019 USA
Tel.: ++1 (305) 289 1121 ext. 230
Fax: ++1 (305) 743 7627
E-mail: drc-vr@dolphins.org
www.dolphins.or

Desc.:   Dolphin Research Center (DRC) is an organisation dedicated to marine mammal research and education. It offers volunteers unique opportunities for learning about dolphins and various aspects of the daily operations of a marine mammal care facility. DRC also offer Internships involving concentration in a specific department. For individuals desiring a more interactive programme, see DolphinLab programme in Notes.

Spp.:   Bottlenose dolphin, Atlantic spotted dolphin, sea lion.

Loc.:   Grassy Key, Florida, USA.

Travel: Flights to Miami then transfer to Marathon.

Dur.:   1 – 4 months for volunteers; 3 – 4 months for internships.

Per.:   Year round.

L. term: Available for local residents.

Age: Min. 18.

Qualif.:   Good physical shape (able to lift 30 lbs/15 kg).

Work: Assist in animal food preparation, monitor visitors and answer questions, assist staff in conducting public interactive programmes, perform various facility maintenance tasks and provide administrative support. Interns duties vary depending upon the specific internship (animal care & training, animal husbandry, medical care, dolphin-child therapy, research, education, visual communications, and guest programmes.

Lang.:   English fluency is a requirement.

Accom.:   Not provided, DRC assists with locating housing/roommates.

Cost: Living expenses can be as much as US$1500/month.

Applic.:   Application available on website or mailed upon request.

Notes: Individuals desiring a shorter, more interactive learning experience may be interested in the week-long DolphinLab class. See website or contact for info: drc-ed@dolphins.org.

DOLPHINS & SEA LIFE AROUND THE MALTESE ISLANDS

The Biological Conservation Research Foundation (BICREF)
P.O. Box 30, Hamrun Malta
Tel./Fax: ++(356) 3290 3049
E-mail: avel@cis.um.edu.mt
http://sites.keyworld.net/bicref

Desc.: Boat and aerial research surveys undertaken in the region throughout the year to analyse the associations between environmental variables and observe different marine organisms. Boat surveys take 1 day, but 3-day research cruises are planned when weather permits.

Spp.: Bottlenose dolphin (*Tursiops truncatus*), common dolphins (*Delphinus delphis*), sea turtles (*Caretta caretta*), sea birds, such as cory shearwaters, large fish, manta rays.

Hab.: Mediterranean coastal and pelagic waters.

Loc.: Maltese Islands.

Travel: Fly to Luqa International Airport, Malta, or ferry from Sicily.

Dur.: Negotiable, inquire with the organisation.

Per.: Year round; summer is most intense.

L. term: Possible, but ask more information to the project.

Age: Min. 18, max. 45.

Qualif.: A background in biology. Sea-faring stamina and interest or experience in marine research and conservation required. Training on basic survey techniques and applications of research is provided.

Work: Observation and data recording during research surveys. Organise information and data after the surveys.

Lang.: English or Italian.

Accom.: Hotels, hostels, etc., are available in Malta. During 3-day trips, volunteers will sleep on board of the sailing or survey boat.

Cost: Contact the organisation for information.

Applic.: Send a brief CV, letter of interest and application form 6–4 months prior to the volunteering period.

Notes: Any special needs should be stated in the application letter.

ECOLODGE SAN LUIS & RESEARCH STATION

Apdo. 36, Santa Elena de Monteverde, Puntarenas Costa Rica
Tel.: ++ (506) 645 5277/645 5890
Fax: ++ (506) 645 5364/645 5890
E-mail: liebermv@racsa.co.cr
www.ecolodgesanluis.com

Desc.: The Ecolodge San Luis & Research Station, which is affiliated with the University of Georgia, is dedicated to research, education, ecotourism, conservation and the community. Field courses, academic programmes and the public are served. Volunteers include Interns and Resident naturalists.

Spp.: Cloud forest flora and fauna, crop species.

Hab.: Tropical cloud forest, tropical agricultural landscape.

Loc.: San Luis de Monteverde, Northwestern Costa Rica.

Travel: Bus from San Jose to Monteverde; then taxi to the Ecolodge.

Dur.: Interns: min. 3 months. Resident Naturalists: min. 5 months.

Per.: Year round.

L. term: Preferred for Resident naturalists (9 months or longer).

Age: Min. 20.

Qualif.: Interns: excellent physical condition, able to interact with scientists, students and the public. Resident Naturalists: BS, tropical experience, natural history background, Spanish.

Work: Working as part of a team in: leading hikes, horseback tours, birdwalks, slide shows, community service; helping with logistics; designing educational programmes; participating in research, education, ecotourism and conservation missions.

Lang.: English; conversational Spanish is essential for Resident Naturalists. Intensive language study can be arranged on site at $280/week, including homestay.

Accom.: Bunkhouse or rustic one-room casitas. Bedding provided.

Cost: Interns pay initial US$480; Resident Naturalists pay no fee. All volunteers receive free room and board.

Applic.: Send e-mail to request application form and further details.

Notes: Intensive training in flora and fauna, language, culture, is provided. Good research potential. University credit possible.

ECOLOGY & CONSERVATION OF DEER IN PATAGONIA

Universidad Nacional del Comahue
JoAnne Smith-Flueck, PhD candidate
C.C. 176 8400 S.C. de Bariloche   Argentina
Tel./Fax: ++54 (944) 467 345
E-mail: joannesmith@infovia.com.ar

Desc.: The project objectives are to estimate population size and to determine the reproductive status, social behaviour, food habits, genetic diversity and degree of genetic isolation from other populations of deer in southern Patagonia in Argentina.

Spp.: Andean huemul deer (*Hippocamelus bisulcus*), naturalised red deer (*Cervus elaphus*).

Hab.: Mountainous temperate rainforest.

Loc.: Southwest Argentina.

Travel: Airplane to Buenos Aires, then airplane or bus to Bariloche.

Dur: 2–5 weeks.

Per.: December to April.

L. term: Only with project leader's approval after regular period.

Age: Min. 18.

Qualif.: Good backpacking and camping experience in mountainous wilderness.

Work: Research includes: counts, habitat surveys, diet, genetic and morphometric analysis and recording location, altitude, vegetation and terrain type and presence of livestock. Direct observations with binoculars and scopes (provided). Radiotelemetry work on red deer.

Lang.: English or Spanish (German also spoken).

Accom.: Sleeping bags and tents during field work. Hostel in town.

Cost: US$50/week with food provided during field work. Room and board in Bariloche is approx. US$20/day.

Agents: Contact project leader directly.

Applic.: A short CV with a letter of introduction is required.

Notes: The climate is harsh and unpredictable even in summer. Expect windy, rainy and even snowy conditions. Supportive hiking boots, warm clothing and rain gear are required.

ECOLOGY OF COMMON DOLPHIN IN ALBORAN SEA

Alnitak Marine Environment Research and Education Centre
Calle Nalón 16,
E–28240 Hoyo de Manzanares, Madrid Spain
Tel./Fax:++34 (619) 108 797
E-mail: alnitak@cetaceos.com
www.geocities.com/tofte2000/

Desc.: Monitoring the distribution and dynamics of cetaceans, in particular the declining common dolphin populations in the region, using photo-ID and bio-acoustic surveys. Research is carried out onboard the *Toftevaag*, an old 1910 Norwegian fishing boat converted into a research vessel.

Spp.: Common dolphin (*Delphinus delphis*), striped and bottlenose dolphins, long-finned pilot whales, Risso's dolphins.

Hab.: Temperate sea (Mediterranean Sea).

Loc.: Southeast Spain.

Travel: Airplane to Almería; bus or taxi to the ship (Almerimar).

Dur.: 10 days.

Per.: November, December, January, Easter, June to October.

L. term: Volunteers can join the project for more than 1 period.

Age: Min. 15.

Qualif.: No particular skills needed.

Work: Volunteers share all duties with the research crew, including navigation, helping with the feeding of computer data, lookout watch, water sampling and analyses and bio-acoustic watch. Volunteers, depending on their experience, can participate in other activities such as inflatable-boat driving, photo-ID and underwater filming. During days of bad weather researchers will show slides, videos and publications.

Lang.: Spanish, English, French and Dutch.

Accom.: In bunks aboard research vessel. Sleeping bag required.

Cost: About US$ 2,125 (GB£1,395) including food.

Agents: Contact the Earthwatch Institute (see Organisation list).

Applic.: Apply on-line at www.earthwatch.org

FOREST HEALTH MONITORING

Tongariro/Taupo Conservancy, Department of Conservation
Sean Husheer, DOC Private Bag, Turangi New Zealand
Tel.: ++64 (7) 386 9248 – Fax: ++64 (7) 386 7086
E-mail: shusheer@doc.govt.nz – sdeverell@doc.govt.nz
www.doc.govt.nz/Community/OO6~Volunteers/
(to obtain the ~ sign press Alt+126 on the numeric keyboard)

Desc.: Forest health assessment in Tongariro National and Forest Parks (101,068 ha) and Kaimanawa Forest Park (77,887 ha). This involves field work establishing and remeasuring of permanent vegetation monitoring plots using standardised techniques to determine the impact of introduced browsing animals.

Spp.: Podocarpaceae and southern beech (Fagaceae) forests.

Hab.: Temperate forest and grassland.

Loc.: Central North Island, New Zealand.

Travel: Volunteers will need to fly to Auckland International Airport.

Dur.: Min. 3 months.

Per.: September to April.

Age: Min. 20.

Qualif.: Good natured, committed to conservation, have an ability to work in a dynamic team environment and a high level of physical fitness. Entire days are often spent walking. Well developed field skills, including experience in camp-craft and living in back-country/mountain huts. A botany degree or equivalent experience is essential. Use of Latin helpful.

Work: Gauging forest health by measuring tree diameters, sapling and seedling heights and abundance in vegetation plots. Vegetation monitoring plots, permanently tagged sample trees and quadrats and fenced ungulate exclosure plots are employed.

Lang.: English.

Accom.: Tent camps or back-country huts. House in Turangi.

Cost: NZ$100/month (approx. US$50).

Applic.: Send CV and hand-written letter. Applications close June 30.

Notes: The project has been suspended for the 2002–2003 Austral summer, contact Sean Husheer or Steve Deverell at the e-mail addresses above for the upcoming seasons.

FOREST RESTORATION

National Park Service, Rock Creek Park
3545 Williamsburg Ln, NW
Washington, DC 20008   USA
Tel.: ++1 (202) 895 6077 – Fax: ++1 (202) 895 6075
E-mail: sue-salmon@nps.gov
www.nps.gov/rocr/

Desc.: This project focuses on exotic plant management, Dutch elm disease management, gypsy moth mitigation and vegetation mapping. Projects depend upon the season. Researchers also may write grant proposals and use Global Positioning software.

Spp.: *Celastrus orbiculatus, Ampelopsis brevipedunculata*, American elm, etc.

Hab.: Eastern deciduous forest.

Loc.: Mid-Atlantic of North America.

Travel: Airplane to Washington DC, USA.

Dur.: Variable.

Per.: Year round.

L. term: Inquire with organisation.

Age: Min. 18.

Qualif.: Familiarity with botany and computer knowledge is welcome. Must be in good shape and fluent in English. Participation or completion in a college level programme required.

Work: Integrated pest management may include vine cutting and work with herbicides, monitoring rare, threatened and endangered species, as well as vegetation plot monitoring and data entry.

Lang.: English.

Accom.: Group housing may be available. Bring sheets or sleeping bag. A small stipend for lunch may be available.

Cost: If a room cannot be provided, the cost will vary, depending on the type of accommodation. Hostels range from US$14–35/day. Volunteers must pay for transportation.

Agents: Contact Sue Salmon at the above address directly.

Applic.: Send CV, 3 references and copy of school transcript.

FRIENDS OF THE SEA OTTER

125 Ocean View Blvd. #204
Pacific Grove, California 93950 USA
Tel.: ++1 (831) 373 2747
Fax: ++1 (831) 373 2749
E-mail: education@seaotters.org – info@seaotters.org
www.seaotters.org

Desc: Friends of the Sea Otter (FSO), a non-profit organisation founded in 1968, is dedicated to the protection of the southern sea otter as well as sea otters throughout the north Pacific range. Goals include maintaining and increasing the current protections for sea otters and sea otter habitat, as well as educating the public about the otter's unique behaviour and habitat. The organisation also facilitates critical scientific research and advocacy work.

Spp: Southern sea otter (*Enhydra lutris*).

Hab: Northern Pacific (California) coast.

Loc.: Central coast California (Monterey Bay Area).

Travel: Airplane to San Francisco, then bus to Monterey.

Dur.: Negotiable, inquire with the organisation.

Per.: Year round.

L. term: Possible, inquire with the organisation.

Age: Min. 18.

Qualif.: A sincere commitment to help the endangered sea otters.

Work: The Otter Spotter programme trains volunteers the necessary observation skills to assess sea otter behaviour and other aspects of their natural history. Volunteers watch otters from observation points. They also serve as a conduit for information on sea otters and sea otter conservation to the public that they meet at various look-out points.

Lang.: English, Spanish useful.

Accom.: In rented apartment or hostel.

Cost: Volunteers are responsible for travel, room and board.

Applic.: CV and references required.

Notes: Other volunteer projects exist. Contact Cindy Murphy, Office of Oil Spill Prevention and Response, tel.: ++1(916) 327 9946.

GALAPAGOS NATIONAL PARK & MARINE RESERVE

GOBI Galapagos On-line Biodiversity Inventory Project
(Unidad de Comunicacion)
Puerto Ayora, Isla Santa Cruz, Galapagos Archipelago Ecuador
Tel.: ++ (593) 4 73 9144 – Fax: ++ (593) 4 73 8134
E-mail: jtb@darwinvest.com.ec – foviedo@spng.org.ec
www.galapagospark.org

Desc.: The Galapagos On-line Biodiversity Inventory is designed to better understand how many species have been identified in the archipelago's park and marine reserve. This Internet directory runs on a computer database: 7,400 species are managed at feasibility study level. GOBI is an international project involving scientists, biology students, on-line photo archivists, as well as local press agents.

Spp.: 7,460 species identified as of December 2001.

Hab.: Terrestrial, freshwater, marine.

Loc.: Galapagos archipelago, 960 km west of coastal Ecuador. 8,010 km^2 land, 133,000 km^2 marine reserve. Both are now UNESCO Natural Heritage Sites.

Travel: Airplane from Guayaquil or Quito to Baltra island airport, bus to Itabaca Canal, ferry or bus to Puerto Ayora.

Dur.: 1-week field inventory expeditions; 15 days–1 mont editorial desk; 2–3 months database management.

Per.: Year round.

L. term: Long-term volunteers with useful skills are welcome.

Age: Min. 18.

Qualif.: On-line database managers, biology students, multimedia, PR and communication experts, computer and biodiversity analysts.

Work.: Construction of on-line database; assist in multimedia activity; join research expeditions; feed and operate digital studio; assist in press relations and PR; join the Galapagos National Park & Marine Reserve Unidad de Comunicacion.

Lang.: English, Spanish useful.

Accom.: In tents, observatories, campus, hotels, boats.

Cost: Volunteers cover travel, room and board (US$300–400/month).

Applic: Contact jtb@darwinvest.com.ec

GENESIS II CLOUDFOREST PRESERVE AND WILDLIFE REFUGE

Apdo. 655
7050 Cartago Costa Rica
Tel./Fax: ++ (506) 381 0739
E-mail: info@genesis-two.com
www.genesis-two.com (click on 'more options')

Desc.: This 47-hectare preserve was established to protect endangered cloud forest habitat. Volunteers assist with planting native trees and trail construction and maintenance.

Spp.: Birds, trees, epiphytes, ferns, butterflies/moths.

Hab.: Cloud forest, recovering pastureland.

Loc.: Central Talamanca mountains of Costa Rica; altitude 2,300 m.

Travel: Airplane to San José, then bus to project site.

Dur.: Min. 4 weeks; max. 9 units of 4 weeks each.

Per.: January to November.

L. term: Possible for specially qualified or highly motivated volunteers.

Age: Min. 21.

Qualif.: Volunteers must be physically fit and motivated; an interest in environmental concerns is especially welcome.

Work: July to October: planting native trees. November to June: constructing and maintaining trail system. Other projects include reforestation, T-shirt design, topographical mapping, bird frequency and observations. In the 4-week commitment, volunteers work for 2, 10-day periods (6 hours/day), with 4 days off after each period.

Lang.: English. Spanish is useful.

Accom.: Facilities are simple; electricity is 120-volt alternating current; there is a short-wave radio, but no TV.

Cost: Min. US$150/week, including room, board and laundry.

Applic.: Request application form to be returned with a deposit of US$150. Balance is due 1 month before joining the project.

Notes: June to December is wet season: expect cool, rainy conditions. Sunburn is possible owing to the high altitude.

GIBBON REHABILITATION PROJECT

Wildlife Animal Rescue (W.A.R.) Foundation
235 Sukhumvit Soi 31
Bangkok 10110   Thailand
Tel. ++66 (2) 662 0898 – Fax: ++66 (2) 261 9670
E-mail: war@warthai.org – info@ecovolunteer.org
www.warthai.org – www.ecovolunteer.org

Desc.: The Sanctuary is located on the island of Phuket, off the South coast of Thailand and has been in operation over 10 years. The project was started in 1992 by the American zoologist Terrance Dillon Morin, who died in 1995. It currently houses over 70 gibbons. The aim of the project is the rehabilitation of suitable captive-raised gibbons (which have been confiscated to illegal owners) back to a natural habitat. This is achieved by releasing them in a small uninhabited island. The process of rehabilitation is very lengthy and only a very small number of gibbons arriving at the sanctuary, due to their experience with humans, become candidate. There is therefore an ongoing need to provide care and protection for the majority of these gibbons, some of which have communicable diseases and will remain at the project for an indefinite period.

Spp.: White-handed gibbon (*Hylobates lar*).

Hab.: Tropical rainforest.

Loc.: Bang Pae Waterfall, Khao Phra Thaew National Park, Phuket, Thailand.

Travel: Airplane to Phuket (or to Bangkok and then bus to Phuket).

Dur.: Min. 3 weeks.

Per.: Year round.

L. term: Students and graduates in biology, anthropology and veterinary medicine are especially welcome to stay for long periods and can do research under the supervision of the project leader (min. availability 2 months). Interesting opportunities also exist for those with an education in tourism or public relations.

Age: Min. 18.

Qualif.: Good physical condition, enthusiastic and able to work without assistance. Experience with animals or skills in construction, tourist assistance, public relations, etc., can be very helpful. Experience can be a criterium for selection.

Work: Depending on the duration of stay, education and experience, volunteers can assist in preparing food and feeding the gibbons, assist in behavioural observation, building, maintaining and cleaning the cages, clearing footpaths, lecturing and showing tourists around the centre. Volunteers work 6 days a week. On days off volunteers can go sightseeing or enjoy the tropical beaches of Phuket.

Lang.: English.

Accom.: Bungalows for 2 or more persons located close to the sanctuary, with toilet, shower and cooking facilities.

Cost: Stays of 3–8 weeks, US$1,170 for the first 3 weeks and US$130 each additional week; for stays longer than 8 weeks, US$975 for the first 3 weeks, US$65 for each additional week (flights, food, visa and insurance not included).

Agents: The Ecovolunteer Network at www.ecovolunteer.org.

Applic.: Through The Ecovolunteer Network (see Organisation list) or the Wild Animal Rescue Foundation of Thailand.

Notes: The Centre can accommodate 8–12 people at a time; couples and groups can be accommodated depending on season and number of volunteers.

GOLDEN BOOMERANG LANDCARE

594 Sunny Corner Road
Touron Springs 2795 Australia
Tel.: ++61 (263) 377 279 – Mob.: ++61 (40) 1093 005
E-mail: earthfix@bigpond.com
www.earthfix.org.au

Desc.: Rejuvenating 125 acres of Australian farmland.
Spp.: Several subtropical plant species.
Hab.: Australian scrubland.
Loc.: Turon Springs in the Central Tablelands, 200 km northwest of Sydney.
Travel: Contact the project for information about travel.
Dur.: Negotiable, there are no set periods.
Per.: Year round.
L. term: Volunteers can join for short or long periods.
Age: Min.18.
Qualif.: No special skills required. Anyone is welcome to join and apply their skills and interests.
Work: The projects considers landcare as care and survival for everyone. The focus is community care, entertainment and land repair.
Lang.: English.
Accom.: In a bunkhouse situation: shared cooking, cleaning, etc. Sometimes sleeping outdoors in swags.
Cost: No cost. Food and expenses are shared: not more than AUS$15 (approx.US$8) per day.
Applic.: An initial membership fee is required. All volunteers become members and are covered by insurance. Apply with expressions of interest by e-mail.

THE GOLDEN EAGLES OF MULL

Earthwatch Europe
267 Banbury Road
Oxford OX2 7HT   UK
Tel.: ++44 (1865) 318 838 – Fax: ++44 (1865) 318 383
E-mail: info@earthwatch.org.uk
www.earthwatch.org/europe

Desc.: One in 10 of all Golden Eagles live in the misty crags of this Inner Hebridean Island. The aims of the project are to discover the mix of environmental conditions that golden eagles and other predatory birds need to thrive here, for example, how these birds use their shared habitat and how land-use practices could impinge on their populations.

Spp.: Golden eagles, buzzards, ravens.

Hab.: Cliffs, heathland.

Loc.: Isle of Mull, Scotland.

Travel: Meeting is at Ben Doran on the coast of the low lying Ross of Mull.

Dur.: 3 – 7 days.

Per.: July to September.

L. term: No long-term volunteer opportunities available.

Age: Min. 16.

Qualif.: No special skills required.

Work: Volunteers will help with habitat mapping and will drive around the island to verify and add to data. Volunteers will also observe individual birds at nest or root sites.

Lang.: English.

Accom.: A secluded 5-bedroom stone cottage, 400 m from the sea.

Cost: Starting from GB£ 395 (approx. EUR/US$600).

Agents: Earthwatch Institute (see organisation list).

Applic.: Call or e-mail Earthwatch Europe.

GREAT WHALES IN THEIR NATURAL ENVIRONMENT

ORES – Foundation for Marine Environment Research
Postfach 756, 4502 Solothurn Switzerland
Tel./Fax.: ++41 (32) 623 6354
E-mail: utscherter@gmx.ch
www.ores.org

Desc.: The coastal ecosystem in the St. Lawrence River estuary in Eastern Canada is known for the near-shore abundance and diversity of its marine life forms, especially of baleen whales. ORES Centre personnel, with the help of volunteers, study their feeding behaviour, distribution, abundance, habitat utilisation and have developed and introduced minimally intrusive research methods. During the course, volunteers not only will have many encounters with different whales and are actively involved in data collecting, they also will learn what the whales are doing and why. Research results, conservation issues and general knowledge on whales are shared during several lectures.

Spp.: Finback whale, minke whale, beluga, harbour porpoise, blue whale, humpback whale, sperm whale.

Hab.: Ocean-river estuary in protected marine waters.

Loc.: Province of Québec, Les Bergeronnes (220 km east of Québec City), St. Lawrence and Saguenay River confluence.

Travel: Airplane to Toronto, Montreal or Québec City, then by bus (or car) to Les Bergeronnes.

Per.: July to October.

Dur.: Two programmes are offered: the General Interest Course (GIC) of 2 weeks to broaden knowledge of the ocean generally and of whales in particular (for general interest students-degree or diploma credit available); the Internship Course (ISC; medium-term 6 weeks, long-term 12 weeks) are open to anybody who has completed the introductory course and who would like to gain deeper insight into the ongoing studies (also suitable for independent study and undergraduate thesis projects).

L. term: Possible for expert volunteers (see previous section).

Age.: Min. 18.

Qualif.: No particular skills or knowledge are needed. ORES personnel teach any skills needed. Strong interest in field work, team work, and outdoors activity. Volunteers must be able to spend 4–6 hours on a open boat.

Work: Observation and data gathering daily (weather permitting) by small research teams from open inflatable boats. Studies carried out among others: feeding strategies and techniques, photo-identification, distribution, echograph recording of prey distributions; ventilation recording, plankton sampling; sound recording, documenting whale/human activity interactions; lab work.

Lang.: English. The language in the province of Québec is French.

Accom.: Participants in introductory course stay at the well-equipped Parc Bon Désir campground overlooking the St. Lawrence. Sleeping tents, cooking tent and infrastructure are provided. Lectures and work take place at the near-by centre, in a converted 100-year-old farmhouse. Internship students are living at the station in cabins with 4 beds.

Cost: Fee for GIC (accommodation included, travel and food excluded) is US$950 (approx. EUR950/GB£630). Fees for ISC on request. Volunteers individually organise their travel to and from the centre. ORES provides exposure/floating suits for the work on boats, land transportation during the course and lectures.

Applic.: Apply directly via e-mail. Due to the high demand, it is recommended to contact ORES early in the year. Specific information and an application form will be sent either by mail, e-mail or fax.

GREAT WHITE SHARK PROJECT

South African White Shark Research Institute (WSRI)
P.O. Box 50775, V & A Waterfront, Cape Town 8001 South Africa
Tel.: ++27 (21) 552 9794
Fax: ++27 (21) 552 9795
E-mail: whiteshk@iafrica.com
www.whiteshark.co.za

Desc.: The history of the project includes an extensive tagging programme from 1990 to 1998, tissue sampling for genetic analysis and blood extraction for hormonal analysis. Currently, the project includes data on environmental parameters, recording of individual markings, sex, size estimation and individual behaviour at the boat. Although the project still conducts extensive data collection, great emphasis is placed on education and conservation programmes.

Spp.: Great white shark (*Carcharodon carcharias*).

Hab.: South Atlantic pelagic, coastal and island waters.

Loc.: Dyer Island & Geyser Rock, 4 miles offshore of Gansbaai, Western Cape, South Africa.

Travel: By airplane to Cape Town, then transport to Gansbaai (190 km, close to Dyer Island) is organised by WSP.

Dur.: 14 days. Volunteers for longer durations are considered after they have completed the 14 day programme.

Per.: Year round.

L.term: With project leader's approval after 2-month trial period.

Age: Min. 18.

Qualif.: Priority is given to applicants who are students of marine biology, filming arts and who are interested in a career in marine tourism. Anyone can apply, all applications are taken on merit.

Work: Field data collection work of free swimming white sharks, recording environmental conditions and white shark activity. Work also includes hands on boat work, on-shore work, cage diving, lectures and working with tourists.

Lang.: English.

Accom.: Students will stay at the WSP lodge in Kleinbaai. Student rooms are comfortable and meals are excellent.

Cost.: US$1,500 for 14 days. This includes accommodation, meals, lectures, field work, cage diving and transport from and to Cape Town.

Applic.: Request an application form.

Notes: The 14-day programme is structured to provide students with an opportunity to work on the ocean with great white sharks under the guidance of some of the most experienced white shark people in the world. The students will have the opportunity of learning from the WSP staff, in aspects ranging from working with free swimming white sharks, to shark tourism, data collection, cage diving, photography and seamanship. The programme works on a team effort and although fun and relaxed, the participants are able to learn a great deal of practical knowledge. The 14 days is intensive, with only 1 day allowed for personal recreation.

GREY WOLF PROJECT

Wolf Education and Research Center (WERC)
517 Joseph Ave, P.O. Box 217, Winchester, Idaho 83555 USA
Tel.: ++1 (208) 924 6960
Fax: ++1 (208) 924 6959
E-mail: werced@camasnet.com
www.wolfcenter.org

Desc.: Public information, education and research concerning endangered species, with an emphasis on the grey wolf, its habitat and ecosystem in the northern Rocky Mountain region. WERC cares for a captive pack of wolves: "The Sawtooth Pack: Wolves of the Nez Perce". WERC is in partnership with the Nez Perce Tribe, which currently handles the wolf management and reintroduction for Idaho.

Spp.: Grey timber wolf (*Canis lupus*).

Hab.: Camas prairie, timber.

Loc.: North-central region of Idaho; near the borders of Idaho, Washington and Oregon, USA.

Travel: From Lewiston, ID take Highway 95 south to Winchester, ID. Follow signs for the Winchester Lake State Park. The centre is approximately 1 mile past the State Park.

Dur.: Varies with prior agreement between individual and WERC.

Per.: Year round; the need is greater from June to September.

L. term: Possible: inquire with the project.

Age: Min.18.

Work: Volunteers are involved in maintenance and/or construction, building, staffing the visitor centre; providing educational programmes, assisting with membership documentation and generally helping where needed.

Lang.: English.

Accom.: Volunteer camp is available depending on number of volunteers on-site and season. Local off-site lodging facilities can be recommended.

Cost: Max. US$20/day; excluding meals and transportation to/from Winchester.

Applic.: Request information and application form via e-mail or mail.

GRIFFON VULTURE CONSERVATION PROJECT

Eco-center Caput Insulae – Beli
E Beli 4, 51559 Beli Croatia
Tel./Fax: ++385 (51) 840 525
E-mail: info@caput-insulae.com
        caput.insulae@ri.tel.hr
www.caput-insulae.com

Desc.: The griffon vulture has disappeared from many European countries and is declining in its southeastern European range. The Croatian population includes approximately 100 breeding pairs. The objective of this project is to study griffon vulture biology and ecology to determine the critical factors for their survival on the islands and to develop new conservation strategies in order to maintain the present breeding population.

Spp.: Griffon vultures (*Gyps fulvus*), golden eagle (*Aquila chrysaetos*), short-toed eagle (*Circaetus gallicus*), peregrine falcon (*Falco peregrinus*), eagle owl (*Bubo bubo*), shag (*Phalacrocorax aristotelis*).

Hab: Mediterrannean sea-cliffs, oak forests and grasslands.

Loc.: Kvarner Archipelago, Northeast Adriatic, Croatia.

Travel: Airplane to Zagreb; bus or train to Rijeka; bus to Cres.

Dur.: Min. 1 week.

Per.: Year round.

L. term: Possible, for extremely motivated and qualified volunteers.

Age: Min. 18 years (16 with parent's permission).

Qualif.: Good physical health.

Work: Recording griffon vulture colonies, noting all sightings and behaviour on the cliffs, documenting visible wing-markers, etc.

Lang.: English, Italian.

Accom.: Eco-center: 26 beds, 2 bathrooms, hot showers, fully-equipped kitchen (volunteers help cook and housekeep).

Cost: From EUR/US$ 80–125 (approx.GB£55–85) for 1 week. Food not included (approx. EUR5/day).

Agents: The Ecovolunteer Network at www.ecovolunteer.org.

Applic.: Application form on website.

Notes: Volunteers can also participate in other activities: interpretation for tourist and locals, dry stone wall or trail reconstruction, etc.

HAWAIIAN FOREST RESTORATION PROJECT

Kokee Resource Conservation Program c/o Natural History Museum
P.O. Box 100, Kekaha, Hawaii, 96752 USA
Tel.: ++1 (808) 335 9975 – Fax: ++1 (808) 335 6131
E-mail: rcp@aloha.net – kokee@aloha.net
www.aloha.net/~kokee/
(to obtain the ~ sign press Alt+126 on the numeric keyboard)

Desc.: In the isolated Hawaiian Islands over 1,000 plant species evolved, and the forests of Kokee State Park contain many species found nowhere else in the world. However, because of invasive weed species introduced to the islands in the last 2 centuries, Hawaii also contains over 50% of the US Federally listed endangered plant species. This programme removes invasive weeds from selected areas of the mountain state park in order to restore those forested areas to their native state.

Spp.: Weed species: strawberry guava, blackberry, kahili ginger.

Hab.: Mesic montane Koa-dominated forests, wet montane Ohia-dominated forests, mixed-bog communities.

Loc.: Kokee State Park, Kauai, Hawaii.

Travel: Airplane to Kauai.

Dur.: 1 week to 1 month.

Per.: Year round.

L. term: Possible, inquire with organisation.

Age: Min. 18.

Qualif.: Must be physically fit. Volunteers are trained and supervised. Priority is given to volunteers with a degree and/or experience in ecology, conservation or botany.

Work: Supervised by programme staff, volunteers use herbicides and hand weed to maintain the nearly native state containing unique, rare and endangered plant species. Volunteers work 8-hour days, often involving strenuous hiking in mountainous areas.

Lang.: English.

Accom.: Rustic housing in historic camp (bunk beds).

Cost: Volunteers pay for their own food and transportation.

Applic.: Request application form to Ellen Coulombe or Katie Cassel.

Notes: Groups are welcome but space is limited to parties of 14.

143

HOWLER MONKEY PROJECT, Mexico

Pithekos
Via Savona 26, 20144 Milano Italy
Tel.: ++39 (02) 8940 5267
Fax: ++39 (02) 7005 94457
E-mail: asspithekos@tiscalinet.it
www.pithekos.it

Desc.: This project started in 1997 in collaboration with the Parque de la Flora y Fauna Sylvestre Tropical (PFFST), in the Los Tuxtlas region, Veracruz, Mexico. The aim of the PFFST – Pithekos collaboration is to study and save *Alouatta palliata* and its habitat. Research on howler monkeys, their habitat and the bio-diversity of the region aims to find the best way to protect them. The programme is now being extended to a wider scope sustainable development project of the area.

Spp.: Mexican mantled howler monkey (*Alouatta palliata*), birds.

Hab.: Tropical rainforest.

Loc.: Los Tuxtlas region, Vercaruz, Mexico.

Travel: Flight to Mexico City or Veracruz, then bus to Catemaco.

Dur.: Min. 2 weeks, max. 1 month.

Per.: January, February, July, August (other periods to be defined).

L. term: Longer period possible with project leaders' approval.

Age: Min. 18.

Qualif.: Must be adaptable, able to work independently and with others, walk medium distances and tolerate heat. Photographers welcome.

Work: Assist with field research and explain project to local population.

Lang.: Spanish (or Italian, Portuguese, French) or English.

Accom.: House with common rooms, toilets and kitchen; a small hotel is also available. Sheets or sleeping bags required.

Cost: Approx. EUR/US$100; inquire with organisation.

Applic.: Apply by e-mail.

Notes: Groups normally do not exceed 10–12 volunteers.

HUMPBACK RESEARCH PROJECT, Brazil

The Ecovolunteer Network
Meyersweg 29   7553 AX Hengelo The Netherlands
Tel.: ++31 (74) 250 8250 – Fax: ++31 (74) 250 6572
E-mail: info@ecovolunteer.org
www.ecovolunteer.org

Desc.:   The Humpback Research Project carries on humpback research cruises in the Abrolhos Marine National Park. Humpbacks winter in this area for reproduction, between July and November. The research focuses on monitoring the humpack whale population and on behavioural studies on humpbacks.

Spp.:   Humpback whale.

Hab.:   Marine habitat with coral reefs and islands.

Loc.:   Caravelas, Bahia and the Abrolhos Archipelago, Brazil.

Travel: Travel to Caravelas, Bahia, Brazil. Meet at airport or bus terminal.

Dur.:   2 – 3 weeks.

Per.:   July to November.

L.term: Not possible.

Age.:   Min. 18.

Qualif.:   No particular skills needed. Volunteers must be in good health.

Work: Volunteers search for whales, operate the GPS and register whale behaviour. Scientists and volunteers participate in all activities, including processing data, computer work, operating the outboard motor, cooking, cleaning and other household duties. Volunteers may be asked to assist in other research projects of the National Park, such as monitoring tourism, protecting seaturtles or counting birds.

Lang.:   English.

Accom.: Shared rooms in a hotel or on the research vessel.

Cost: US$1,295 for 2 weeks; US$325 for 1 extra week.

Agents: The Ecovolunteer Network at www.ecovolunteer.org.

Applic.: The Ecovolunteer Network (see Organisation list).

INTERNATIONAL TRUST FOR TRADITIONAL MEDICINE (ITTM)

Vijnana Niwas, Madhuban, Kalimpong 734 301
West Bengal   India
Tel.: ++91 (3552) 56459/53502
E-mail: ittmk@vsnl.com
www.kreisels.com/ittm

Desc.: ITTM is a non-profit Trust based in northeastern Himalayas, with the objective to promote study on Indo-Tibetan medicine and associated medical cultures of this Himalayan region. Activities include, among others: biodynamic cultivation of medicinal plants of the Eastern Himalaya; yoga and art classes for local children, social work with impoverished children.

Spp.: Medicinal plants of the Darjeeling.

Hab.: Tropical, temperate and alpine ecological zones.

Loc.: Kalimpong, northeastern Himalayas, Darjeeling District.

Travel: From Delhi or Kolkata by plane to Bagdogra or by train to North Jalpaiguri, then jeep, bus or taxi to Kalimpong.

Dur.: Mini. 4 weeks, max. 6 months to 1 year.

Per.: Year round.

L. term: 6 months to 1 year.

Age: Min. 20.

Qualif.: Skills depend on projects: from biodynamic gardening, to lab science, steam distillation for essential oils, Tibetan language, computer pagination, Hatha yoga or teaching crafts to children.

Work: General activities are to assist in: preparing and spraying of BD preps and preparing compost; working in the laboratory (essential oils, chromatography, herbal teas); identifying, labelling, collecting medicinal plants; preparing a database of the medicinal plants; assisting in office and computer work.

Lang.: English, willingness to learn Tibetan or Sanskrit is appreciated.

Accom.: Double rooms, communal bathroom with hot shower; separate guest-flat for long-term volunteers with 2 rooms.

Cost: Approx. US$10 per day.

Applic.: E-mail CV with expression of interest and photograph.

Notes: Volunteers have access to the library and a computer.

IONIAN DOLPHIN PROJECT, Greece

Tethys Research Institute
c/o Civic Aquarium, Viale G.B. Gadio 2
20121 Milano Italy
Tel.: ++39 (02) 7200 1947 – Fax: ++39 (02) 7200 1946
E-mail: tethys@tethys.org
www.tethys.org

Desc.: This is the first long-term project on cetaceans in Ionian Greece, initiated in 1993 by the Tethys Research Institute (see Organisation list), with the goal to study the socio-ecology of common and bottlenose dolphins that live in the coastal waters of the island of Kalamos. Common dolphins are now declining in the Mediterranean, owing to overfishing, by-catches, pollution and human disturbance. By monitoring this community, researchers hope to find proper conservation measures. Methods of investigation include photo-ID and behavioural sampling, respiration sampling and biopsy sampling from free-ranging identified dolphins.

Spp.: Common dolphin (*Delphinus delphis*), bottlenose dolphin (*Tursiops truncatus*); sea turtles (*Caretta caretta*) and monk seals (*Monachus monachus*) may be also observed.

Hab.: Coastal waters of the central Ionian Greece.

Loc.: Island of Kalamos, Greece.

Travel: Airplane to Athens or Preveza, then bus to Mytika. Transfer to Kalamos is provided by the researchers. Patras can also be reached by ferry from the Italian ports of Venice, Ancona or Brindisi.

Dur.: 10 days.

Per.: May to September.

L. term: Successive shifts can be booked. For logistic reasons, volunteers cannot stay at the field station before the beginning or after the end of the shift(s).

Age: Min. 18.

Qualif.: No particular skills are required. Volunteers should be interested and very motivated.

Work: The work consists of observations from the inflatable craft and from the land; volunteers will shift between the 2 on a daily basis. With good weather 1 group of volunteers conduct boat-based surveys of dolphins, while the other group makes land based observations. Volunteers at the observation point on the land are in constant contact with the boat via VHF, in order to give information on the presence of dolphins. With bad weather volunteers stay at the base, entering and analysing data and matching the catalogued slides. Lectures on the dolphin biology are also carried out by the researchers.

Lang.: English, Italian, Greek helpful.

Accom.: The base is located in the village of Episcopi. Supplies are made on the mainland. The house has 5 bedrooms, 1 of which is equipped with 6 beds for the volunteers. Everyone takes part in cooking and housekeeping. The base is equipped with a computer, a basic scientific library, photographic archives, slide projector, telephone, fax and VHF.

Cost: EUR620–780 (approx. GB£410–520), depending on the season, including food. Volunteers are required to carry travel insurance, covering medical expenses, which can be made when booking. Fees do not include travel.

Agents: Tethys Research Institute (see Organisation list).

Applic.: Request a standard application form to be completed and returned to the Tethys Research Institute Volunteer Programme. Given the high number of applications, early booking is suggested.

Notes: Only 6 volunteers can participate in each shift. From 3–4 researchers reside at the field station with the volunteers. The small size of the boat and the low-noise engine allow an easy approach of the dolphins and their following at close range without major modifications of their behaviour.

IRACAMBI ATLANTIC RAINFOREST RESEARCH AND CONSERVATION CENTER, Brazil

Fazenda Iracambi, Rosário da Limeira
36878–000 Minas Gerais Brazil
Tel.: ++55 (32) 3721 1436 – Fax: ++55 (32) 3722 4909
E-mail: iracambi@iracambi.com
www.iracambi.com

Desc.: Amigos de Iracambi is a non-profit organisation that promotes the conservation of the Atlantic Rainforest, while helping the local farmers to develop sustainably. The organisation aims to reverse the process of land degradation and deforestation, by restoring land fertility, productivity and economic viability.

Spp.: Inventories of flora and fauna are being carried out.

Hab.: Semi-deciduous rainforest.

Loc.: Southeastern Brazil in the State of Minas Gerais.

Travel: Fly to Rio de Janeiro, bus to Muriaé and Rosário da Limeira.

Dur.: 3 months, but shorter periods are negotiable.

Per.: Year round.

L. term: Visa allows max. 180 days. Longer stays require special visa.

Age: Min.18, no max.

Qualif.: General hands with no skills are welcome. IT, GIS and mapping specialists, carpenters, teachers (in Portuguese), tropical botanists, and zoologists, are especially needed.

Work: Extremely various: wildlife surveys, nature interpretation, cartography, construction, graphic and web design, marketing, fundraising, reforestation , socio-economic research, building and maintaining trails, medicinal plants farming, environmental education for local school children, farmers outreach, etc. Iracambi encourages individuals to use at best their skills.

Lang.: English, Portuguese is extremely helpful but not essential.

Accom.: Shared room in traditional farm cottages (a few km apart) with electricity and gas stoves for individual cooking.

Cost: US$500 for first 3 months or less, US$150 per month thereafter; includes all food and accommodation, not transport.

Applic.: Send CV via e-mail. No deadlines or forms to fill in.

Notes: Full information from the volunteer page on the website.

ISCHIA DOLPHIN PROJECT

Studiomare
Via D'Abundo 82
80075 Forio d'Ischia (NA) Italy
Tel./Fax: ++39 (081) 989 578 – Mob.:(on board) ++ 39 (349) 5749927
E-mail: studiomare@pointel.it
www.mare.it/studiomare

Desc.: The submarine canyon of Cuma is an important habitat where a particular pelagic community can be found very close to the coast. The constant presence of whales and dolphins, pelagic fishes and marine birds is related to the geological and ecological characteristics of the area. The research objectives are to include the canyon into the perimeter of the future Marine Protected Area of Ischia, Procida and Vivara Islands proposed by the Italian Ministry of Environment. The study area is an important breeding and feeding ground for the endangered short-beaked common dolphin and for all Odontocetes species. The submarine canyon is also used as feeding ground by fin whales. The strong impact of the boats on cetaceans is becoming a growing problem in the busy summer days: it causes distress and disorientation and occasionally death by propeller strike. Management measures to protect cetaceans in this key area are urgently needed.

Spp.: Common dolphin (*Delphinus delphis*), striped dolphin (*Stenella coeruleoalba*), bottlenose dolphin (*Tursiops truncatus*), Risso's dolphin (*Grampus griseus*), pilot whale (*Globicephala melas*), finback whale (*Balaenoptera physalus*).

Hab.: Coastal and pelagic Mediterranean waters, submarine canyon.

Loc.: Mediterranean sea, Ischia Island, Italy.

Travel: Airplane or train to Naples, then bus to Beverello, then ferry or hydrofoil to Ischia island.

Dur.: 1 week.

Per.: June to October.

L. term: Maximum stay is 2 weeks with project leader approval.

Age: Min. 18.

Qualif.:   No particular skills required just good physical health.

Work: Daily course of cethology (evolution, adaptation to the sea, classification, bio-acoustic, social behaviour, relations with fisheries); practical lessons on cetacean watching; during sightings volunteers carry out precise tasks, such as timing the divings or photo-identifying the animals. The recording system allows volunteers to get confidence with cetaceans' vocalisations and background noises of the sea. Cooking, dish washing, cleaning, steering and watching shifts are shared among the volunteers.

Lang.:   English or Italian/French/Spanish.

Accom.: On board of 'Jean Gab', a 17.70 m wooden cutter built in 1930 in Marseille, transformed in a laboratory on the sea, the boat is provided with a 10-years database and a recording system to collect bio-acoustic data and underwater videos. Available on board are books and scientific literature on cetaceans.

Cost: EUR625–725 (approx. GB£410–480). Price inlcudes: food and beverages, accommodation, fuel for the research vessel and the inflatable craft, port fees, lectures and training by StudioMare researchers, certificate of attendance. Travel, insurance (EUR13.50), membership fee (EUR30), and the first dinner, are not included.

Agents: StudioMare.

Applic.:   Send and e-mail to above address. A 50% deposit to reserve the place is needed with the application.

Notes: StudioMare works in the area since 1991 thanks to the volunteers' help.

JATUN SACHA, Ecuador

Fundación Jatun Sacha
Eugenio de Santillán N34 –248 y Maurián
Casilla 17–12–867 Quito Ecuador
Tel.: ++593 (2) 243 2173 – Fax: ++593 (2) 243 2240
E-mail: volunteer@jatunsacha.org
www.jatunsacha.org

Desc.: Jatun Sacha Foundation is an Ecuadorian NGO whose main objective is conservation of the environment. Jatun Sacha has 5 biological stations located in different areas of Ecuador: Amazon, coast and highlands.

Spp.: Various species of Ecuadorian fauna and vegetation.

Hab.: Andean cloud forest, tropical rainforest, dry forest, premontane forest, humid forest, mangrove forest.

Loc.: Ecuadorian coast, highlands and Amazon.

Travel: By airplane to Quito, bus or truck from Quito to the stations.

Dur: Min. 15 days.

Per.: Year round.

L.term: Possible, inquire with the organisation.

Age: Min. 18.

Qualif.: Volunteers must be dynamic and interested in conservation.

Work: Reforestation, agroforestry, organic agriculture and farming, community extension projects, general mainteinance, meteorological and other environmental data collection, trekking, visits to communities, aquaculture work.

Lang.: English, basic Spanish is highly recommended, but not required.

Accom.: Shared cabins, in some cases without electricity, with toilets outside.

Cost: Application fee US$30. Food and accommodation US$300 per month.

Applic.: Send by regular mail: CV, a cover letter, 2 passport size photos, medical certificate, police record, and a US$30 application fee.

THE KANHA NATIONAL PARK ECOSYSTEM, India

The Krishna Jungle Resort, Village Mocha
Kanha national park, Madhyapradesh India
Tel.: ++ 91 (761) 310 318/504 023/24
Fax: ++ 91 (761) 315 153
E-mail: hotelkrishna@vsnl.com
www.indiamart.com/krishnaresort

Desc: Volunteers are needed as educational/ecotourism interpreters to the lodge guests of the ecosystem of Kanha National Park.

Spp.: A wide variety of mammals, birds and reptiles.

Hab.: Moist deciduous forest, dry deciduous forest, valley meadows and plateau meadows.

Loc.: Central India; n the state of Madhya Pradesh also known as the Kiplings country.

Travel: Nearest rail station and airport is Jabalpur, 165 km from Kanha National Park. There are direct trains and flights from Delhi to Jabalpur.

Dur.: 6 months.

Per.: November to April.

L. term: Yes.

Age: Min. 15.

Qualif.: No particulars skills needed. A strong interest towards wildlife and nature and good interpretation skills are needed.

Work: Interacting with the guests and leading them in game drives.

Lang.: English.

Accom.: Room in the Resort.

Cost: US$500 for 6 months. Cost of food and accommodation included. Transportation to the project site not included.

Applic.: Via e-mail directly to the resort.

Notes: Volunteers from the UK are especially welcome.

LEATHERBACK SEATURTLE TAGGING PROGRAMME

Ocean Spirits Inc.

P.O. Box 1373, Grand Anse, St.George's, Grenada, West Indies

Tel.: ++ (473) 442 1055

Fax: ++ (473) 442 1055 (call ahead)

E-mail: oceanspirits@caribsurf.com

www.oceanspirits.homestead.com/oceanspirits.html

Desc.:	Ocean Spirits Inc. is a non-profit NGO dedicated to the conservation of marine life and the marine environment. Through 3 programmes: Education, Research and Conservation and Community Development the NGO is working to change attitudes towards the sustainable use of resources in Grenada.
Spp.:	Leatherback sea turtle (*Dermochelys coriacea*); Hawksbill sea turtle (*Eretmochelys imbricata*).
Hab.:	Tropical beaches.
Loc.:	Grenada, West Indies.
Travel:	Plane to Grenada, volunteer are met at the airport.
Dur.:	Volunteers must commit for a period of 6 weeks.
Per.:	March to September.
L. term:	Volunteers may stay for more than1 period.
Age:	Min. 18.
Qualif.:	Previous experience of field work and data collection is an advantage. Good physical condition as the work involves long hours, beach walks and some cycling, in all weather conditions. Enthusiasm and flexibility are also important
Work:	Night beach patrolling for nesting sea turtles, applying tags and collecting other data. Morning beach surveys to determine turtle nesting activity. Conducting educational field trips, manning the public information desk and camp maintenance activities.
Lang.:	English.
Accom.:	Dormitory style accommodation, sheets and towels needed.
Cost:	GB£750/US$1,275 for 6 weeks. Price includes accommodation, food and airport transfers.
Applic.:	Standard application form available via e-mail on request. Apply no later than 6 weeks prior to requested voluntary period.

LEOPARDS OF PHINDA, South Africa

Dept. of Biological Sciences, Monash University
P.O. Box 18.Victoria, 3800 Australia
Tel.: ++61 (3) 9905 5602
Fax: ++61 (3) 9905 5613
E-mail: luke.hunter@sci.monash.edu.au
www.wildaboutcats.org/internship.htm

Desc.: The research investigates the conservation ecology of leopards in a region where land-use varies from wildlife reserves (where protection is strict) to livestock farms where leopards are heavily persecuted. The research will provide data essential to ensure the species survival in the region.

Spp.: Primarily leopards; additional monitoring of lions, cheetahs and spotted hyaenas as well as counts of prey species.

Hab.: Woodland-savannah mosaic.

Loc.: Northern KwaZulu-Natal province, South Africa.

Travel: Airplane to Johannesburg then to the field site by a 90-minute flight in a light passenger plane.

Dur.: 2 weeks.

Per.: Year round.

L. term: Only for a third week for an extra cost of US$1,000.

Age: Under 18 must be accompanied by a guardian. No upper limit.

Qualif.: No particular skills needed but volunteers must be physically fit and will need to be able to put in long hours under physically demanding field conditions.

Work: Volunteers assist in live-capture of wild leopards to fit with radio-collars and to collect data on physical measurements, weight, tissue sampling. Long hours are spent radio-tracking and observing leopards. Monitoring of other carnivore species (lions, cheetahs and spotted hyaenas), intermittent counts of prey species and entering data onto computer databases.

Lang.: English.

Accom.: Accommodation is in a large comfortbale farmhouse.

Cost: US$2,660; includes room, board and inland flight from Jo'burg.

Applic.: Contact Dr. Luke Hunter for an application form.

Notes: Only 2 volunteers can join each expedition.

LIBANONA ECOLOGY CENTRE, Madagascar

BP 42, Fort Dauphin–614 Madagascar
Tel.: ++ 261 (20) 922 1242
E-mail: libanonaecology@hotmail.com
www.andrewleestrust.org.uk/libanona.htm

Desc.: The Libanona Ecology Centre (LEC) is a Malagasy NGO working in the field of conservation and training in Southeast Madagascar. Current projects are themed on: community forest management, GIS, conservation education, applied biodiversity, anthropological research and community tourism.

Spp.: Various species of Malgasy flora and fauna.

Hab.: Malagasy spiny forest, littoral forest, humid forest, transitional forest, coastal ecosystem.

Loc.: Madagascar, off the coast of Africa.

Travel: Flight to Antananarivo and internal flight to Fort Dauphin.

Dur.: From a few weeks to 8–9 months.

Per.: Year round.

L.term: Possible, inquire with organisation.

Age: Min. 18, no max.

Qualif.: Depend on particular placement and project. An ability to work in extremely challenging conditions is a must.

Work: In the following skill areas: GIS, eco tourism, conservation education, TEFL, apiculture, forestry, biodiversity research. Placements are designed with specific volunteers in mind.

Lang.: English, French required for field and office activities.

Accom.: Very basic. Ranges from rough camping to rooms in wooden huts to a comfortable house in LEC. No hot water.

Cost: Depends on placement, concrete contribution to a LEC development project is requested (financing materials for local development associations, or for the lab and library) as a goodwill gesture. A typical 3-month placement costs approx. GB£2,750 (approx. EUR/US$4,100), but it can vary.

Applic.: Send CV and letter of interest via e-mail to Barry Ferguson. Specify area of expertise, availability and theme of interest.

LIFELINE CAT RESEARCH AND REHABILITATION CENTRE, Belize

P.O. Box 86 San Ignacio
Cayo   Belize
E-mail: pm@li-feline.com – lifelinebelize@yahoo.co.uk
www.li-feline.com

Desc.: A Belizean non-profit, NGO dedicated to the conservation of endangered wild cats, with special emphasis on the rehabilitation of confiscated cats to the wild.

Spp.: Jaguar, puma, ocelot, margay, jaguarundi.

Hab.: Broadleaf forest, tropical pine forest.

Loc.: Central Belize, Central America.

Travel: By air to Belize International Airport then by minibus to LiFeline.

Dur.: Courses last a minimum of 10 days.

Per.: Year round.

L.term: 3-, 6- or 12-month periods for outstanding volunteers.

Age: Min. 18.

Qualif.: Ability to work in tropical rainforest, clean driving licence. Must have reasonable standard of physical fitness. A degree in zoology or associated subject would be an advantage.

Work: Helping to build and maintain cat enclosures, monitoring released cats by radio telemetry, behavioural studies. Caring for rescued cats (feeding them and helping with veterinary procedures). Occasionally act as guide to visiting school parties.

Lang.: English, some Spanish useful.

Accom.: At local ranch for courses; in a house on site for long-term volunteers.

Cost: Courses cost US$1,795 for 10 days excluding flights. Long-term volunteers food: approx. US$70 per week.

Applic.: Request application form via e-mail.

Notes: See website for more information.

LIVING AND WORKING WITHIN A SUSTAINABLE VILLAGE

BTCV
36 St. Mary's Street Wallingford, Oxfordshire OX10 0EU   UK
Tel.: ++ 44 (1491) 821 600
Fax: ++ 44 (1491) 839 646
E-mail: information@btcv.org.uk
www.btcv.org

Desc.: Gomorszolos is a sustainable village that integrates sustainable agriculture, traditional handicrafts, eco-tourism, education in alternative technologies and nature protection into the development scheme of the region. The project is a partnership between BTCV and Green Action.

Spp: Orchids set in a rich habitat.

Hab.: Traditionally cultivated land and orchards surrounding the village.

Loc.: Gomorszolos village in northern Hungary, 2 km from the Slovakian border, close to the World Heritage Aggtelek and Bukk National Parks.

Travel: Airplane to Budapest, bus to Kelemer (Meeting point Kelemer bus stop).

Dur.: 9 days.

Per.: Throughout thesummer.

L. term: Contact organisation for details.

Age: Min. 18.

Work: Ecological grassland management, helping in the orchards and the option of helping on the organic study farm. Work takes place in mornings only giving time to visit the unique cave system in Aggtelek National Park and Eger town, with it's thermal baths, learn Hungarian folk dances, try traditional felt making, take archery lessons and sample local cuisine.

Lang.: English.

Accom.: A new traditional-styleguest house in the Education Centre, which incorporates energy-saving techniques.

Cost: GB£355 (approx. EUR/US$530) flight not included.

Agents: BTCV at www.btcv.org.

Applic.: BTCV (see Organisation list).

LOGGERHEAD SEA TURTLES IN LINOSA, Italy

CTS – Centro Turistico Studentesco e Giovanile
Via A. Vesalio 6
00161 Rome Italy
Tel.: ++39 (06) 4411 1473/4 – Fax.: ++39 (06) 4411 1401
e-mail: ambiente@cts.it
www.cts.it

Desc.: Loggerhead sea turtles come to nest on the island of Linosa, south of Sicily. Their survival in the Mediterranean is threatened by water pollution, habitat destruction and human activities. CTS researchers, with funding from the EU, are trying to protect the rare nesting beaches by collecting data, patrolling these areas and informing tourists and local people about the importance of habitat and species protection. Monitoring and tracking of turtles by advanced satellite technology are among the activities carried out.

Spp.: Loggerhead sea turtle (*Caretta caretta*).

Hab.: Mediterranean coast.

Loc.: Island of Linosa, Sicily, Italy.

Travel: Airplane to Palermo and Linosa or ferry from Agrigento.

Dur.: 10 days.

Per.: June to September.

L. term: Inquire with organisation.

Age: Min. 18 (16 with parent's authorisation).

Qualif.: Volunteers must be flexible and willing to work during the night.

Work: Participants will observe and count nesting females, nests, eggs or hatchlings and rescue injured animals. Volunteers will also give information to local people and tourists. Lectures on flora, fauna and geology of the island and excursions are scheduled.

Lang.: Italian, Spanish accepted.

Accom.: Apartment with kitchen.

Cost: EUR 280–350 (approx.GB£ 180–230), food and travel not included.

Agents: CTS regional offices in Italy (see Organisation list).

Applic.: Request application form. Membership to CTS required.

MANAGEMENT PLAN FOR PILOS LAGOON

Hellenic Ornithological Society (HOS)
Vas. Irakleiou 24, 10682   Athens   Greece
In the field: HOS, Hotel Pilos, Gialova, 24001 Pilos Greece
Tel./Fax: ++30 (723) 41 634 – Mob.: ++30 (997) 948 644
E-mail: jobogi@otenet.gr
www.ornithologiki.org

Desc.: The goal of the project is the implementation of a management plan for the Pilos lagoon. The goals are wetland restoration, providing visitor facilities and educating local people about the value of the site. A very important and sensitive section of the project is the research and protection of the African chameleon, found exclusively in this region.

Spp.: African chameleon (*Chamaeleo africanus*).

Hab.: Mediterranean coastal lagoon.

Loc.: Greece, southwestern coast of the Peloponnese peninsula.

Travel: Airplane to Athens or by ferry from Italy to Patras; bus, train or airplane to Kalamata or Kiparissia; bus to Pilos.

Dur.: 1–2 months.

Per.: June to October.

L. term: Only with project leader's approval after regular period.

Age: Min. 20, max. 35, depending on the experience.

Qualif.: No particular skills required.

Work: Beach patrolling to prevent collection and disturbance of the chameleons and helping with field research.

Lang.: English, Greek.

Accom.: In tents in a public campsite. Volunteers can bring their own tent. Sleeping bag and mat are a must.

Cost: About EUR100 (approx. GB£65) for a month stay. This fee covers the expenses of the camping and of the material used.

Agents: Contact project leaders (Marilia Kalouli or Andrea Bonetti).

Applic.: An application form needs to be filled out.

Notes: Field work and beach patrolling is hard work, especially during the summer. Volunteers must be motivated.

MANATEE RESEARCH PROJECT, Belize

Oceanic Society Expeditions
Fort Mason Center, Building E
San Francisco, California 94123   USA
Tel.: ++1 (415) 441 1106 – Fax: ++1 (415) 474 3395
E-mail: info@oceanic-society.org
www.oceanic-society.org

Desc.: The goal of this project is to collect biological data necessary for manatee protection and habitat management. The research objectives are to determine distribution and abundance of manatees at Turneffe Atoll, their behavioural ecology, and environmental parameters of microhabitats used consistently.

Spp.: Manatee (*Trichechus manatus*).

Hab.: Tropical sea.

Loc.: Turneffe Atoll, Belize.

Travel: Volunteers can reach Belize by airplane using group airfare from some US gateway cities (Houston, Los Angeles, Miami).

Dur.: 8 days.

Per.: June, July.

L. term: Inquire with organisation.

Age: Min. 18.

Qualif.: No particular skills required.

Work: By small boat, volunteers visit zones of manatee concentration, map positions, note individual markings, and log behavioural information.

Lang.: English.

Cost: US$1,490.

Accom.: Beachfront cabanas with porch, double rooms with private bath.

Applic.: Request application form to be returned with a deposit of US$300.

Notes: Max. group size is 8. Volunteer can have free time for beach snorkelling.

MANGA DEL MAR MENOR
RESTORATION AND RESEARCH PROJECT

Instituto de Ciencias Sociales y Ambientales & Amigos de la UNESCO
Plaza Cetina 6, Entlo.1, 30001 Murcia Spain
Tel.: ++34 (968) 220 596 – Fax: ++34 (968) 220 597
E-mail: unesco@ctv.es
www.ctv.es/USERS/murban/volunt.htm

Desc.: The project includes cultural and natural resource restoration and research in different zones in the Manga del Mar Menor; ecological research in the coastal landscapes and wetlands of the Calblanque Park; prehistoric and archaeological research in the Cueva Victoria, antiquities site; coastwatching and research activities around the wetlands.

Spp.: Seabirds, raptors, marine mammals, endemic species.

Hab.: Coastal Mediterranean wetland.

Loc.: La Manga del Mar Menor, Spain.

Travel: A brochure with information will be provided upon request.

Dur.: 15 days to 3 months.

Per.: July to September.

L. term: Max. 3 months.

Age: Min.16.

Qualif.: No special qualifications required. Volunteers must have a strong motivation to work for nature conservation.

Work: Activities include data collection, cleaning caverns, filming videos, observation of submarine zones and plants, informing the visitors to the park, environmental education with children.

Lang.: Spanish, English, French. Other languages are welcome. Spanish lessons can be provided.

Accom.: Tents in First Touristic Camping, tents in the park.

Cost: 15 days, without accommodation cost EUR145; tents in the park and meals cost EUR375; tents in a First Class Camping cost EUR330 without meal (in both cases participants must provide their own tent and sleeping bag). Fees include transportation from the airport, half board and insurance.

Applic.: Request application form, or download it from the website.

THE MARINE MAMMAL CENTER (TMMC)

Marin Headlands, GGNRA
Sausalito, California 94965 USA
Tel.: ++1 (415) 289 7325 /979 4357 (volunteer inquiries)
Fax: ++1 (415) 289 7333
E-mail: volunteer@tmmc.org
www.tmmc.org – www.marinemammalcenter.org

Desc.: The Marine Mammal Center is a leading rescue, rehabilitation and release facility for marine mammals. It treats almost 600 animals a year. Volunteer crews work on a 24-hour shift, 365-days a year.

Spp.: Marine mammals, primarily pinnipeds.

Hab.: Pacific coast.

Loc.: Northern California (San Francisco).

Travel: Airplane to San Francisco, then by car.

Dur.: Flexible.

Per: Volunteers are accepted year round but are needed most during high season (March to August).

L. term: Volunteers can remain as long as they like.

Age.: Min. 18.

Qualif.: Ability to work as part of a team and with wild animals.

Work: Volunteers prepare food, feed animals, restrain animals for tube feeds and physical exams, clean pens, wash dishes, do laundry, administer medication, weigh animals and chart all observations. The shifts run from 6–12 hours depending on the season. Training is provided.

Lang.: English.

Accom.: No accommodation available.

Cost: Volunteers must provide accommodation, food and transportation. There is no public transportation to the site. Volunteers can reach the site by bicycle.

Applic.: After admission volunteers must attend an orientation upon arrival and complete a liability waiver.

Notes: This physically demanding work requires good health.

MARINE TURTLE & YOUTH ENVIRONMENTAL EDUCATION

Grupo Ecologico de La Costa Verde
827 Union Pacific
PMB 078–253, Laredo, Texas 78045–9452   USA
Tel.: ++52 (311) 258 4100 (in Mexico)
E-mail: tortuga@pvnet.com.mx – grupo-eco@project-tortuga.org
www.project-tortuga.org

Desc.: Grupo Ecologico de la Costa Verde is a Mexican Non-profit, Civil Association dedicated to the protection of the natural environment, with special interest in the protection of the marine turtles and in Youth Environmental Education.

Spp.: Olive Ridley (*Lepidochelys olivacea*); leatherback (*Dermochelys coriacea*); eastern Pacific green turtle (*Chelonia agassizi*).

Hab.: Marine, tropical, coastal.

Loc.: Central Pacific coast of Mexico.

Travel: By airplane to Puerto Vallarta ; bus from Puerto Vallarta, north to San Francisco or San Pancho.

Dur: Min. 2 months; 5–6 months is ideal.

Per.: June 15 to November 15.

L. term: Possible for outstanding volunteers.

Age: Min. 22.

Qualif.: Volunteers must be able to work in occasional heavy rain and operate a Volkswagen dune buggy over rough, muddy roads; they also should have a fair understanding of rural environment problems and of preservation of natural resources, and be able to do public work with children.

Work: Collect marine turtle nests between 9am–6pm, 5–7 nights/week; maintain records on relocation and/or collection of nests, temperatures, hatchlings released and nest cleaning; teaching and lectures.

Lang.: English (with some Spanish) is needed for Marine Turtle Project. Spanish (with some English) for teaching.

Accom.: See Cost section below.

Cost: Rooms rent for US$80–120/month, single apt. US$225–400/month. Food is US$35–45/week. Volunteers pay for travel.

Applic.: By e-mail .

MEDITERRANEAN FIN WHALE PROGRAMME

Tethys Research Institute
c/o Civic Aquarium, Viale G.B. Gadio 2
20121 Milano Italy
Tel.: ++39 (02) 7200 1947 – Fax: ++39 (02) 7200 1946
E-mail: tethys@tethys.org
www.tethys.org

Desc.: Since 1987 the Tethys Research Institute has conducted research on fin whales that concentrate during the summer in the western Ligurian Sea and in the Corsican Sea. The Mediterranean Fin Whale Programme conducts studies of the ecology, habitat use and population dynamics and behaviour of these cetaceans. Research techniques include photo-ID, biopsy sampling and photogrammetry.

Spp.: Fin whales (*Balaenoptera physalus*), striped dolphin (*Stenella coeruleoalba*), Risso's dolphin (*Grampus griseus*) sperm whale (*Physeter catodon*), long-finned pilot whale (*Globicephala melas*).

Hab.: Pelagic and coastal waters.

Loc.: Ligurian Sea, Mediterranean Sea.

Travel: Departure and arrival is in San Remo, Italy. Airplane to Nice, Genoa or Milan, then train to San Remo.

Dur.: 7 days (6 nights on board).

Per.: June to October.

L. term: Volunteers can book successive cruises.

Age: Min. 18 years.

Qualif.: No qualifications required. Volunteers should be able to swim. Flexibility, enthusiasm and willingness to help with all research and household activities are necessary.

Work: Volunteers will be trained at the beginning of the cruise and then will assist with research activities (photo-ID, data collection and filing, observations, etc.) and will share cooking and cleaning duties. Lectures and slide projections on marine biology and cetaceans are scheduled.

Lang.: Italian, English.

Accom.: On board the 19-metre ketch *Gemini Lab*, participants will be hosted in 3 double and 1 quadruple cabin, with bunk beds. Sleeping bags required. There are 2 showers and 2 toilets.

Cost: Costs range from EUR570–730 (approx. GB£ 380–485) for a 6–day cruise depending on the season. Food and fuel (except for the first evening) are included. Travel to San Remo and a compulsory insurance (EUR15 for each period) are not included.

Agents: Tethys Research Institute (see Organisation list).

Applic.: Download from the website the application form to be completed and returned to the Tethys Research Institute Volunteer Programme. Early booking is necessary for July and August.

Notes: Participants should be aware that this is a scientific research project rather than a vacation programme. Also take note of the following: in bad weather it will not be possible to conduct the field research activities; it is strictly forbidden to smoke inside the boat and on the inflatable; it is possible that volunteers share the cabin with a person of the opposite sex.

MONITORING OF OLIVE RIDLEY SEA TURTLE POPULATIONS

Regional Wildlife Management Program
Universidad Nacional
Apdo. 1350–3000 Heredia Costa Rica
Tel.: ++ (506) 237 7039/277 3600 – Fax: ++ (506) 237 7036
E-mail: clee@una.ac.cr – prmvs@una.ac.cr
www.una.ac.cr/ambi/prmvs/

Desc.: This is a 16-year old ongoing project that monitors the population of olive ridley sea turtles at Nancite Beach, on the northwestern Pacific coast of Costa Rica. Nancite is 1 of the few known 'arribada' beaches in the world, where 10s of 1,000s of turtles emerge to nest over a 1–7 day period. The project estimates numbers of nesting turtles, predation rates on nests and hatchlings, hatching success, and develops management plans for this unique population. Unlike other arribada beaches, Nancite is well-protected from poachers due to its inaccessibility and because it is part of a national park. Data collected over the past several years shows that the turtle population at Nancite is declining sharply. The project also aims to promote environmental awareness and to find ways of minimizing negative human impact on sea turtles.

Spp.: Olive ridley sea turtle (*Lepidochelys olivacea*).

Hab.: Tropical coast, tropical dry forest.

Loc.: Northwestern Pacific coast of Costa Rica, inside Santa Rosa National Park, Guanacaste Province.

Travel: Airplane to San José International airport, then bus to Santa Rosa National Park (4.5 hours), then a 10-mile hike over uneven terrain to Nancite biological station.

Dur.: Min. 4 months; 6–12 months desirable.

Per.: Year round.

L. term: Long-term volunteers are preferred. Principal researcher will not spend long periods of time at the site, so volunteers will receive training to perform all duties independently.

Age: Min. 21.

Qualif.: Bachelor's degree in biology, environmental sciences or related field required. Volunteers must be outdoor-oriented, well organised and independent, be physically fit and willing to live in a remote yet pristine natural area. Must be physically fit enough to endure the long hike in hot and humid climate, over uneven terrain. Knowledge of Windows software (word processor, spreadsheet) is desirable.

Work: Count turtles with 2 different methods (quadrats and transects) during arribadas, mark nests, register predation and hatching rates, measure and tag adult turtles, translocate nests, take environmental parameters, remove debris from beach and free turtles caught in vegetation or in debris. A team of 2 volunteers is usually present at Nancite all year round. Volunteers are expected to spend a minimum of 23 days a month in Nancite, then have 7 days off.

Lang.: Spanish, English, Portuguese (Spanish highly desirable).

Accom.: Nancite biological station houses up to 25 people. It has bunk beds with a few individual rooms, bathrooms with running water and kitchen. There is no electricity but a solar panel and a gas generator are available for recharging batteries. Bed sheets, pillowcase and a mosquito net are required. Additionally, volunteers prepare their own meals and help to keep the biological station clean.

Cost: Housing is provided by the project. Additional money is needed for food, buses and personal expenses while in town. Room and board in town may range from US$15–35/day.

Agents: Prospective volunteers should contact Professor Claudette Mo (Principal investigator) or Susana Cruzela at the above address.

Applic.: Send a CV and 2 letters of recommendation from former supervisors or professors who can attest personal qualifications, especially concerning willingness to work under difficult conditions, self-reliance, motivation, human relations, intellectual capacity. No deadline.

Notes: In the past 8 years, the project has had more than 17 volunteers, from Costa Rica, Panama, US, Spain, Switzerland and Germany.

MONK SEAL PROJECT, Turkey

The Ecovolunteer Network
Meyersweg 29   7553 AX Hengelo The Netherlands
Tel.: ++31 (74) 250 8250
Fax: ++31 (74) 250 6572
E-mail: info@ecovolunteer.org
www.ecovolunteer.org

Desc.: The Mediterranean monk seal is 1 of the 12 most endangered species in the world and needs immediate protection. In the Aegean Sea there are only 150–180 individuals left. This project was initiated in 1993 with help from WWF and AFAG, a Turkish nature conservation organisation.

Spp. Mediterranean monk seal (*Monachus monachus*).

Hab.: Mediterranean Sea.

Loc.: Foca, 80 km north of Izmir, Turkey.

Travel: Airplane to Izmir, then transfer to Foca.

Dur.: Min. 2 weeks.

Per.: Year round.

Age: Min. 18, max. 40.

Qualif.: Volunteers must speak English, be in good physical health, able to walk on difficult ground and swim well. Diving and boating experience, knowledge of biology and other languages is useful. Volunteers with birdwatching experience can contribute to the inventory of bird species.

Work: Volunteers assist biologists in surveys of caves, land observations, collecting data on animals, plants and weather conditions and help in public awareness activities (slide shows, T-shirt sales, daily talks on tour boats).

Lang.: English, knowledge of other languages is welcome.

Accom.: Small pension or campsite depending on the period.

Cost: EUR420 (approx. GB£ 280) for 2 weeks; EUR195 (approx. GB£120) for every additional week.

Agents: The Ecovolunteer Network at www.ecovolunteer.org.

Applic.: The Ecovolunteer Network (see Organisation list).

THE MONKEY SANCTUARY

Looe
Cornwall PL13 1NZ   UK
Tel./Fax: ++44 (1503) 262 532
E-mail: info@monkeysanctuary.org
www.monkeysanctuary.org

Desc.: The Monkey Sanctuary is home to a natural colony of woolly monkeys and rescued capuchins. It was founded in 1964 as a reaction against the pet trade in primates. The Sanctuary is open to the public during the summer and the main emphasis is to encourage an attitude of caring and respect toward primates and the environment. The Sanctuary gardens and meadows contain many native species of plants and animals.

Spp.: Woolly monkeys (*Lagothryx lagothricha*) and capuchins.

Hab.: N/A.

Loc.: Looe, Cornwall, UK.

Dur.: 2–4 weeks.

Per.: Year round.

L. term: Invitation to stay long term if the initial visit proves successful.

Age: Min. 18.

Qualif.: No specific skills required, although applicants should have an interest in the field and practical skills are always welcome.

Work: Maintaining and cleaning the enclosures, preparing food for the animals, providing information to the public.

Lang.: English.

Cost: A voluntary donation for room and board is requested. Volunteers must provide transportation to the Sanctuary.

Applic.: Write for further details (please enclose international postage coupon or stamped SAE for UK residents), then fill out an application form. Owing to the large number of applicants, please apply at least 6 months in advance.

MONTE ADONE WILDLIFE PROTECTION CENTRE

Via Brento, 9
40037 – Sasso Marconi (BO) Italy
Tel./Fax: ++39 (051) 847 600
E-mail: info@centrotutelafauna.org
www.centrotutelafauna.org

Desc.: A voluntary non-profit institution working in the rescue and rehabilitation of wild animals found injured. Emergency service is active 24hrs/day. The Centre also takes care of different exotic animals found abandoned or others that have been confiscated from Government authorities. Guided visits for schools and families also play an important socio-educational role in the Centre's activities.

Spp.: Local wildlife (ungulates, mammals, raptors) and exotic fauna (primates, felines, reptiles, etc.).

Hab.: Temperate mountain woodland.

Loc.: Monte Adone, Sasso Marconi, near Bologna, Italy.

Travel: From Bologna by train to Pianoro or to Sasso Marconi.

Dur.: Min. 20 days, after a 1-week trial period.

Per.: Year round, busiest months during the spring (April to June).

L. term: To be arranged with Centre's Director after intial period.

Age: Min. 20.

Qualif.: A true love for animals, attitude to live and work in community, willingness to work in close contact with animals, goodwill and spirit of adaptation, sense of responsibility.

Work: Work (8–10hrs/day) depends on the season. Feeding, cleaning and caring of animals. Day and night rescuing operations of wounded fauna. Maintenance and building activities. Volunteers will give a little help in the housekeeping.

Lang.: Italian, English is also spoken by centre coordinators.

Accom.: In shared rooms in the Centre.

Cost: A EUR80 (approx. GB£55) payment is required to cover food and insurance for the first trial week. The Centre will offer free full board for the remaining period. Travel not included.

Notes: Anti-tetanus and B hepatitis vaccinations are required.

MORAY FIRTH DOLPHIN MONITORING PROJECT

The Moray Firth Wildlife Centre
Spey Bay
Moray, Scotland IV32 7PJ   UK
Tel.: ++44 (1343) 820 339 – Fax: ++44 (1343) 829 109
E-mail: inquiries@mfwc.co.uk
www.mfwc.co.uk

Desc.: Long term monitoring of the dolphins using the southern Moray Firth coast. Based on shorewatch monitoring and photo-ID studies to compile a record of individuals that utilise the area together with movements and behavioural studies.

Spp.: Bottlenose dolphin (*Tursiops truncatus*).

Hab.: North Sea coast.

Loc.: Northeast Scotland.

Travel: Airplane (or bus or train) to either Aberdeen or Inverness; bus or train to Fochabers. Spey Bay lies 5 km north of Fochabers.

Dur.: Min. 1 week.

Per.: June to September.

L. term: Support workers may book extra weeks subject to availability.

Age: Min. 18.

Qualif.: Project Officer: qualified marine biologist preferably with cetacean work experience. Boat handling and photography are useful skills. Ability to work alone or with others. Support volunteers require no previous experience or qualifications.

Work: Project officer: photo-ID work, update records, supervise volunteers, public interpretation. Support volunteers: assist project officer; shore monitoring and estuary wildlife surveys.

Lang.: English. Other languages useful for interpretation work.

Accom.: Project Officer has caravan. Support volunteers stay at a B&B.

Cost: Project Officer must be self-sufficient for food. Support volunteers pay GB£550/week (approx. EUR/US$800) for full board. Travel to Spey Bay not included.

Applic.: Send for further details and application form.

Notes: To board the boat volunteers climb ladders on a harbour wall.

MUNDA WANGA WILDLIFE PARK AND SANCTUARY

P.O. BOX 38267, Kafue Rd,
Lusaka Zambia
Tel.: ++260 (1) 278 456
Fax: ++260 (1) 278 529
E-mail: environment@zamnet.zm

Desc.: Munda Wanga is a botanical garden, wildlife park and sanctuary. In the 1980s it was left to decay, resulting in many animals dying in their old zoo-style cages. It has been recently taken over by a new charitable trust and the process of rehabilitation is well underway. The new management is in the process of renovating the old cages into new spacious enclosures, giving the animals a quality of life that was lacking. A function of the new Munda Wanga is environmental education, as well as conservation by conducting captive breeding and release programmes of endangered species.

Spp.: A variety of African birds and mammls, including wild dogs.

Hab.: Wetland, woodland and grassland. A river runs through the area.

Loc.: Approx.15km outside of Lusaka, the capital of Zambia.

Travel: Airplane to Lusaka, volunteers are met at the airport.

Dur.: 3 weeks. Volunteers can stay for longer or shorter periods.

Per.: Year round.

L. term: Possible at reduced rate after approval of the project manager.

Age: Min. 18, no max.

Qualif.: No particular skills needed other than enthusiasm to work hard.

Work: Designing enrichment material, monitoring animals, giving tours, working with school groups, fundraising, hand-rearing orphaned animals, cleaning enclosures, giving out flyers, construction, etc. Work is 6 days/week, 8 hours/day.

Lang.: English.

Accom.: Basic dorm style room, with bathroom and cooking area.

Cost: US$600 (approx. GB£ 400) includes accommodation, food, trips to wildlife ranches and transport to and from the airport.

Applic.: Request via e-mail, fax or mail a standard from to fill in.

Notes: Volunteers' contributions help projects undertaken at the time.

NOAH'S ARK

Noah's Ark Animal Shelter
P.O. Box 241, Agia Triada, Akrotiri, Chania
Crete, TK 73100   Greece
Tel.:   ++30 (821) 66 146
Mob.:++30 (946) 88 1155
www.archenoah-kreta.com

Desc.: Noah's Ark is the only animal shelter in Crete, caring for about 600 animals, operating on donations and small foreign grants only. The project is aimed at rescuing, treating, caring for and when possible re-homing animals.

Spp.: Domestic cats, dogs, donkeys; birds (budgerigars, canaries, parrots, owls, hawks).

Hab.: Mediterranean.

Loc.: Western Crete, Greece.

Travel: Plane to Chania airport (10 minutes from the shelter), Heraklion (2   hours away) or Athens (then night boat to Chania).

Dur.: 2 weeks to 1 year.

Per.: Year round.

L. term: Long term encouraged, inquire with organisation.

Age: Min.16, max. 60.

Qualif: Volunteers should love animals and be strong enough to handle the sight of animal cruelty, starvation, illness.

Work: Nursing cleaning, feeding, diet control, treating small animals under supervision; assisting in building new quarantine quarters.

Lang.: English, German, Greek.

Accom.: Local villa accommodation at reasonable rates.

Cost: Volunteers pay for accommodation. Noah's Ark will assist in obtaining accommodation and local transportation.

Agents: Contact Ms. Silke Wrobel at Noah's Ark.

Applic.: No official form needed, send letter of inquiry.

Notes: High summer is very hot; winter months are wet and muddy.

THE OCEANIA RESEARCH PROJECT

The Oceania Project
P.O. Box 646
Byron Bay NSW 2481 Australia
Tel.: ++61 (2) 668 58128 – Fax: ++61 (2) 668 58998
E-mail: expedition@oceania.org.au
www.oceania.org.au

Desc.: The Oceania Project is a non-profit research and education organisation dedicated to raising awareness of Cetacea and the Ocean Environment through research and education. The Oceania Project is in the seventh year of a 10-year study of the abundance, distribution and behaviour of humpback whales in the Whale Management & Monitoring Area of the Hervey Bay Marine Park, off the northeast coast of Queensland, Australia. The study is being undertaken in conjunction with the Queensland Department of Environment. A further research permit has been granted to The Oceania Project to extend the study into the Mackay/Capricorn Section of the Great Barrier Reef Marine Park for the next 3 years. The Hervey Bay Study is conducted from a vessel during the 10 weeks of the annual humpback migration from August to October. The research platform is funded by paying volunteers who join the expedition for a week at a time. As well as participating in the on-board research programme, expedition participants are provided with in depth interpretation and education programmes about cetaceans. Involvement in the Barrier Reef Programme is limited; details are available on request.

Spp.: Humpback whale (*Megaptera novaeangliae*), brydes tropical whale (*Balaenoptera edeni*), minke-piked whale (*Balaenoptera acutorostrata*), common dolphin (*Delphinus delphis*), bottlenose dolphin (*Tursiops truncatus*), Indo-pacific humpback dolphin (*Sousa chinensis*).

Hab.: Tropical coast/ocean bay/Great Barrier Reef.

Loc.: Hervey Bay, northeast coast of Queensland, Australia.

Travel: Airplane to Brisbane (capital of Queensland). The expedition departure point is Urangan Boat Harbour, Hervey Bay (approx. 400 km north of Brisbane, with access by car or daily bus, train or intrastate airline).

Dur.: 1–10 weeks, Sunday to Friday.

Per.: July to October.

L. term: Volunteers can join the expedition for a max. of 10 weeks.

Age: Min. 14.

Qualif.: No particular skills needed, previous field experience in marine mammal research useful. Common sense, a committed interest in whales and dolphins and willingness to work long hours as part of a small highly motivated and focused field research team.

Work: Assist with observations and with collection and collation of spatial and environmental data. General duties associated with daily operation of the expedition aboard the vessel.

Lang.: English.

Accom.: Ship-style bunk. The present expedition vessel is a 17-metre sailing catamaran. Information about what to bring, etc., will be provided to applicants.

Cost: Volunteers from 14–18 years of age pay AUS$750/week (approx. US$400). Graduate or post graduate students or teaching staff from an eligible educational institution pay AUS$950/week (approx. US$500), otherwise AUS1150/week (approx. US$620). Cost includes living aboard the expedition vessel, a bunk, all meals, participation in field research and on-board interpretation and education programmes. Transportation or accommodation to and from the departure point or personal insurance is not included.

Applic.: Application is by registration form, which will be provided on request. The web-site of the Oceania Project provides information about the Annual Whale and Dolphin Expedition, including the means to register and pay for the weekly segment or segments required by applicants.

Notes: Students or under-graduates may be able to receive credit towards marine science or environmental studies courses.

OPERATION OSPREY, Scotland

RSPB – The Royal Society for the Protection of Birds
The Lodge, Sandy
Bedfordshire SG19 2DL UK
Tel.: ++44 (1767) 680 551
Fax: ++44 (1767) 692 365
www.rspb.org.uk

Desc.: Within its Residential Voluntary Warden Scheme, RSPB (see Organisation list) offers special projects such as Operation Osprey, an opportunity for bird protection and conservation work. Ospreys are an endangered species in Scotland.

Spp.: Osprey (*Pandion haliaetus*).

Hab.: Scots pine woodland, lochs, moors.

Loc · Abernethy Forest Reserve, Loch Garten, Scotland.

Travel: Travel details are given to selected applicants.

Dur.: Min. 1 week (Saturday to Saturday); max. 2 weeks.

Per.: Late March to early September.

Age: Min. 18.

Qualif.: Good spoken English and willingness to be part of a team.

Work: Osprey nest site protection and surveillance, information to visiting public.

Lang.: English.

Cost: Accommodation is provided free. Food and travel expenses are not included.

L. term: N/A.

Accom.: In chalets.

Applic.: Write to the Volunteer Unit at the above address for further details and for an application form. Enclose a self-addressed label with 2 first class stamps (in the UK) or 2 International Postage Coupons. Information is also available on www.rspb.org.uk/vacancies/

THE ORANGUTAN FOUNDATION

7 Kent Terrace, London, NW1 4RP   UK
Tel.: ++ 44 (20) 7724 2912
Fax: ++44 (20) 7706 2613
E-mail: info@orangutan.org.uk
www.orangutan.org.uk

Desc.: The Orangutan Foundation is a charity that works to protect and study orangutans and their habitat in Indonesia and Malaysia. The Foundation also cares for and reintroduces orangutans back into the wild. It has a volunteer programme in Tanjung Puting National Park, Kalimantan.

Spp.: Bornean and Sumatran Orangutan (*Pongo spp.*).

Hab.: Tropical rainforest.

Loc.: Indonesia and Malaysia on the islands of Borneo and Sumatra. The volunteer programme is located in Kalimantan, Borneo.

Travel: By airplane to Indonesia, train or flights to Semerang. From Semerang flight or boat to Pangkalan Bun.

Dur: Min. 6 weeks.

Per.: 4 teams of 12 people, from April to November.

L. term: Max. 6 weeks.

Age: Min. 18.

Qualif.: Previous experience in the field is desirable but not necessary. Good health and willingness to do manual work are necessary.

Work: The main target area of the programme will be Camp Leakey, the historical research site of Dr. Biruté Galdikas, situated within Tanjung Puting National Park. Help is needed to continue the ongoing renovation and expansion project. Proposed activities include repairing existing structures, increasing boundaries of the study area, trail cutting, installing walkways and signs and developing facilities for conservation education.

Lang.: English or Indonesian.

Accom.: Very basic. In huts on the floor or hammocks in the forest.

Cost: About GB£470 (approx. EUR/US$700) for food and accommodation, volunteers are responsible for their travel.

Applic.: Contact the UK office for an application form.

ORANGUTAN HEALTH

Dr Ivona Foitova – Principal Investigator
Tengger Bungalows
Bukit Lawang 20774, Sumatra Indonesia
E-mail: chrisb@indo.net.id
www.orangutan-health.org

Desc.:	The project investigates the way that orangutans self-medicate in order to treat illness and eradicate parasites. It appears that orangutans, like humans, take medicinal plants to treat their illnesses. Apes using plants to treat a 'dodgy gut' is a fairly new finding, and questions arise about how they know which plants to select for which ailments and which plant treats which parasite.
Spp.:	Orangutan (*Pongo pygmaeus*).
Hab:	Tropical rainforest.
Loc.:	Bukit Lawang, Sumatra, Indonesia.
Travel:	By airplane to Medan via Jakarta, Kuala Lumpur, Singapore or Penang. Volunteers are met at the airport.
Dur.:	Min. 17 days.
Per.:	Year round.
L. term:	Possible, inquire with the organisation.
Age:	Min. 18.
Qualif.:	A good level of fitness – able to hike 10km during 1 day in difficult terrain, without health problems, allergies or phobias. Volunteers are required to be patient and attentive.
Work:	Work will be split between 3–4 day treks in the jungle, and computer/lab work at base camp. This will be rotated and will depend on people's strengths in certain areas.
Lang:	English.
Accom.:	Accommodation is very basic: a bed, a mosquito net and a basic Asian toilet. No shower, but a supply of water to wash.
Cost:	US$1,170 (approx. GB£780) excluding travel.
Applic.:	Request an application form via e-mail.
Notes:	There is no physical contact whatsoever with orangutans. A medical certificate of good health is mandatory.

ORKNEY SEAL RESCUE CENTRE

Dyke End, South Ronaldsay
Orkney, KW17 2TJ, Scotland   UK
Tel./Fax: ++44 (1856) 831 463
E-mail: selkiesave@aol.com

Desc.: The care of 50 seal pups every year with a variety of problems. Most of the seals that come into the centre have been separated from their mothers. Others have been injured by discarded fishing nets or have been injured by gun shot.

Spp.: Marine mammals: grey seals (*Halichoerus grypus*); common and harbour seals (*Phoca vitulina*).

Hab.: Marine/coastal.

Loc.: Northern Islands of Scotland.

Travel: By airplane to London, Glasgow, Edinburgh, Inverness or Aberdeen; bus or train by sea from Thurso or from Aberdeen to Orkney.

Dur.: Min. 4 weeks.

Per.: Year round except April and May.

L. term: Possible after intial period and approval.

Age: Min. 18.

Qualif.: A strong motivation to work with animals.

Work: Cleaning, food preparation and feeding the seals at the centre; possible involvement with rescue and release of seals; participate in cooking (vegetarian) and house cleaning.

Lang.: English.

Accom.: Shared in a house with 2 attic bedrooms with bathroom.

Cost: GB£15–20/week (approx.EUR/US$22–30) for the cost of food.

Appilc.: Send an application form to Orkney Seal Rescue (the Green Volunteers application form is accepted).

Notes: The work at Orkney Seal Rescue can at times be wet and cold with long hours. It is a very rewarding job especially when the seals are released back into the wild.

PANDRILLUS FOUNDATION

Drill Monkey Rehabilitation & Breeding Center
H.E.P.O. Box 826 Calabar   Nigeria
Tel.: ++234 (87) 234 310
E-mail: drill@infoweb.abs.net   –   pandrillus@msn.com
(many websites describe the project: type"Pandrillus" in a search engine;
see http://limbewildlife.org for Limbe Wildlife Centre, see Notes)

Desc.: Founded in 1991, the centre recovers captive drill orphans and rehabs them into breeding groups: 110 drills born to date. The project is closely involved in conservation of Afi Mountain Wildlife Sanctuary where wild drills, gorillas and chimps survive. Project also maintains 20 non-breeding chimpanzees. Animals are kept in enclosures of natural habitat of up to 9 ha. The Project also runs the Limbe Wildlife Center in Cameroon.

Spp.: Drill (*Mandrillus leucophaeus*), chimpanzee (*Pan troglodytes*).

Hab.: Tropical rainforest.

Loc.: Southeast Nigeria.

Travel: Flight to Lagos then to Calabar.

Dur.: Min. 1 year.

Per.: Year round.

L. term: Highly encouraged.

Age: Min. 25.

Qualif.: Mature persons with 1) animal, veterinary or medical experience/skills or practical skills (carpentry, electrical, etc.); 2) appropriate educational background; 3) developing country experience; 4) sincere interest in conservation; 5) good human relations ability ; 6) administrative or management experience.

Work: Staff management and training, animal management and record-keeping, administration, public relations, education, construction and maintenance. Versatility is a must.

Lang.: English.

Accom.: House at urban site, open-walled cabins at field site.

Cost: Room and board provided. Travel to project, not provided.

Applic.: Send CV with references, a photograph and a letter of intentions. Interview with an appointed person will follow.

Notes: Volunteers may also apply for the Limbe Wildlife Center.

PIONEER MADAGASCAR

Azafady UK
Studio 7, 1a Beethoven Street, London W10 4LG UK
Tel.: ++44 (20) 8960 6629
Fax: ++44 (20) 8962 0126
E-mail: mark@azafady.org – azafady@easynet.co.uk
www.madagascar.co.uk

Desc: Azafady is a registered UK and Madagascar-based NGO. Through Pioneer Madagascar, volunteers can experience working with a grass-roots organisation fighting the problems of extensive deforestation and extreme poverty on this unique island. The programme focuses on integrated conservation and development working closely with the Malagasy people.

Spp.: Primates, reptiles and birds eg. brown collared lemur (*Eulemur fulvus collaris*), loggerhead turtle (*Caretta caretta*).

Hab.: Littoral forest (tropical coastal forest), coastal zone.

Loc.: Southeast Madagascar.

Travel: Airplane to Antananarivo, then to Fort Dauphin.

Dur.: Project placements are 10 weeks.

Per.: Year round; schemes start in January, April, July and October.

L. term: Long-term stay as a coordinator or specialist can be arranged.

Age: Min. 18, no max.

Qualif.: No special skills needed; enthusiasm and sensitivity are a must; practical and research experience welcome.

Work: Work varies depending on the time of year, project programme and schedules of co-ordinators. Projects include counts of lemurs and birds in fragmented forest areas, conservation of loggerhead turtles, building facilities, pharmacies and schools.

Lang.: English or French; intensive course in Malagasy is given.

Accom.: Very basic under canvas, located near the rural village of Saint Luce; occasional use of other Azafady residences.

Cost: Successful applicants must cover live costs (flight, insurance, medical expenses, visa and equipment) and raise a minimum donation to the charity of GB £2,000 for UK applicants and GB£2500 (approx: EUR/US$ 3,800) for overseas applicants.

Applic.: Fill in forms available from the website.

PROJECT DELPHIS

Earthtrust
1118 Maunawili Road, Kailua, Hawaii 96734 USA
Tel.: ++1 (808) 254 2866 (ext. 1)
Fax: ++1 (815) 333 1158
E-mail: sue@flipperfund.com
www.earthtrust.org

Desc.: Photo-Identification and data analysis of ID's of wild spinner and spotted dolphins off Oahu. In seasons in which field work takes place, ID is made using underwater video and overflights for data collection. Most of the work is using computers to analyse data, uploading of the photo collection.

Spp.: Bottlenose dolphin, spinner and spotted dolphins.

Hab.: Coastal waters off Oahu.

Loc.: Oahu, Hawaii.

Travel: Airplane to Honolulu.

Dur.: Min. 1 month; longer is preferred.

Per.: Year round. The wild work is seasonal, mainly May to October.

L. term: Length of time is unlimited.

Qualif.: Photo-identification and data analysis experience. In seasons when field work takes place, volunteers must have life saving skills and ability to handle rough ocean water sustained swimming. Field study requires video data underwater collection skills. Some seasons there is field work but this may not be the case in any given season.

Work: Act as research assistant to the project co-ordinator in the field study of the wild dolphins.

Lang.: English.

Accom.: Volunteers will find their own rental.

Cost: In addition to a contribution (contact the project for information) volunteers find and pay their own rental and food (average US$900/month).

Applic.: Contact: via e-mail: sue@flipperfund.co. Send CV and letter of intent. State intended length of stay and qualifications.

PROJECT TAMAR

Fundação Pro-Tamar
Caixa postal 2219
Rio Vermelho Salvador BA, 40210–970 Brazil
Tel.: ++55 (71) 676 1045 – Fax: ++55 (71) 676 1067
E-mail: protamar@e-net.com.br
www.tamar.com.br

Desc.: This non-governmental, non-profit organisation was created in 1988 to provide financial support for research and conservation of sea turtles in Brazil. This project aims to re-establish the natural reproductive cycle of sea turtles by transferring a portion of the nests to a protected hatchery, releasing the hatchlings, tagging the nesting females and organising public awareness activities. About 350 people are now working with the Foundation for the protection of turtles.

Spp.: Leatherback, hawksbill, olive ridley, loggerhead, green seaturtles.

Hab.: Tropical coast.

Loc.: Various beaches along the Brazilian coast.

Travel: Airplane to Rio de Janeiro or other Brazilian airports.

Dur.: Min. 2 weeks.

Per.: October to February.

L. term: Inquire with organisation.

Age: Min. 18.

Qualif.: Good health and ability to walk long distances (10–15 km/day) on loose sand and to stand the heat of neo-tropical climate.

Work: Night surveys, nest ID, egg transfer, hatchling count and release, adult female tagging. Work with local fishermen.

Lang.: Portuguese (helpful to work with local people), English.

Accom.: Project stations near or in small fishing villages; each station has a kitchen, hot and cold running water.

Cost: US$650 for 2 weeks; additional weeks possible at lower cost.

Applic.: Apply via e-mal and be prepared to send reminders since messages do get overlooked.

Notes: The project does not take volunteers every year; inquire with the organisation to verify.

PROJECTO JUBARTE DO CABO VERDE

Swiss Whale Society
Via Nolgio 3, CH–6900 Massagno Switzerland
Tel.: ++41 (91) 966 09 53
Fax: ++41 (91) 966 09 53
E-mail: jann@dial.eunet.ch
www.isuisse.com/cetaces

Desc.: The project's objective is to study the distribution and behaviour of Humpback whales around the Cabo Verde islands, and to identify the threats faced by the whales during their stay in the waters of the archipelago (fisheries, traffic, pollution, etc.).

Spp.: Humpback whale (*Megaptera novaeangliae*).

Hab.: Coastal waters and open ocean.

Loc.: Cabo Verde Islands, Atlantic Ocean.

Travel: Flight to island of Sal (international airport) and meet the ship or continue with domestic flight to another island where the ship may be located. Meeting point to be confirmed in advance.

Dur.: Min. 2 weeks.

Per.: February to April.

L. term: Max. length of stay is 2 months.

Age: Min.18.

Qualif.: No particular skills needed; photography welcome; relatively good physical condition to be able to live and work on a boat.

Work: Help in observation work; recording data on behaviour under supervision of scientists; photography.

Lang.: English (German, Italian, Dutch, Portuguese are also spoken).

Accom.: On board a research ship.

Cost: About EUR1,600 (approx. GB£ 1,100) for 2 weeks on board the ship. Flight from Europe costs about EUR 700.

Agents: Alfred Mandl Alsatour, Cabo Verde, tel. ++(238) 231 213, fax: 231 520, e-mail: alfred@alsatour.de; Chris Schlegel chrisschlegel@hotmail.com; Scheepszaken, e-mail: sparks@scheepszaken.nl, www.scheepszaken.nl

Applic.: Contact Beatrice Jann of the Swiss Whale Society at the address above, or one of the agents.

PROVCA – PROGRAMA DE VOLUNTARIOS PARA LA CONSERVACION DEL AMBIENTE

San José Avs. 8 y 10, calle 21 casa 815 C
P.O. Box 085–3007, Heredia   Costa Rica
Tel.:/Fax: ++(506) 222 7549
E-mail: mam271@racsa.co.cr

Desc.: Provca works with Costa Rican National Parks developing environmental projects, according to the parks' needs.
Spp.: Various species of flora and fauna of Costa Rica.
Hab.: Tropical rainfrest or cludforest; tropical coast.
Loc.: National parks of Costa Rica.
Travel: Airplane to San José, then by bus to the National Park.
Dur: Min. 2 weeks.
Per.: Year round.
L. term: 1–3 or more months depending on the project.
Age: Min.18 for individual participants; min. 16 for groups accompanied by a group leader.
Qualif.: Ability to work in occasional difficult conditions, have a fair understanding of rural environmental problems and preservation of natural resources and the capacity to deal with the public.
Work: Depends on the project; some activities are, for example, general maintenance at facilities, cleaning of beach, providing information to tourists or language classes to park personnel, assisting on different duties at turtles nesting sites, support on administrative duties, etc.
Lang.: English, some Spanish knowledge helpful.
Accom.: At the park facilities (volunteers often have to share rooms).
Cost: US$12 per day to cover room and board.
Applic.: By e-mail or fax.

PROYECTO CAMPANARIO

Campanario Biological Reserve
Apdo. 56–6151 Santa Ana 2000 Costa Rica
Tel.: ++(506) 282 5898 – Fax: ++(506) 282 8750
E-mail: campanar@sol.racsa.co.cr

Desc.: Founded in 1990, Proyecto Campanario maintains a tropical rainforest biological reserve in southwest Costa Rica. Through tropical ecology courses and eco-tourism, funds are generated to keep the reserve in its natural state. In addition, the programme offer opportunities for eco-tourists, student groups (of all ages) and researchers to learn more about the biodiversity and ecology of the Osa Peninsula to then promote the cause of rainforest protection in their own communities.

Spp.: Rainforest and tropical coastal flora and fauna.

Hab.: Tropical rainforest; mangrove forest, coastal zone.

Loc.: Osa Peninsula, southwest Costa Rica (near Corcovado NP).

Travel: Flight to San Jose, bus to Palmar, then boat to Campanario.

Dur.: Min. 3 weeks.

Per.: Year round.

L. term: Possible with project leader's approval.

Qualif.: No particular skills are needed, only enthusiasm and a positive attitude. Every effort is made to utilize skills of volunteers. They should be able to swim, be able to work without supervision and be in good physical and emotional health.

Work: Variable; includes manual labour restoring trails, taking species inventories, building observation points, sometimes under hot or wet conditions.

Lang.: English, Spanish helpful but not essential.

Accom.: In a rustic field station (no hot water) or in a tent cabin close to the beach. Shared room or tent with at least 1 other volunteer.

Cost: Volunteers give a non-refundable US$300 contribution for food, prior to arrival. Each additional week costs US$100.

Applic.: Request application form via e-mail or fax.

Notes: A medical, accident and evacuation insurance is compulsory.

PRZEWALSKI HORSE REINTRODUCTION PROJECT

The Ecovolunteer Network
Meyersweg 29,   7553 AX Hengelo The Netherlands
Tel.: ++31 (74) 250 8250
Fax: ++31 (74) 250 6572
E-mail: info@ecovolunteer.org
www.ecovolunteer.org

Desc.: The main objectives of the project are to reintroduce Przewalski horses in the Hustain Nuruu Nature Reserve, to protect the biological diversity of the Mongolian steppe ecosystem and to implement social-economic programmes. During the 90s, several harems of horses were released in the reserve after being kept under semi-wild conditions in acclimation areas. They are monitored to ensure they adjust to their new environment and to study their behaviour. The project hopes to build a self-sustaining viable population.

Spp.: Przewalski horse (Tahki).

Hab.: Mountain steppe.

Loc.: Hustain Nuruu Nature Reserve, Mongolia.

Travel: Travel by plane or train to the Mongolian capital Ulaanbatar; meeting at the airport or train station.

Dur.: Min. 3 weeks.

Per.: June to September. Rest of the year by request only.

L. term: Inquire with the organisation.

Age.: Min. 18.

Qualif.: Familiarity with horse riding; good health.

Work: Monitoring and making behavioural observations of mares before, during and after birth; 2-year-olds before and during separation from the harem and following the release of a harem. Homerange research is done. Observation trips on horseback with a Mongolian Ranger.

Lang.: English.

Accom.: In shared Mongolian tents in the steppe.

Cost: US$1,090 for 3 weeks; US$52 for every extra day.

Agents: The Ecovolunteer Network at www.ecovolunteer.org.

Applic.: The Ecovolunteer Network (see Organisation list).

PUNTA BANCO SEA TURTLE PROJECT, Costa Rica

Sea Turtle Restoration Project
P.O. Box 400/40 Montezuma Avenue
Forest Knolls, California 94933 USA
Tel.: ++1 (415) 488 0370 – Fax: ++1 (415) 488 0372
E-mail: info@tortugamarina.org – seaturtles@igc.org
www.tortugamarina.org – www.seaturtles.org

Desc.: Each year more than 350 olive ridley sea turtles nest on the beach of Punta Banco, Costa Rica. The hatchery and research project is in co-operation with the Tiskita Foundation.

Spp.: Olive ridley sea turtle (*Lepidochelys olivacea*).

Hab.: Subtropical coast, rainforest jungle.

Loc.: Punta Banco, Pacific coast of Costa Rica, near Panama.

Travel: Flight to San José, then plane or truck to Tiskita Jungle Lodge.

Dur.: Min. 2 weeks.

Per.: August to December.

L. term: Long term encouraged with a decrease of fee.

Age: Min. 18.

Qualif.: Experience in biology, education or photography helpful. Volunteers should be in reasonably good health.

Work: Night beach patrols for nesting turtles, moving eggs into a hatchery and participating in environmental education programmes. Tag and measure adult turtles, record data on hatching success and work with community and local biologists.

Lang.: Spanish very helpful but not strictly necessary.

Accom.: Rustic cabins operated by local community members, or by the Tiskita Jungle Lodge accomodating 1–6 people.

Cost: From US$500 for 2 weeks up to US$ 1,200 for 2 months including meals and lodging; transportation not included.

Agents: Contact STRP directly. Local office: STRP, Apdo.1203–1100, Tibas, San José, Costa Rica, tel.: ++(506) 241 5227, fax: ++(506) 236 6017, e-mail: info@tortugamarina.org

Applic.: Contact STRP; Todd Steiner in USA; Randall Arauz in CR.

Notes: Leisure activities include jungle hikes, swimming, bird watching (over 230 species recorded), etc. The Lodge also operates an experimental fruit farm with over 100 varieties of fruit.

RE-AFORESTATION PROJECT, Ghana

Save the Earth Network

P. O. Box CT 3635, Cantonments – Accra Ghana

Tel.: ++233 (21) 667 791 – Fax: ++233 (21) 669 625

E-mail: ebensten@yahoo.com – eben_sten@hotmail.com

www.worldsurface.com/browse/tour.asp?tourid=449

www.idealist.org (type:'Save the Earth Network' in search window)

Desc.: The purpose of the project is to plant trees on 50 acres of land, to restore a tropical rain forest destroyed by excessive lumbering for timber, firewood and charcoal. An additional objective of the project is to protect the watershed and to restore the habitat for wildlife and birds, and to rejuvenate 50 acres of farmlands through nursing and planting of Leucaena trees, 'the miracle tree'.

Spp.: Leucaena, Mahogany and Teak trees.

Hab.: Tropical rain forest, villages and farms.

Loc.: Western region of Ghana, West Africa.

Travel: Plane to Accra, bus to Takoradi and to the project area.

Dur.: 4 weeks to 1 year.

Per.: Year round.

L. term: Volunteers can join for up to 1 year, with project leader's approval, after the regular volunteer period.

Age: Min. 18, max. 60, or older if in good physical condition.

Qualif.: No particular skills needed.

Work: Nursing and planting of trees and weeding. Volunteers work 4 days a week for 2 hours per day.

Lang.: English.

Accom.: In a house with water and electricity.

Cost: US$250/month. Room and board are included. Volunteers provide transportation to the project site.

Applic.: A standard form must be requested from the project to be completed and returned. There are no deadlines or membership requirements.

Notes: There are many small villages near the project area where volunteers can visit on their free time for cultural exchange.

REEF CHECK GLOBAL CORAL REEF MONITORING

Headquarters, c/o Institute of the Environment
University of California at Los Angeles
1362 Hershey Hall, 149607, Los Angeles, CA 9005–1496 USA
Tel.: ++1 (310) 794 4985 – Fax: ++1 (310) 825 0758
E-mail: rchck@UCLA.edu
www.ReefCheck.org

Desc.: Reef Check is an international programme working with communities, governments and businesses to scientifically monitor, restore and maintain coral reef health. Reef Check objectives are to: educate the public about the coral reef crisis; to create a global network of volunteer teams trained in Reef Check's scientific methods who regularly monitor and report on reef health; to facilitate collaboration that produces ecologically sound and economically sustainable solutions; and to stimulate local community action to protect remaining pristine reefs and rehabilitate damaged reefs worldwide.

Spp.: Coral reef organisms, include fish, invertebrates and coral.

Hab.: Tropical and subtropical coral reefs.

Loc.: Volunteers are needed in Australia, Korea, Palau, Hawai'i, Tanzania, Mexico, Egypt, Indonesia, United States and others.

Travel: Travel arrangements are the responsibility of the participant.

Dur.: Min.1 week.

Per.: Year round.

L. term: To be arranged with Headquarters.

Age: Min. 18

Qualif.: Participants must be confident swimmers and comfortable with snorkeling for long periods of time. SCUBA may be used at some locations. Non-divers help organizing Reef Check activities, sponsorship, training sessions, etc.

Work: Volunteers will be trained in RC methods and carry out coral reef surveys in water no deeper than 10m.

Lang.: Language used in country of choice.

Accom.: Accommodations vary with location.

Cost: Cost vary with location.

Applic.: See website or contact e-mail address above for information.

REHABILITATION AND RELEASE OF WILDLIFE

Programa Regional en Manejo de Vida Silvestre
Universidad Nacional
Apartado 1350, 3000 Heredia   Costa Rica
Tel.: ++(506) 277 3600/237 7039 − Fax: ++(506) 237 7036
E-mail: cdrews@una.ac.cr   −   prmvs@una.ac.cr
www.una.ac.cr/ambi/prmvs/

Desc.: The Programa Regional en Manejo de Vida Silvestre puts interested volunteers in contact with Wildlife Rescue Centres for injured animals, undesired pets and wild animals confiscated by Costa Rican authorities. There is an urgent demand for places to keep this wildlife with adequate conditions and clear policies regarding the fate of these animals (euthanasia, perpetual captivity, release into the wild).

Spp.: Mammals and birds; occasionally reptiles and amphibians.

Hab.: Lowland rainforest, tropical dry forest, cloud forest, rural areas.

Loc.: Costa Rica.

Travel: Flight to San José, then bus to the Rescue Centre of choice.

Dur.: Min. 3 months to several months or longer.

Per.: Year round.

L. term: To be arranged with the Rescue Centre of choice.

Age: Min. 18.

Qualif.: Veterinary knowledge and/or experience in handling captive wildlife are highly desirable.

Work: May involve cleaning enclosures, feeding animals, rehabilitation, research, education programmes, fund-raising, administration.

Lang.: Spanish, English.

Accom.: Very basic.

Cost: Transportation not included. Room and board provided.

Agent: Dr. Carlos Drews, Programa Regional en Manejo de Vida Silvestre.

Applic.: Send via e-mail a brief outline of skills and preferences. The applicant will receive a list of addresses. A full application should then be sent (exclusively via e-mail) to the preferred project/s.

Notes: Only a small fraction of the applicants is accepted. Applicants are therefore encouraged to apply also to other organisations.

RE-HYDRATION OF THE EARTH, Kenya

Westerveld Conservation Trust
Flevolaan 34, 1399 HG Muiderberg The Netherlands
Tel.: ++31 (294) 261 457
Fax: ++31 (294) 262 080
E-mail: mg.vanwesterop@ncd.nl
www.westerveld.nu

Desc.: Re-hydration and water conservation project. Recreation of water catchments and rehabilitation of sunken water table.

Spp.: Rhino, elephant.

Hab.: Semi-arid area in sub-saharan Africa; bush country.

Loc.: Rhino release area, Tsavo East National Park, among others.

Travel: By air to Nairobi, Kenya. Meeting point at Nairobi railway station; train or car to project location.

Dur.: Min. 2 weeks.

Per.: Year round.

L. term: Possible. Students and initiatives from engineers, biologists, etc. welcome. Volunteers must cover their stay.

Age: Min. 18.

Qualif.: Good health and physical condition. Willing to work in the field for long hours with hot temperatures.

Work: Assist staff of Westerveld Safari and rangers of Kenya Wildlife Service with the construction of water catchments in the Tsavo and Amboseli Region. Clean, cook and shop for camp.

Lang.: English.

Accom.: Tented shelter in Westerveld Tented Camp in Tsavo. Beds, covers and sheets are available.

Cost: EUR/US$ 800 (approx. GB£550) for 2 weeks and EUR/US$ 315 (approx. GB£210) for every extra week. Transport to and from project and during fieldwork. Meals, entry and camping fees for the National Parks included. WCT membership, EUR 16/person, is required.

Applic: Westerveld Conservation Trust for information and booking.

Notes: Fieldwork dates at request. Take old and sturdy clothing and shoes because thorny bushes cannot be avoided in these rocky areas. Participants must have personal insurance.

RHINO RESCUE PROJECT, Swaziland

The Ecovolunteer Network
Meyersweg 29,   7553 AX Hengelo The Netherlands
Tel.: ++31 (74) 250 8250
Fax: ++31 (74) 250 6572
E-mail: info@ecovolunteer.org
www.ecovolunteer.org

Desc.: Protecting wildlife against poaching is the priority of the Mkhaya Game Reserve, located in Swaziland. In this protected area live black and white rhinos, which are poached for their horns. Many other species, such as elephants, buffalos, antelopes, crocodiles, hippopotamus, zebra, giraffes, monkeys, leopards, etc., can be observed in the Reserve. Volunteers are needed to help with maintenance work in the Reserve and assist with anti-poaching activities. Financial contributions raised through this volunteer programme are essential to the project.

Spp.: White rhinoceros (*Ceratotherium simum*), black rhinoceros (*Diceros bicornis*).

Hab.: African savannah.

Loc.: Mkhaya Game Reserve, Lowveld, Swaziland, Africa.

Travel: Airplane to Mbabane; a visa and a passport valid for at least 6 months after leaving Swaziland are necessary.

Dur.: Min. 2, max. 5 weeks.

Per.: Year round.

L. term: Max. 5 weeks; inquire with organisation for possible exceptions.

Age: Min. 18.

Qualif.: Volunteers must speak English, be able to walk long distances and tolerate heat. Some knowledge of wildlife and birds is helpful. Volunteers must also be prepared to abide by the specific rules and conditions laid down by the Reserve.

Work: Participation in daily monitoring of endangered species, nightly detecting of poaching activities from watchtowers, animal surveys, maintenance work. Most working days start before sunrise. Half or full days off from work may be requested to recover from fatigue. Cooking and cleaning tasks are rotated amongst volunteers on a daily basis. Volunteers will always work together with a Swazi ranger, who has absolute authority. The safety of people and animals is the first consideration during all activities.

Lang.: English.

Cost: 2 weeks, US$980; 3rd week, US$210; 4th week, US$133 (fifth week is free.) Flights, visa, local taxes and insurance not included.

Accom.: Simple huts or tents close to the working area. Overnight camping is very primitive with cold-water shower, pit latrine, mattresses, bedding and mosquito nets.

Agents: The Ecovolunteer Network at www.ecovolunteer.org.

Applic.: The Ecovolunteer Network (see Organisation list).

Notes: Volunteers can explore nearby parks and accommodation is offered when available. Where possible opportunities will be offered to participate in white-water rafting trips and guided game drives. Volunteers are required to take full precautions against malaria and tick-bite fever.

RINGING PROGRAMME OF MIGRATORY PASSERINES

Estacion Biologica de Doñana (Csic)
Charo Cañas (Reserva biologica de Doñana) Apartado de Correos 4
21760 Matalascañas, Almonte, Huelva   Spain
Tel: ++34 (59) 440 032/440 036 – Fax: ++34 (59) 440 033
E-mail: jilam-1@teleline.es   –   joseluis@ebd.csic.es
www.ebd.csic.es/ringing/ – www-rbd.ebd.csic.es

Desc.: The Estacion Biologica de Doñana has developed a ringing station in the national park of Doñana, which is active during the migratory season (autumn) to study the migration of passerine species across the Sahara (trans-Saharian migrants).

Spp.: An incredible variety of European migrating birds.

Hab.: National Park of Doñana.

Loc.: Manecorro area (near El Rocio village), Spain.

Dur: Contact organisation for details.

L. term: Contact organisation.

Age: Min. 18.

Qualif.: Previous bird capturing and ringing experience.

Work: Volunteers participate in the ringing activities form dawn to dusk. There are 2 days off for each working day. Volunteers will also assist school children visiting the Centre. During the days off volunteers are encouraged to join any of the research teams working in the area.

Lang: English, Spanish.

Accom.: Shared rooms with shared bathroom and shower; kitchen facilities, refrigerator and washing machine available. Cleaning rooms, beds, etc., is the responsibility of the volunteers. A contribution for room and board is required.

Cost: Contact the organisation for information.

Applic.: Contact the organisation.

RIVER OTTER PROJECT, Brazil

Projecto Lontra, Brazil
The Ecovolunteer Network
Meyersweg 29   7553 AX Hengelo The Netherlands
Tel.: ++31 (74) 250 8250 − Fax: ++31 (74) 250 6572
E-mail: info@ecovolunteer.org
www.ecovolunteer.org

Desc.: This project involves the volunteer in field activities related to the study and conservation of river otters in southern Brazil. Research work has offered insight towards the ecology and conservation of otters and their habitat.

Spp.: American river otter.

Hab.: Streams and lakes, estuaries, coastal lagoons, mangroves.

Loc.: Piri Lake, Island of Santa Catarina, Atlantic Ocean, about 1,000 km south of Rio, Brazil.

Travel: Flight to Florianopolis, Santa Catarina State.

Dur.: Min. 1 week.

Per.: Year round.

L. term: Long-term encouraged; price decreases for longer stays.

Age: Min. 18.

Qualif.: Good health and physical condition. Willing to work in the field for long periods under varying weather conditions. Able to walk for long periods and spend evenings in the forest at wildlife observation posts.

Work: Activities vary and include analysis of the otter's frequency at the shelters, monitoring of nests, ethological studies and food habits. Most of volunteers' work is in the field, but also some laboratory analysis is involved. Work involves treks through the Atlantic forest, dunes, use of canoes and kayaks and nocturnal observations. Approx. 10 hours/day.

Lang.: English, Portuguese, Spanish.

Accom.: Research bases have toilets and hot water; 2 meals per day.

Cost: US$365, 320, 275, 230, for first, second, third and every extra week respectively.

Agents: The Ecovolunteer Network at www.ecovolunteer.org.

Applic.: The Ecovolunteer Network (see Organisation list).

SCOTTISH WHALE & DOLPHIN PROJECT

The Hebridean Whale and Dolphin Trust, HWDT
28 Main Street, Tobermory
Isle of Mull, Argyll PA75 6NU Scotland UK
Tel. ++44 (1688) 302 620 – Fax: ++44 (1688) 302 728
E-mail: hwdt@sol.co.uk
www.hwdt.org – www.gn.apc.org/whales/

Desc.: Various conservation-related projects on whales, dolphins and porpoises inhabiting the waters of western Scotland. Educational and research projects are conducted by the Trust.

Spp.: Cetaceans (whales, dolphins), seals, otters, basking sharks.

Hab.: Temperate marine and coasts.

Loc.: Western Scotland.

Travel: Train or bus from Glasgow or London to Oban; ferry from Oban to Isle of Mull.

Dur.: Min. 1 month.

Per.: April to November.

L. term: Long-term positions possible for outstanding volunteers.

Age: Min. 18.

Qualif.: Education experience (for education projects); administration/marketing skills (for fund-raising/campaigning projects); student/graduate in a biological science (for research projects).

Work: Two days working in education centre; 2–3 days working on individual projects (research or education based).

Lang.: English.

Accom.: Hostel or caravans, depending on volunteer budget. Trust staff will help with booking and arrangement.

Cost.: Accommodation and food is approx. GB£75–100/week (approx. EUR/US$ 110–150)

Applic.: CV and detailed cover letter. Interviews (can be by telephone) for short–listed applicants. Send self–addressed envelope to the Volunteer Coordinator to receive a placement pack.

Notes: Volunteers must have a sense of humor, be enthusiastic, efficient, willing to work as part of a team and able to deal with the public.

SCOTTISH WILDLIFE RESCUE

Hessilhead Wildlife Rescue Trust
Hessilhead, Gateside, Beith Ayrshire KA15 1HT Scotland UK
Tel.: ++44 (1505) 502 415
E-mail: hessilhead@hessilhead.netlineuk.net
        hessilhead@hessilhead.supanet.com
www.geocities.com/RainForest/Vines/5227/

Desc.: Rescue, repair, rehabilitate and release all native species of wild birds and mammals. Hand rearing, cleaning and feeding animals; maintenance and construction work and monitoring the casualties after release. Some groups of birds will be ringed, and hopefully some species will be radio-tracked.

Spp.: All Scottish wild birds and mammals.

Hab.: Urban, woodland, farmland, coast, moorland.

Loc.: West central Scotland.

Travel: The Centre is within easy travelling distance from Glasgow.

Dur.: Min. 2–3 weeks.

Per.: March to October.

L. term: Suitable volunteers may be able to stay for 6 months or more.

Age: Min. 18.

Qualif.: Ability to work as part of a team. Training will be given. Experience of radio tracking could be useful. Veterinary experience useful.

Work: Volunteers may help with all aspects of the Trust's work. This includes rescue, treatment, feeding, cleaning, preparing birds and animals for release and post-release monitoring. Educational work with the public may be possible.

Lang.: English.

Accom.: Caravans.

Cost: Caravan are free. Food must be provided by the volunteer. A donation towrds cost of accommodation would be appreciated. Volunteers must arrange their own transport, though can be collected from Glasgow.

Applic.: Apply directly to HWRT with relevant details and a contact number or address. More information will be supplied.

SEA TURTLE CONSERVATION PROGRAM, Cost Rica

Asociación ANAI Apdo. 170–2070,
Sabanilla de Montes de Oca, San José   Costa Rica
Tel.: ++ (506) 224 3570/ 224 6090
Fax: ++ (506) 253 7524
E-mail: volunteers@racsa.co.cr – anaicr@racsa.co.cr
www.anaicr.org

Desc.: Asociación ANAI has over 15 years of experience working in the Caribbean coastline of Costa Rica, mainly in the region of Talamanca; one of the biologically richest areas of the planet with over 2% of the entire world's biodiversity. The Sea Turtle project was started in 1986 in Gandoca Beach and the success of that project has lead to its expansion in year 2000 to cover Playa Negra. Before an unknown beach for sea turtles nesting, now the most important beach for the Hawksbill sea turtle, which is critically endangered worldwide.

Spp.: Seaturtles: Leatherback (*Dermochelys coriacea*), Hawksbill (*Eretmochelys imbricata*), and Green (*Chelonia Mydas*).

Hab.: Caribbean, tropical coast.

Loc.: Gandoca and Playa Negra Beaches, region of Talamanca, Caribbean coastline of Costa Rica.

Travel: Airplane to San Jose, then bus to Talamanca.

Dur.: Min. 1 week, max. 6 months.

Per.: March to July; peak nesting period in April to May.

L.Term.: Generic volunteers can stay for the entire nesting season. Professional volunteers typically come for 8–12 months.

Age: Min. 18.

Qualif.: ANAI has 2 kinds of volunteers: generic and professional. For generic volunteers no specific skills are required, but a strong motivation is a must. Ability to walk long hours at night and to withstand hot tropical temperatures. Professional volunteers have skills in fields such as economy, business administration, accounting, agriculture, and forest management work and in the process developing new skills and experiences.

Work: Generic volunteers help patrol the beach to protect the turtles, assist with the scientific monitoring of the species, guard nests and work with the hatchlings on their journey to the ocean. Professional volunteers will put their skills at the disposal of the organisation while helping in the tasks of generic volunteers.

Lang.: English, Spanish useful.

Accom.: In Gandoca with local families; in Playa Negra in the project camp.

Cost: For generic volunteers there is a registration fee of US$25. Full room and board costs US$15/day, or US$6/day with own tent in camp, with cooking facilities (food can be purchased in the nearby village). Optional services include US$7/night lodging in ANAI office in San José and US$30 airport pick up. For professional volunteers there is no registration fee and housing is provided, both in San José and in the field. Basic work expenses are covered. Professional volunteers cover their own food, transportation and other personal expenses.

Agents: Contact Asociación ANAI directly.

Applic.: Use on-line application form.

Notes: Gandoca Beach is in the Gandoca-Manzanillo Wildlife Refuge, a protected area that also includes mangrove, coral reefs and tropical rainforest. Playa Negra is within the Cahuita National Park. Volunteers at both projects sites will be able to explore the amazing marine and land wildlife of the region during their stay.

SEA TURTLE PROJECT, Rhodes Island

CHELON, Marine Turtle Conservation and Research Program
Viale Val Padana, 134/B
00141 Rome Italy
Tel./Fax: ++39 (06) 8125301
E-mail: chelon@inwind.it
www.tiscali.it/chelon_ea/

Desc.: This project, in the southern part of the Island of Rhodes, focuses on loggerhead turtle nest census and protection, nesting behaviour observation and tagging of nesting females. Vegetation and bird studies are also conducted.

Spp.: Loggerhead sea turtle *(Caretta caretta)*.

Hab.: Mediterranean coast.

Loc.: Fourni beach, an isolated and beautiful beach at the southwest of Rhodes, Greece.

Travel: Airplane to Athens; airplane or ferry to Rhodes.

Dur.: 2 weeks.

Per.: July to August.

L. term: Inquire with the organisation.

Age: Min. 18.

Qualif.: No specific skills required.

Work: Volunteers assist researchers in data gathering on nests, nesting behavioural observations, tagging and botanical census. In the night work focuses on turtle nesting behaviour observation. Lessons on sea turtle conservation and biology are also scheduled.

Lang.: English, Italian. Greek is helpful.

Accom.: In own tents.

Cost: EUR 500 for 2 weeks (approx. GB£ 350). Price includes meals and camping. Travel and personal expenses and insurance are not included.

Applic.: Contact Chelon for further information and application form.

Notes: Max. group size is 12.

SEA TURTLE PROJECT, Thailand

Naucrates 'Conservation Biology'
Via Corbetta 11
22063 Cantù (CO)   Italy
Tel.: ++39 (333) 430 6643 – Fax: ++39 (031) 716 315
E-mail: naucrates12@hotmail.com – naucrates12@tiscalinet.it
www.naucrates.org

Desc.: The sea turtle project focuses on nest protection, satellite tracking and application of conservation strategies, educational programming for the local community and on conservation awareness activities for visitors.

Spp.: Olive ridley (*Lepidochelys olivacea*), leatherback (*Dermochelys coriacea*), green (*Chelonia mydas*) and hawksbill (*Eretmochelys imbricata*) turtles.

Hab.: Tropica coast.

Loc.: Phra Thong and Khao Island, Phang-Nga province, Thailand.

Travel: Airplane to Phuket Island or to Ranong (via Bangkok), then bus or car to Kura Buri pier and boat to Phra Thong Island.

Dur.: Min. 10 days.

Per.: December to April.

L. term: Inquire with the organisation.

Age: Min. 18.

Qualif.: Volunteers must be prepared for long walks in hot and humid conditions on the beach. Research assistant position (unpaid) available based on academics and experience.

Work: Beach patrols (day or night) for turtle nest monitoring. Visits to the local schools for the educational programme. Lectures on biology and conservation are given to tourists. Rescuing turtles caught in fishing nets.

Lang.: English, Italian.

Accom.: In huts on the beach at the Golden Buddha Beach resort.

Cost: EUR 760 (approx. GB£500) in huts for 2 weeks including 3 meals per day. Travel expenses, trip to neighbouring islands and insurance not included.

Applic.: Contact the organisation for an application form.

Notes: For Research Assistant position send CV before October.

SEA TURTLE RESCUE CENTRE, Greece

Archelon – Sea Turtle Protection Society of Greece
Solomou 57, GR–104 32 Athens Greece
Tel./Fax: ++30 (210) 523 1342
E-mail: stps@archelon.gr
www.archelon.gr

Desc.: Archelon is a non-profit organisation that conducts sea turtle conservation projects in Greece with the support of international volunteers. This project focuses on treatment and rehabilitation of injured, sick or weak turtles. Raising of public awareness is part of the activities, as well as expanding and improving the Sea Turtle Rescue Network in Greece.

Spp.: Sea turtles.

Hab.: Mediterranean coast.

Loc.: Glyfada, about 20 km from Athens, Greece.

Travel: Airplane to Athens. Inquire with the organisation for further instruction.

Dur.: Min. 4 weeks.

Per.: Year round.

L. term: After the initial stay of 4 weeks.

Age: Min. 18.

Qualif.: A strong motivation.

Work: Treatment of turtles, construction and maintenance work, painting, building, cleaning.

Lang.: English. German and Greek are useful.

Accom: At the Centre.

Cost: Participation fee is approximately EUR70 (approx.GB£45). Volunteers must also pay for their own travel expenses and pay a min. of EUR9/day to cover food costs.

Applic.: Prospective volunteers must fill out an application form.

Notes: Participation fee includes a 1-year subscription to the newsletter *Turtle Tracks* as a Archelon supporter. Volunteers must carry international health insurance.

SEA TURTLE SUMMER FIELD WORK, Greece

Archelon – Sea Turtle Protection Society of Greece
Solomou 57, GR–104 32 Athens Greece
Tel./Fax: ++30 (210) 523 1342
E-mail: stps@archelon.gr
www.archelon.gr

Desc.: Archelon is a non-profit organisation that conducts sea turtle conservation projects in Greece with the support of international volunteers. Summer field work includes monitoring turtle nesting activities on the beaches, tagging nesting female turtles, protecting nests and raising public (visitor and local) awareness.

Spp.: Loggerhead sea turtle *(Caretta caretta)*.

Hab.: Mediterranean coast.

Loc.: Peloponnesus and the islands of Zakynthos and Crete, Greece.

Travel: Airplane to Athens, then bus or ferry boat.

Dur.: Min. 4 weeks.

Per.: May to October.

L. term: Volunteers applying for long term are particularly welcome.

Age: Min. 18.

Qualif.: On-site training provided. Tolerance for hot weather necessary.

Work: Based upon project requirements; include beach surveys, nest relocations, on-site nest protection as well as tagging nesting female turtles at night and raising public awareness through information stations, slide shows and beach patrolling.

Lang.: English. German, Italian, Dutch, Swedish and Greek useful.

Accom: Designated free campsites in tents. Basic sanitary and cooking facilities with limited water supply.

Cost: Participation fee is approximately EUR70 (approx.GB£45) plus a min. EUR9/day to cover food costs. Travel expenses paid by volunteer.

Applic.: Prospective volunteers must fill out an application form.

Notes: Participants receive a 1-year subscription to *Turtle Tracks* newsletter. International health insurance required. Groups (over 2 persons) not accepted for the same area.

SEA TURTLES OF THE PACIFIC COAST OF COSTA RICA

Universidad Nacional de Costa Rica
P.O. Box 1350–3000, Heredia Costa Rica
Tel.: ++ (506) 237 7039/231 4986
Fax: ++ (506) 237 7036
E-mail: carlosmarioo@hotmail.com – corrego@una.ac.cr

Desc.: Determining the causes of mortality of marine turtles occurring in their nesting beaches along the Pacific Coast of Costa Rica, and to provide educational programmes to the local communities promoting the conservation of marine turtles.

Spp.: Marine turtles: olive ridley (*Lepidochelys olivacea*), eastern Pacific green (*Chelonia mydas agassizzi*), leatherback (*Dermochelys coriacea*).

Hab.: Tropical marine, coastal.

Loc.: Pacific Coast of Costa Rica.

Travel: Fly to San José, Costa Rica; bus from San José to sites.

Dur.: Min. 1 month; 3 months is ideal.

Per.: August to December. Educational programmes may extend into February.

L. term: Encouraged.

Age: Min. 18.

Qualif.: Able to work in tropical coastal weather conditions with occasional heavy rain and walking long stretches of marine turtle nesting beaches. Photography skills are welcome. Spanish necessary for surveys and educational programmes.

Work: Data collection includes performing standard necropsies on dead turtles, collecting morphometric measurements of the turtles and recording environmental parameters. Participation in community surveys and educational workshops.

Lang.: English and Spanish.

Accom.: Rooms for rent or lodging with a local family.

Cost: Food and lodging between US$250–300.

Applic.: By e-mail to Dr. Orrego Vasquez.

SIBERIAN/EAST RUSSIAN VOLUNTEER PROGRAM

Building the Great Baikal Trail
Earth Island Institute
300 Broadway, Suite 28, San Francisco, California, 94133 USA
Tel.: ++1 (415) 788 3666 – Fax: ++1 (415) 788 7324
E-mail: baikalwatch@earthisland.org
www.earthisland.or

Desc.: Earth Island and the Buryat Federation for Ecotourism and Mountain-climbing are now planning to build the Great Baikal Trail (GBT). The GBT will be the first system of hiking trails in Russia. It will lead some 1,600 km around Lake Baikal, through 3 national parks and 3 nature reserves. Starting in 2003, multiple teams of volunteers will be organised to help build the trail. Teams will be international, with many local Siberians mixing with foreign participants. At least 5 project sites are planned. Examples would be: 1) in Zabaikalski National Park, where a 40-mile trail extension needs to be constructed from the foot of the Barguzin Mountains, along the shores of Baikal, to the wooden Siberian village of Ust-Barguzin; 2) in Baikalski Nature Reserve, where a 3-mile trail needs improving from the Reserve's visitor centre up into an old-growth forest and right up to the edge of a secluded waterfall; 3) along the southern shores of Baikal, where the Round Baikal Railroad is now being partially converted to a hiking and biking trail, leading through tunnels, gables, and many cliff-front passages that face Baikal. For more information on all the work sites for volunteers in the summer, please www.baikal.eastsib.ru/gbt/index_en.html

Spp.: Varies greatly: along the trail one might see Baikal seal, bears, eagles, sable or red deer. Divers may see many exotic species of fish and even coral.

Hab.: Lakeshore habitat, temperate mountain forests, wetlands and meadowlands.

Loc.: Lake Baikal region of south central Russia, near the Mongolian border.

Travel: Airplane to Irkutsk (via Moscow or the Far east) or the Trans-Siberian train, which takes 3 days of travel from Moscow.

Dur.: 2–4 weeks.

Per.: Summer, from May to September.

L. term.: Opportunities for volunteering for several projects around Baikal are available for those who wish to stay on longer.

Age: Min.18.

Qualif.: Helpful (but not required) trail-building experience. Good health and ability to do hard work are a must, since some heavy tools will be used, with training provided.

Work: Mostly physical, all outdoors, with opportunities to assist design and strategy teams as they choose the best sites and methods for building each trail.

Lang.: Some knowledge of Russian would be helpful but not required. At least 1 English-language interpreter will be working on every team.

Accom.: Field work involves sleeping on boats or in tents; sleeping bag required.

Cost: Earth Island charges no fees for referring to the trail-building crews. However, the Federation is a non-profit group and will depend on international volunteers to pay for their own travel costs to reach the field site at Baikal. Food and tents will be provided for volunteers at the site. Volunteers should also bear the cost of insurance and accommodations in Russia before and after the work period.

Agents: Prospective volunteers can communicate directly with Earth Island's staff (at baikalwatch@earthisland.org) or with the Russian partners at the national parks and nature reserves, through their colleagues at the Federation (baikal@eastsib.ru), who are fluent in English.

Applic.: No application form to fill out, simple inquiries will be sufficient.

Notes: There are many other volunteer and internship opportunities with Siberian environmental groups available, where knowledge of Russian is a requirement. For more information on these programmes, contact Earth Island Institute.

SINAI WILDLIFE CLINIC (SWC)

c/o Domina Club and Hotel,
Coral Bay, South Sinai
Sharm El Sheikh   Egypt
Tel.:   ++20 (62) 601 610 (ext. 1039)
Mob.: ++20 (10) 520 6514
E-mail: wildlifeclinic@sinainet.com.eg

Desc.: SWP is an NGO involved in environmental and wildlife conservation, village-level health care programmes, environmental education programmes for children, operation of wildlife rehabilitation centres and human health services for desert-dwelling bedouin clans.

Spp.: White stork *(Ciconia ciconia)*, gazelle, ibex, sea turtles, birds.

Hab.: Desert, tropical seas.

Loc.: Southern tip of Sinai at entrance to Gulf of Aqaba and junction of Red Sea.

Travel: Airplane to Sharm-el-Sheik, Egypt.

Dur.: Medical doctors/veterinarians min. 6 months; all others min. 1 year.

Per.: Year round, arriving either January or August.

L. term.: Strongly encouraged.

Age: Min. 18, max. 60.

Qualif.: The following professions are preferred: medical doctors, veterinarians, conservationists, nurses, environmental education teachers as well as post- or undergraduate students in related disciplines. Persons working with SWP must be able to live outdoors and to tolerate hot weather, as much of the work takes place in the desert and mountains along the coast of the Red Sea. Scuba diving is useful.

Work: Wildlife rescue and rehabilitation, environmental education.

Lang.: Fluent English mandatory. Arabic helpful but not required.

Accom.: Air-conditioned houses.

Cost: No fee required for MDs and veterinarians. US$300/month for all others. Full room and board is provided. Volunteers must provide their own transportation to Egypt.

Applic.: Via fax or e-mail.

SKAFTAFELL NATIONAL PARK, Iceland

BTCV
36 St. Mary's Street Wallingford
Oxfordshire OX10 OEU   UK
Tel.: ++44 (1491) 821 600 – Fax: ++44 (1491) 839 646
E-mail: information@btcv.org
www.btcv.org.uk

Desc.:   Skaftafell National Park is a dramatic landscape of green oasis surrounded by black sand, dark rivers and white glaciers. When the park opened to the public erosion soon became a serious problem. Constructing footpaths directs visitors to certain areas and helps to conserve this unique landscape.

Spp.:   Subarctic flora and fauna (arctic fox, ptarmigan).

Hab.:   Glacier area, subarctic tundra.

Loc.:   Skaftafell National Park, southeast Iceland.

Travel: Airplane from Heathrow Airport (meeting point).

Dur.:   2 weeks.

Per.:   June – July.

L. term: Contact organisation for details.

Age: Min. 18.

Qualif.:   No specific skills required but work can be quite arduous.

Work: Constructing footpaths.

Lang.:   English.

Accom.:   Local Campsite.

Cost: GB£595 (including flight from the UK) (approx. EUR/US$900).

Agents: BTCV at www.btcv.org.

Applic.:   BTCV (see Organisation list).

SOUTHWESTERN RESEARCH STATION

American Museum of Natural History
P.O. Box 16553 Portal, Arizona 85632 USA
Tel./Fax: ++1 (520) 558 2396
E-mail:swrs@amnh.org
http://research.amnh.org/swrs/

Desc.: The volunteer programme offers students in biological sciences outstanding opportunities to observe and become involved with scientists doing field research. Food and lodging are provided to volunteers in exchange for 24 hours per week of routine chores, with the remaining time available for research activities. The programme is open to both undergraduate and graduate students; the latter may pursue their own research projects. The programme is open to non-students as well, particularly in the spring and fall.

Spp.: Birds, reptiles, amphibians, mammals, insects.

Hab: Five life-zones are encountered, from desert to alpine.

Loc.: Portal, southeastern Arizona.

Travel: Airplane to Tucson, then shuttle to Douglas (meeting place).

Dur.: Generally 6-week commitment, although shorter commitments are allowed in the spring and the fall.

Per.: Mid-March through the end of October.

L. term: Possible with the Station director's approval, after intial period.

Age: Min. 17, no max.

Qualif.: Some biological background is helpful, but not necessary.

Work: Volunteers work 24 hours on routine Station chores, e.g., housekeeping, grounds keeping, assisting in the kitchen/dining room, in exchange for room and board. Remaining time is available for research activities.

Lang.: English.

Accom.: Shared rooms are provided. All linens are provided. Meals are in a common dining room.

Cost: There is no cost to volunteers, other than transportation.

Applic.: Contact the Director, Wade C. Sherbrooke, Ph.D. An application must be submitted with letter(s) of reference.

SUSTAINABLE MANAGEMENT OF THE AGUARONGO

Fundación Ecológica Mazán
Casilla Postal 01–01–844
Agustin Cueva 735 y Julio Matovelle, Cuenca Ecuador
Tel.: ++593 (7) 882 753/815 796/815 896
Fax: ++593 (7) 815 723
E-mail: mazan@etapa.com.ec – marmosqs@yahoo.es

Desc.: The Aguarongo Protected Forest is located in one of Ecuador's areas of high deforestation. In 1993, the Foundation initiated the Sustainable Management of the Aguarongo Forest project. Main project activities include reforestation, environmental education and alternative agriculture.

Spp.: Initial studies of the forest have identified 127 plant species including 31 trees, 64 shrubs, 20 herbs, 6 epiphytes and 5 vines, 11 mammal, 33 bird, 2 amphibian and 2 reptile species.

Hab.: Andean forest (2,800–3,200m of altitude).

Loc.: Southern Ecuadorian Andes.

Travel: Airplane to Quito or Guayaquil, then bus to Cuenca and surrounding communities.

Dur.: No limits, depending on the experience and adaptability to the projects goals and personnel.

Per.: Year round.

L. term: Volunteers staying over 1 year are preferred. Short-term (1–3 months) work is mainly manual labour.

Age: Min. 21.

Qualif.: Various qualifications relevant to the activites listed below.

Work: Accounting and bookkeeping, tree nursery, agroforestry, community training, environmental education, small business management and various other positions.

Lang.: All volunteers must have an intermediate Spanish level.

Accom: Apartment (or rented room). Room and board in Cuenca starts at US$300/month.

Cost: No charge, however, no services (room and board, transportation, etc.) are provided. The Foundation will help volunteers with logistic details and cultural assimilation.

Applic.: Interested volunteers may send a CV and cover letter.

TAITA DISCOVERY CENTRE

The Savannah Group
P.O. Box 48019, Nairobi   Kenya
Tel.: ++254 (2) 331 191 – 222 075
Fax: ++254 (2) 330 698 – 216 528
E-mail: tsavo@savannahcamps.com
www.savannahcamps.com/tdc

Desc.: Tsavo is Kenya's largest national park. It forms a vital migratory corridor across the Taru Desert for elephants and lions, between the Galana River in Tsavo East to south to the foothills of Mt. Kilimanjaro and Lake Jipe in Tsavo West. A purpose-built African Village of 16 traditional rondavels is dedicated to environmental education. Scientists, educators, local communities, students, volunteers and conservationists have access to work, study and explore.

Spp.: Large mammals.

Hab.: Savannah and acacia woodlands.

Loc.: 60 km southeast of Voi at Bachuma, adjacent to southeast boundary of Tsavo East National Park.

Travel: 400 km, 7–8 hour drive via Voi to Nairobi on the Nairobi/Mombasa Trans African Highway. 100 km, 1–2 hour drive via Bachuma to Mombasa. Voi Railway Station has daily service between Nairobi and Mombasa. Flights available to Mombasa, Kenya

Dur.: Education programmes: 10 days. Volunteer work: 1–3 months.

Per.: Year round.

L. term: Possible. Inquire with the organisation.

Age: Min. 12; under 18 must be accompanied by an adult.

Qualif.: No particular skills required. However, the TDC has often opportunities for skilled volunteers, such as computer trainers, who can apply for a reduced fee. See website for details.

Work: Monitoring wild game movement; land management and community service projects.

Lang.: English.

Accom.: Tents at Galla Research Camp; full board.

Cost: Cost start at US$180/week. Park fees are payable directly.

Applic.: Download form from website.

TALKING LEAVES RANCH, Inc.

HC 31 Box 398
Prescott, Arizona 86303 USA
Tel.: ++1 (928) 899 0313
E-mail: tlr@radiolink.net
www.radiolink.net/tlr

Desc.: This is an earth-friendly building project in the wilderness of the Bradshaw Mountains in central Arizona. The lodge is strawbale with earthen exterior and interior plastering.

Spp.: Southwestern US Alpine vegetation.

Hab.: Surrounded by Prescott National Forest (pine, oak, etc.).

Loc.: Southwestern US.

Travel: Airplane to Phoenix, then van shuttle to Prescott.

Dur.: No minimum volunteer commitment.

Per.: Best time for volunteers is spring (May to July 4) and fall (September to November 15) Sometimes there is unseasonably warm fall weather until Dec. Summer monsoon activity is approx. July 4th to end of August.

L. term: Hostile winter weather precludes year-round camping.

Age: No minimum or maximum but fitness for activity at 7000 ft. (2,100m) elevation is essential.

Qualif.: No particular skills needed. Plastering can be taught. Those with building trades or experience are appreciated.

Work: Volunteers may participate in different aspects of the greenbuilding process. There is also an organic orchard to be planted, a hydroponic greenhouse project and a trail building project.

Lang.: English.

Accom.: Camping accommodation, outside solar shower facility. Some tents available if needed, but volunteers must provide their own bedding.

Cost: No fees. Volunteers must provide own transportation and food.

Applic.: Apply via Internet, telephone or mail.

Notes: See website for basic information and contact the project for further questions.

TAMBOPATA RESIDENT NATURALIST PROGRAM, Peru

TReeS
P.O. Box 33153, London NW3 4DR UK
www.geocities.com/treesweb/

Desc.: Several lodges along the Tambopata River offer Resident Naturalist (RN) programmes. RNs are volunteer guides/nature interpretes who guide turists of the lodges to visit the Tambopata Nature Reserve.

Spp.: Tropical rainforest species.

Hab.: Sub-tropical moist forest.

Loc.: Tambopata region, southeastern Peruvian province of Madre de Dios. The lodges are located along the Tambopata River.

Travel: Airplane to Lima, then to Puerto Maldonado, then river boat.

Dur.: Min. 3 months; 6 months preferred.

Per.: Year round. Applicants should arrive 1 week earlier to be trained by the departing RN.

L. term: RNs who wish to stay at least 6 months are preferred.

Age: Min. 22.

Qualif.: Graduation in natural sciences, biology or related disciplines.

Work: RN duties include: giving advice and training to Peruvian staff on conservation issues; daily recordings of weather data; maintaining sightings logs; helping maintain the trail system; meeting and orientating arriving guests; guiding tours and giving lectures; writing a final report.

Lang.: English, Spanish useful but not essential.

Accom.: Shared room in one of the lodges.

Cost:: Most lodges offer free room and board in return for guiding tourist groups. RNs pay for their travel to Puerto Maldonado.

Applic.: Contact TRees for details. UK applicants must send an A4 SAE.

Notes: RNs may also be able to undertake their own research during their stay. As 2–6 RNs are simultaneously present in each lodge, the duties can be distributed at their discretion, by informing the General Manager.

TEMPERATE RAINFOREST RESEARCH PROJECT (TRRP)

Box 905 Bella Coola
British Columbia V0T 1C0 Canada
Tel.: ++1 (250) 799 5810
Fax: ++1 (250) 799 5830
E-mail: trrp@envirolink.org
www.trrp.org

Desc.: TRRP is a non-profit society whose objective is to facilitate research on the unique biology of the coastal temperate rainforest on the mid-coast of British Columbia and to investigate the relationships between endangered species and the ancient forest ecosystems they inhabit.

Spp.: Goshawk, marblet murlet, tailed frog, grizzly bear, salmon.

Hab.: Northern coastal temperate rainforest.

Loc.: Mid-coast of British Columbia.

Travel: Airplane from Vancouver International airport or ferry from Port Hardy to Bella Coola. Cars must be stored at Gnome's Home RV park for CAD$1(approx. US$.67)/foot of car/month).

Dur.: Up to 4 months.

Per.: May to August.

L. term: Fundraising and awareness projects in various communities.

Age: Min. 18.

Qualif.: Researchers are considered on an individual basis. A University degree is preferred and senior researchers and thesis students are welcome. Ability to live in wilderness setting.

Work: Assist researchers and develop research projects.

Lang.: English.

Accom.: Volunteers must bring tent, sleeping bag, rain gear, etc.

Cost: CAD$50/week (approx. US$34) for general costs; senior researchers CAD$80 (approx. US$54). Funding possibilities.

Applic.: Contact TRRP for guidelines.

Notes: TRRP does not offer the volunteer programme every season, as alternative summer internships are offered; see website.

THE TIGER PROJECT, India

Timeless Excursions, Pvt. Ltd.
215, Somdutt Chambers II
9. Bhikaji Cama Place, New Delhi–110016   India
Tel.: ++91 (11) 6161198/6174206 – Fax: ++91 (11) 6193784
E-mail: timeless@vsnl.com
www.timelessexcursions.com

Desc.: Project Tiger was started in 1973 by the Indian Government. Its conservation success has been widely recognised. Activities originating by the project have created several jobs from senior technical officers and field professionals to staff for protection and enforcement.

Spp.: Tiger and all large Indian mammals, including elephant, rhino, leopard, sloth bear, etc.

Hab.: Tropical dry and humid forest.

Loc.: Wildlife Reserves throughout India.

Travel: Meeting in Delhi where transfer to the designated reserve is arranged.

Dur.: From 2–3 weeks to 6 months.

Per.: October to May.

L. term: Max. 6 months.

Age: Min. 18, max. 60.

Qualif.: Basic education, relevant field experience helpful.

Work: Volunteers will assist forest department staff in their fieldwork and various day to day activities or in any other way they consider productive for the project. They will also occasionally have the opportunity to interact with wildlife conservation experts from India and abroad.

Lang.: English.

Accom.: In huts, forest lodges or tents; sleeping bag required.

Cost: Depends on destination. Contributions start from US$990.

Applic.: Contact directly the organisation.

Notes: The organisation is a tour operator providing placements at different projects. Prospective volunteers should verify well conditions and the work activities offered.

TOLGA BAT HOSPITAL

Tolga Bat Rescue & Research, Inc.
P.O. Box 685 Atherton 4883 Australia
Tel.: ++61 (7) 4091 2683
Fax: ++61 (7) 4091 2683
E-mail: jenny.maclean@iig.com.au
www.athertontablelands.com/bats

Desc.: Tolga Bat Hospital works with tick paralysis in spectacled flying foxes. It also rescues flying foxes with the more usual problems from barbed wire, electrocution, shotguns, car accidents, etc.

Spp.: Spectacled flying foxes and little red flying foxes (*Pteropus spp.*), sometimes microbats.

Hab.: Tropical rainforest (Mabi rainforest).

Loc.: Tolga Scrub, Northeastern Australia, Atherton Tablelands.

Travel: Airplane to Cairns, then bus to Atherton.

Dur.: Minimum 4 weeks in busy season; 1 week for rest of year.

Per.: Year round but especially from October to December.

L. term: A stay of 2-3 months in the busy season is welcome.

Age: Min. 20 years, no max.

Qualif.: Ability to work well in teams and for long hours. Good cooking skills are welcome. Experience with bats not necessary, though experience with wildlife is a bonus. Veterinarians welcome.

Work: Work is extremely varied. In tick season it involves searching the colony daily; hospital treatments; feeding babies; preparing food for adults and babies; cleaning; washing; cooking; weighing and measuring bats; computer work. Work in the vegetable and bush gardens.

Lang.: English necessary.

Accom.: Excellent tourist accommodation (Pteropus House). Single, twin or triple room available. Some form of 'soft volunteering' is possible where people can pay more and work less.

Cost: AUS$20 per day for food and accommodation.

Applic.: Send CV highlighting experience in volunteering and any formal qualifications. Vaccination for rabies is mandatory for volunteers from October to December, although Australian Bat Lyssavirus is extremely rare in Spectacled flying foxes.

TREE PLANTERS FARM

Willing Workers on Organic Farms
2 Deserio Rd., Cedar Pocket, Gympie
Queensland 4570 Australia
Tel.: ++61 (7) 5486 6147
E-mail: forest@spiderweb.com.au

Desc.: This privately owned organic working farm aims to establish rainforest tree species through rainforest regeneration and tree planting on former rainforest sites. Special interest on the farm is in rare rainforest tree species. Adjoining the state forest, the farm has large rainforest trees, walking trails, swimming holes, a creek, a camping cave, an isolated visitors hut and an small orchard of tropical fruit trees.

Spp.: Rainforest trees.

Hab: Rainforest.

Loc.: Southeast Queensland.

Travel: Train or bus to Gympie, about 160 km north of Brisbane,the meeting point.

Dur.: 2 nights to make sure that both parties are happy and after that by negotiation.

Per.: Any time of the year.

L. term: Longer terms can perhaps be arranged.

Age: Min. 18.

Qualif.: No specific qualifications required, just enthusiasm.

Work: To assist with the establishment of the forests and perhaps some other farm jobs.

Lang: Only English is spoken but the project manager will assist those that wish to improve their English.

Accom.: Either in a spare bedroom in the house or a self-contained old converted dairy behind the house. Sleeping bags are required.

Cost: No cost. Work is done in return for keep.

Applic.: Contact Bob Whitworth, owner, directly either by telephone or writing to the above address.

TURTLES OF TORTUGUERO, Costa Rica

Caribbean Conservation Corporation
4424 NW 13th Street, Suite A-1
Gainesville, Florida 32609 USA
Tel.: ++1 (352) 373 6441 – Fax: ++1 (352) 375 2449
E-mail: resprog@cccturtle.org – ccc@cccturtle.org
www.cccturtle.org

Desc.: Caribbean Conservation Corporation (CCC) has been tagging and monitoring the green turtles of Tortuguero for over 40 years. CCC is now in its third year gathering information also on leatherback turtles, which nest at Tortuguero beach in impressive numbers.

Spp.: Green turtles (*Chelonia mydas*).

Hab.: Tropical coast.

Loc.: Tortuguero, Costa Rica.

Travel: Airplane to San José Costa Rica.

Dur.: 1–2 weeks.

Per.: June to September.

L. term: Volunteers can stay longer than 2 weeks with prior approval.

Age: Min. 18.

Qualif.: Volunteers must be in good physical condition, be able to live in rustic setting and tolerate harsh weather.

Work: Volunteers assist researchers tagging turtles and collecting data on size, tag numbers, nest location, etc.

Lang.: English. Spanish may be useful.

Accom.: Volunteers stay in local lodges at Tortuguero.

Cost: US$1,360 for 1 week; US$1,820 for 2 weeks. Cost includes 2 nights in San José, transfers to Tortuguero, all room, meals and training while at Tortuguero. A deposit is required. Flight to San José not included.

Agents: Holbrook Travel, tel. 1 (800) 451 7111 in North America.

Applic.: Contact Daniel Evans at CCC or agent to confirm dates.

WAKULUZU, FRIENDS OF THE COLOBUS TRUST

Wakuluzu Trust
P.O. Box 5380, Diani Beach Kenya
Tel.: ++ (254) 127 3519 − Fax: ++ (254) 127 2412
E-mail: wakuluzu@colobustrust.org   −   colobus@dianibeach.org
www.dianibeach.com/colobustrust/ −   www.colobustrust.org

Desc.: The trust is a local organisation committed to saving the Angolan Colobus monkey and preserving the coastal forest habitat.

Spp.: Primates; Angolan colobus (*Colobus angolensis*), olive baboons, sykes, vervets, bush babies.

Hab.: Tropical coral rag forest.

Loc.: Diani Beach, South Mombasa Coast, Kenya.

Travel: Airplane to Nairobi or Mombasa, or train from Nairobi to Mombasa.

Dur.: Min. 6 weeks.

Per.: Year round.

L. term: Subject to prior approval.

Age: Min. 22.

Qualif.: Preferably undergraduates or graduates with experience in conservation, education, zoology, journalism, ecology or veterinary medicine.

Work: Administration, research-field work, injury care and rescue, building colobridges, public awareness and education.

Lang.: English. German, French, Swahili useful but not essential.

Accom.: In a house with shared rooms and facilities. Mosquito net required. Bed linen provided.

Cost: Accommodation costs US$300/month. Food costs approx. US$20/week.

Agents: Born Free Foundation, 3 Grove House, Founary Lane, Horsham, W.Sussex, Rh13 5PL, England.

Applic.: There is a standard form to be completed and a CV required with 2 references.

WHALE AND DOLPHIN PROJECT, La Gomera

M.E.E.R. e. V.
Bundesallee 123
12161 Berlin Germany
Tel./Fax: ++49 (30) 8507 8755
E-mail: meer@infocanarias.com
www.m-e-e-r.de

Desc.: Observation of cetaceans. Scientific study aboard a small whale-watching vessel. Documentation of the behaviour of cetaceans and the kind of interaction between the vessel and the whales.

Spp.: Dolphins, whales, other marine mammals, turtles, sharks.

Hab.: Coastal and offshore subtropical waters of the Atlantic Ocean.

Loc.: Southwest of La Gomera (Canary Islands, Spain).

Travel: Airplane to Tenerife, then ferry to La Gomera.

Dur.: 2 weeks.

Per.: March to April; October to November.

L. term: Not possible.

Age: Min. 18.

Qualif.: No particular skills needed. Previous experience in marine mammal research or ethology is welcome.

Work: Volunteers participate in the whale watching trips, gather data and enter it in a database. A full training programme is provided.

Lang.: English, German.

Accom.: Tourist apartments (2–4 persons).

Cost: EUR875 (approx. GB£ 600).

Agents: The Ecovolunteer Network at www.ecovolunteer.org.

Applic.: Apply directly or through The Ecovolunteer Network (see Organisation list) website.

Notes: During the 14 days stay there are 7 whale watching trips (4-hours trips and one 8-hours day trip).

WHALE RESEARCH IN THE ST.LAWRENCE ESTUARY

Swiss Whale Society Felsbergstr. 3, CH–8625 Gossau, Switzerland
Centre Mériscope, 64 rue du Barrage, Longue-Rive, Québec Canada
Tel.:++1 (418) 231 2033 (summer) – ++41 (1) 930 4491 (winter)
Fax:++1 (418) 231 2033 (summer) – ++41 (1) 930 4491 (winter)
E-mail: dzbinden@dplanet.ch
www.isuisse.com/cetaces – www.meriscope.com

Desc.:   The 'Mériscope' is a small research base on the North shore
of the St. Lawrence estuary. Research projects include the
bioacoustics of minke, finback and blue whales and habitat
utilisation and social behaviour of baleen whales (by means
of photo-identification). Work is conducted with 2 rigid-hulled
inflatable boats; day trips typically last 5–6 hours. Slide talks
and land excursions complete the courses in marine biology.

Spp.:   Baleen whales: blue whales (*Balaenoptera musculus*), finback
whales (*B. physalus*) and minke whales (*B. acutorostrata*).

Hab.:   Subarctic estuary (coastal waters).

Loc.:   St. Lawrence estuary, about 350 km northeast of Québec City.

Travel: Flight to Montreal, then bus to St.Anne-de-Portneuf, via Quebec.

Dur.:   Courses last 2 weeks, 7 courses (max.10 people) per summer.

Per.:   June to September.

L. term: Marine mammal researchers may join for an entire season.

Age: Min.18 (younger participants only accompanied by parents).

Qualif.:   No particular skills needed; reasonably good physical condition
(living in prospector tents and working on board inflatable boats
for several hours); photography and computer skills welcome.

Work: All work under supervision of staff biologists: data collection
at sea; observation and identification of marine mammals;
behavioural sampling; navigation (GPS); sound recording;
photo-ID. Data entry and sound analysis in the lab.

Lang.:   English, German or French.

Accom.:   2 large tents by the sea; cooking in a big kitchen tent.

Cost: US$950 (approx.GB£620), includes accommodation, lectures
and thermo suit; food (approx.US$100/week) excluded.

Agents: Contact Dany Zbinden, project coordinator directly.

Applic.:   A standard form is also available from the website.

WHALES AND DOLPHINS OFF CÔTE D'AZUR, France

Swiss Cetacean Society (SCS)
Max-Olivier Bourcoud
Case postale 1430, CH–1001 Lausanne   Switzerland
Tel.: ++41 (21) 403 2114   – Fax: ++41 (21) 635 5858
E-mail: mbourcou@worldcom.ch   –   cetacean@ip-worldcom.ch
www.oenology.ch/scs   –   www.swisswhales.com

Desc.: Study of the distribution, abundance and dynamics of cetaceans in the Mediterranean Sea, between Côte d'Azur and Corsica.

Spp.: Cetaceans.

Hab.: Mediterranean French coast.

Loc.: South of France (Provence-Côte d'Azur).

Travel: Airplane to Nice; bus or train to Hyères or Toulon (depending on the research ship).

Dur.: Min. 6 days.

Per.: June to September

L. term: Negotiable (max. 4 months).

Age: Min. 18.

Qualif.: Strong interest in cetacean research and conservation, strong willingness to work and learn, navigation experience, photography, good hearing and sight, ability to swim and not prone to seasickness.

Work: Navigation watches, scanning the horizon for whales and dolphins. Assisting the researchers with bio-acoustic watch, skin and feces sampling, photo-ID, recording specific data, etc. Cooking, dishwashing and ship cleaning.

Lang.: French (good knowledge required).

Accom.: On the ship. Volunteers must bring sheets or sleeping bags.

Cost: Approx. EUR800 (approx. GB£ 520) for 6 days and nights for accommodation and food.

Applic.: Send a CV and a statement of purpose (explain interest in the position and expected outcome). Only the cover letter must be written in french. Please apply via e-mail.

WILD DOLPHIN SOCIETIES

Earthwatch Institute
3 Clock Tower Place – Suite 100, Box 75
Maynard, MA 01754   USA
Tel.: ++1 (978) 461 0081 – (800) 776 0188 (toll free in US/Canada)
Fax: ++1 (978) 461 2332
E-mail: info@earthwatch.org – www.earthwatch.org

Desc.: Much of what is known today about bottlenose dolphin society, population dynamics and physiology comes from this hallmark study of the roughly 100 Sarasota Bay individuals, now in its 32nd year (and 22nd year with Earthwatch volunteers). The project has served as a model for other cetacean studies.

Spp.: Bottlenose dolphin *(Tursiops truncatus)*.

Hab.: Tropical sea.

Loc.: Sarasota Bay, central west coast of Florida.

Travel: Airplane to Tampa or Miami. Meeting site is Sarasota.

Dur.: 12 days.

Per.: Year round.

L. term: No long-term opportunities available.

Age: Min. 16.

Qualif.: No special skills required. Photography and boat handling skills may be useful.

Work: Activities include: observing dolphins, documenting behaviour and visible marks, collecting environmental data and filing photos. Volunteers may even help care for stranded dolphins at Mote Marine Lab's dolphin hospital. Participants also share household duties such as shopping, cooking and cleaning.

Lang.: English.

Accom.: A comfortable, 2-bedroom duplex.

Cost: US$1,895 (approx. GB£1,160). Volunteers must cover the cost of their travel to and from Sarasota.

Agents: Earthwatch Institute (see Organisation list).

Applic.: A deposit of GB£200 (US$250) is required.

WILDLIFE TRAUMA CLINIC AND REHABILITATION CENTRE, South Africa

Wild at Heart
15 Plantation Road, Hillcrest, 3610 Kwazulu/Natal South Africa
Tel.: ++ 27 (31) 765 1818 – Fax: ++ 27 (31) 765 1818
E-mail: claude@wah.co.za
www.wah.co.za/volunteer.asp

Desc.: A Wildlife Clinic rescuing and caring for a variety of animals.
Spp.: Various African mammals and birds.
Hab.: The wild animals come from all over South Africa.
Loc.: Kwazulu/Natal, near Durban
Travel: Airplane to Durban.
Dur.: Min. 3 weeks.
Per.: Year round.
L. term: Long-term positions available.
Age: Min. 18, no max.
Qualif.: No particular skills other than a true interest in helping wildlife.
Work: Help injured and neglected wildlife. Work together with Wildlife rehabilitation specialists and the South African Parks Board Ideal for those pursuing veterinary careers. Assist in chores such as: regular check-ups on operated and recovering animals; feeding and preparation of food for the animals; bottle feeding and caring of baby wild animals; wildlife trapping and capturing; relocation of rehabilitated wildlife; researching certain species such as mongoose and monkeys; rehabilitating birds of prey; cleaning cages and enclosures and assisting in creating public awareness about the centre.
Lang.: English.
Accom.: House near the centre.
Cost: US$300 (approx.GB£200), food and accommodation included. Travel and mandatory health insurance not included.
Agents: Contact Claude Fourie at Wild at Heart.
Applic.: Application and Indemnity forms must be completed
Notes: Wild at Heart is an adventure travel agency providing placements at different projects. Prospective volunteers should verify the conditions and the work activities offered.

WOLF TRACKING, Slovakia

BTCV
36 St. Mary's Street Wallingford
Oxfordshire OX10 OEU UK
Tel.: ++44 (1491) 821 600
Fax: ++44 (1491) 839 646
E-mail: information@btcv.org – www.btcv.org.

Desc.: Nizke Tatry National Park in the Carpathian Mountains has extensive forests and caves. The mountains are home to around 200–400 wolves, 850 bears and 380–480 lynx. Volunteers assist with research by tracking wolves and red deer, collecting droppings and looking for wolf kills. The aim is to ensure the long-term conservation of the wolf and to encourage greater understanding of the animal and its role within the forest ecosystem.

Spp: Wolves, brown bear, red and roe deer, lynx, wild boar, eagles.

Hab: Forest.

Loc.: Nizke Tatry National Park, Carpathian Mountains, Slovakia.

Travel: Airplane to Vienna (meeting point at the airport).

Dur.: 2 weeks.

Per.: April to September.

L. term: Contact organisation for details.

Age: Min. 18.

Qualif.: No specific skills required.

Work: Activities include radio tracking, scat collecting and snow tracking.

Lang.: English.

Accom.: Wooden lodges in the heart of the forest, meals will be in a nearby hotel.

Cost: GB£630 excluding flight (approx. EUR/US$950).

Agents: BTCV at www.btcv.org.

Applic.: BTCV (see Organisation list).

WOLF AND BROWN BEAR RESEARCH, Russia

The Ecovolunteer Network
Meyersweg 29,   7553 AX Hengelo The Netherlands
Tel.: ++31 (74) 250 8250
Fax: ++31 (74) 250 6572
E-mail: info@ecovolunteer.org
www.ecovolunteer.org

Desc.: The main goal of this research is to collect data on the activities, number and migration routes of the wolves living in a territory of 1,000 km² in and around the Central Forest Reserve and Biological Station Cisty Les. The brown bear research started in 1970. Its main purpose is to study the ecology, diet and behaviour of these large predators. A rehabilitation project of bear cubs is also ongoing since 1985.

Spp.: Wolf (*Canis lupus*), brown bear (*Ursus arctos*). Other animals of the Reserve include lynx, European mink, moose and many bird species such as cranes, black grouse and black stork.

Hab.: Typical southern taiga.

Loc.: The Central Forest Nature Reserve (CFNR) is situated in the southern taiga of Central European Russia. The reserve is about 350 km northwest of Moscow.

Travel: Airplane to Moscow then train to Staraya Toropa, meeting is at the train station. Private transportation by car from Moscow can be arranged for an extra cost of US$100.

Dur.: 2 weeks. Additional weeks options are available at a lower cost.

Per.: January –March, May–September, and November–December.

L. term: Research opportunities exist for students interested in an independent research project; minimum stay is 1 month, which can be extended upon agreement.

Age: Min. 18, max. 50.

Qualif.: Volunteers must be in good physical condition and able to walk long distances and ski (in winter). Participants should be committed to nature conservation and animal protection.

Work: Volunteers participate in the research on the distribution and the feeding behaviour of wolves and bears. Activities mainly consist of taking long walks through the forest in search of trails that indicate the resting and meeting places of wolves. Volunteers will be looking for faeces or for footprints of wolves and brown bears or for leftovers of prey. In winter, locating of wolf trails is done by using skis. Overnight stays at wooden ranger houses in the forest (with no facilities) are possible.

Lang.: English, Russian.

Accom.: Simple double and single rooms at the research station. During fieldwork a small wooden house or, in summer, a tent is used (sleeping bag necessary). Sometimes volunteers stay with Russian families (employees of the reserve), a unique opportunity to learn more about the Russian way of life. Living conditions are rather primitive and allow little privacy.

Cost: US$818 for 2 weeks, US$273 for the 3rd week, US$214 for 4th week. Students less than 24 years old can have special discounts. Travel/flight to and from Moscow, visa, cancellation insurance and personal expenses not included.

Agents: The Ecovolunteer Network at www.ecovolunteer.org.

Applic.: The Ecovolunteer Network (see Organisation list).

Notes: As the Russian people in the reserve have limited knowledge of English, it is necessary for the volunteers to show initiative.

ORGANISATION ALPHABETICAL INDEX

PROJECT ALPHABETICAL INDEX

GEOGRAPHICAL LOCATION INDEX

Projects are listed in italics. Organisations with projects in many locations are listed in the index under each of the respective geographical areas.

Africa

À Pas De Loup 'Volunteers For Nature'
African Conservation Experience
African Conservation Trust, South Africa
African Experience
Black Rhino, Kenya
Brathay Exploration Group
CERCOPAN Forest Based Research and Education Centre (Nigeria)
Cheetah Conservation Fund, Namibia
Fondo per la Terra - Earth Fund
Frontier
Global Service Corps
Great White Shark Project (South Africa)
Involvement Volunteers Association, Inc.
Leopards of Phinda, South Africa
Libanona Ecology Centre, Madagascar
Munda Wanga Wildlife Park and Sanctuary (Zambia)
Operation Crossroads Africa, Inc.
Pandrillus Foundation (Nigeria)
Projecto Jubarte do Cabo Verde (Cabo Verde)
Raleigh International
Re-aforestation Project, Ghana
Re-hydration of the Earth, Kenya
Rhino Rescue Project, Swaziland
SANCCOB - South African Fundation for the Conservation of Coastal Birds
Taita Discovery Centre (Kenya)
Trekforce Expeditions
Wakuluzu, Friends of the Colobus Trust (Kenya)
Whale and Dolphin Project, la Gomera (Spain)
Wilderness Trust, the
Wildlife Trauma Clinic and Rehabilitation Centre, South Africa

Asia

Ayutthaya Elephant Camp, Thailand
Bohorok Environmental Centre (Indonesia)
Brathay Exploration Group
BTCV
Coral Cay Conservation
Frontier

Asia, con't.
Gibbon Rehabilitation Project (Thailand)
Global Service Corps
i to i
International Trust for Traditional Medicine (India)
Involvement Volunteers Association, Inc.
Kanha National Park Ecosystem, the, India
Operation Wallacea
Orangutan Foundation, the (Indonesia)
Orangutan Health (Indonesia)
Przewalski Horse Reintroduction Project (Mongolia)
Raleigh International
Sea Turtle Project, Thailand
Siberian/East Russian Volunteer Program (Russia)
Tiger Project, the, India
Trekforce Expeditions

Europe
À Pas De Loup 'Volunteers For Nature'
Arcturos
Beluga Research Project, Russia
Bieszczady Wolf Project, Poland
Black Vulture Protection, Bulgaria
Bonelli Eagle Project, Portugal
Brathay Exploration Group
BTCV
BTCV Scotland
CARAPAX - European Center for Conservation of Chelonians
Carpathian Large Carnivore Project (Romania)
Centre for Alternative Technology
Cetacean Research & Rescue Unit (Scotland)
Chantiers de Jeunes Provence Côte d'Azur
Coordinating Commitee for International Volunteer Service
Coral Cay Conservation
Cotravaux
CTS - Centro Turistico Studentesco e Giovanile
Europarc Deutschland
Golden Eagles of Mull, the (Scotland)
Griffon Vulture Conservation Project (Croatia)
Hellenic Ornithological Society
International Otter Survival Fund
Involvement Volunteers Association, Inc.
IUCN - The World Conservation Union

Legambiente
LIPU - Lega Italiana Protezione Uccelli
Living and Working in a Suatainable Village (Hungary)
Monkey Sanctuary, the (UK)
Monte Adone Wildlife Protection Centre (Italy)
Moray Firth Dolphin Monitoring Project (Scotland)
National Trust, the
Noah's Ark (Greece)
Operation Osprey, Scotland
Orkney Seal Rescue Centre (Scotland)
Ringing Programme of Migratory Passerines (Spain)
RSPB - The Royal Society for the Protection of Birds
SCI - Service Civil International
Scottish Whale &Dolphin Project (Scotland)
Scottish Wildlife Rescue (Scotland)
Skaftafell National Park, Iceland
Wilderness Trust, the
Wolf Tracking, Slovakia
Wolves and Brown Bear Research, Russia
WWF - Italy

Mediterranean
Adriatic Dolphin Project (Croatia)
Bottlenose Dolphin Project, Italy
BTCV
Chantiers de Jeunes Provence Côte d'Azur
CTS - Centro Turistico Studentesco e Giovanile
CVG - Conservation Volunteers Greece
Dolphins and Sea Life Around the Maltese Islands (Malta)
Ecology of Common Dolphin in the Alboran Sea (Spain)
Griffon Vulture Conservation Project (Croatia)
Ionian Dolphin Project, Greece
Ischia Dolphin Project (Italy)
Legambiente
Loggerhead Sea Turtles in Linosa (Italy)
Management Plan for Pilos Lagoon (Greece)
Manga del Mar Menor Restoration and Research Project (Spain)
Mediterranean Fin Whale Programme (Italy)
Monk Seal Project, Turkey
Sea Turtle Project, Rhodes Island (Greece)
Sea Turtle Rescue Centre, Greece
Sea Turtle Summer Field Work, Greece

Mediterranean, con't.
Tethys Research Institute
Whales and Dolphins off Côte d'Azur, France
WWF - Italy

Middle East
Sinai Wildlife Clinic (Egypt)

Oceania
BTCV
Cape Tribulation Tropical Research Station (Australia)
CVA - Conservation Volunteers Australia
Forest Health Monitoring (New Zealand)
Golden Boomerang Landcare (Australia)
i to i
Involvement Volunteers Association, Inc.
NZTCV - The New Zealand Trust for Conservation Volunteers
Oceania Research Project (Australia)
Oneworld Volunteers
Tolga Bat Hospital (Australia)
Tree Planters Farm (Australia)

South America
Amargal Tropical Rainforest Research, El (Colombia)
ARFA - Asociacion de Rescate de Fauna (Venezuela)
Association for the Conservation of the Southern Rainforests
Black Howler Monkey Project, Argentina
Black Sheep Inn, Ecuador
Charles Darwin Foundation, Galapagos (Ecuador)
Ecology & Conservation of Deer in Patagonia (Argentina)
Fondo per la Terra - Earth Fund
Galapagos National Park and Marine Reserve (Ecuador)
Humpback Research Project, Brazil
Iracambi Atlantic Rainforest Research and Conservation Center, Brazil
Jatun Sacha, Ecuador
Project Tamar (Brazil)
Raleigh International
River Otter Project, Brazil
Sustainable Management of the Aguarongo (Ecuador)
Tambopata Resident Naturalist Program, Peru

Central America and Mexico
ARCAS - Asociaciòn de Rescate y Conservaciòn de Vida Silvestre
ASVO - Asociacion de Voluntarios para el Servicio en las Areas Protegidas
Birds of Tortuguero, Costa Rica
Bottlenose Dolphin Project, Belize
Cano Palma Biological Station, Costa Rica
Chocoyero - el Brujo Co-managemet Project, el (Nicaragua)
Coral Cay Conservation
Costa Rican Sea Turtles (Costa Rica)
CTS - Centro Turistico Studentesco e Giovanile
Ecolodge San Luls & Research Station (Costa Rica)
Genesis II Cloudforest Preserve and Wildlife Refuge (Costa Rica)
Global Service Corps
Howler Monkey Project, Mexico
i to i
Leatherback Seaturtle Tagging Programme (Grenada)
Legambiente
Lifeline Cat Research and Rehabilitation Centre, Belize
Manatee Research Project, Belize
Marine Turtle and Youth Environmental Education (Mexico)
Monitoring of Olive Ridley Sea Turtle Populations (Costa Rica)
Oneworld Volunteers
Operation Wallacea
PROVCA - Programa de Voluntarios para
    la Conservacion del Ambiente (Costa Rica)
Proyecto Campanario (Costa Rica)
Punta Banco Sea Turtle Project, Costa Rica
Rehabilitation and Release of Wildlife (Costa Rica)
Sea Turtle Conservation Program, Costa Rica
Sea Turtles of the Pacific Coast of Costa Rica (Costa Rica)
Trekforce Expeditions
Turtles of Tortuguero, Costa Rica
YCI - Youth Challenge International

USA and Canada
Acorus Restoration Native Plant Nursery (Canada)
American Bear Association
American Littoral Society
Appalachian Trail Conference
Bimini Lemon Shark Project, Bahamas
Brathay Exploration Group
Caretta Research Project (USA)
Central Coast Cetacean Project (Canada)

USA and Canada, con't.
Dolphin Research Center (USA)
Forest Restoration (USA)
Friends of the Sea Otter (USA)
Great Whales in their Natural Environment (Canada)
Grey Wolf Project (USA)
Hawaiian Forest Restoration Project (USA)
Marine Mammal Center, the (USA)
Mingan Island Cetacean Research Expeditions
Oceanic Society Expeditions
Project Delphis (USA)
San Gorgonio Wilderness Association
SCA - Student Conservation Association, Inc.
Sousson Foundation
Southwestern Research Station (USA)
Talking Leaves Ranch, Inc. (USA)
Temperate Rainforest Research Project (Canada)
U.S. Department of Agriculture - Forest Service
U.S. Fish and Wildlife Service
U.S. National Park Service
Volunteer for Nature
Volunteers for Outdoor Colorado
Whale Research in the St. Lawrence Estuary (Canada)
Wild Dolphin Societies (USA)
Wilderness Trust, the

Worldwide
Biosphere Expeditions
CEDAM International
Coordinating Committee for International Volunteers
Cotravaux
Earthwatch Institute
Ecovolunteer Network, the
Greenforce - Careers in Conservation
IUCN - The World Conservation Union
Reef Check Global Coral Reef Monitoring (USA)
SCI - Service Civil International
United Nations Volunteers
University Research Expeditions Program

SPECIES INDEX

Organisations and projects with no particular focus on any species are not listed in this index. Projects are listed in italics.

African herbivores
African Conservation Experience
African Conservation Trust, South Africa
African Experience
Black Rhino, Kenya
Ecovolunteer Network, the
Re-hydration of the Earth, Kenya
Rhino Rescue Project, Swaziland
Taita Discovery Centre (Kenya)
Wildlife Trauma Clinic and Rehabilitation Centre, South Africa

Bats
Cape Tribulation Tropical Research Station (Australia)
Oneworld Volunteers
Tolga Bat Hospital (Australia)

Bears
American Bear Association
Arcturos
Carpathian Large Carnivore Project (Romania)
Ecovolunteer Network, the
Wolves and Brown Bear Research, Russia

Primates
ARCAS - Asociaciòn de Rescate y Conservaciòn de Vida Silvestre
ARFA - Asociacion de Rescate de Fauna (Venezuela)
Black Howler Monkey Project, Argentina
Bohorok Environmental Centre (Indonesia)
CERCOPAN Forest Based Research and Education Centre (Nigeria)
Ecovolunteer Network, the
Gibbon Rehabilitation Project (Thailand)
Howler Monkey Project, Mexico
Monkey Sanctuary, the (UK)
Orangutan Foundation, the (Indonesia)
Orangutan Health (Indonesia)
Pandrillus Foundation (Nigeria)
Treckforce Expeditions
Wakuluzu, Friends of the Colobus Trust (Kenya)

Felines

ARCAS - Asociaciòn de Rescate y Conservaciòn de Vida Silvestre
ARFA - Asociacion de Rescate de Fauna (Venezuela)
Cano Palma Biological Station, Costa Rica
Carpathian Large Carnivore Project (Romania)
Cheetah Conservation Fund, Namibia
Fondo per la Terra - Earth Fund
Kanha National Park Ecosystem, the, India
Leopards of Phinda, South Africa
Lifeline Cat Research and Rehabilitation Centre, Belize
Rehabilitation and Release of Wildlife (Costa Rica)
Tiger Project, the, India

Wolves

Bieszczady Wolf Project, Poland
Biosphere Expeditions
BTCV
Carpathian Large Carnivore Project (Romania)
Ecovolunteer Network, the
Grey Wolf Project (USA)
Wolf Tracking, Slovakia
Wolves and Brown Bear Research, Russia

Other Mammals

Ayutthaya Elephant Camp, Thailand
Biosphere Expeditions
CTS - Centro Turistico Studentesco e Giovanile
Earthwatch Institute
Ecology & Conservation of Deer in Patagonia (Argentina)
Ecovolunteer Network, the
Fondo per la Terra - Earth Fund
International Otter Survival Fund
Kanha National Park Ecosystem, the, India
Monte Adone Wildlife Protection Centre (Italy)
Munda Wanga Wildlife Park and Sanctuary (Zambia)
Noah's Ark (Greece)
Oneworld Volunteers
Przewalski Horse Reintroduction Project (Mongolia)
Rehabilitation and Release of Wildlife (Costa Rica)
River Otter Project, Brazil
SCA - Student Conservation Association, Inc.
Scottish Wildlife Rescue (Scotland)
Taita Discovery Centre (Kenya)

Tambopata Resident Naturalist Program, Peru
Temperate Rainforest Research Project (Canada)
Wildlife Trauma Clinic and Rehabilitation Centre, South Africa

Whales & Dolphins
Adriatic Dolphin Project (Croatia)
Beluga Research Project, Russia
Bottlenose Dolphin Project, Belize
Bottlenose Dolphin Project, Italy
Central Coast Cetacean Project (Canada)
Cetacean Research & Rescue Unit (Scotland)
CTS - Centro Turistico Studentesco e Giovanile
Dolphin Resercah Center (USA)
Earthwatch Institute
Ecology of Common Dolphin in the Alboran Sea (Spain)
Ecovolunteer Network, the
Galapagos National Park and Marine Reserve (Ecuador)
Great Whales in their Natural Environment (Canada)
Humpback Research Project, Brazil
Ionian Dolphin Project, Greece
Ischia Dolphin Project (Italy)
Marine Mammal Center, the (USA)
Mediterranean Fin Whale Programme (Italy)
Mingan Island Cetacean Research Expeditions
Moray Firth Dolphin Monitoring Project (Scotland)
Oceania Research Project (Australia)
Oceanic Society Expeditions
Project Delphis (USA)
Projecto Jubarte do Cabo Verde (Cabo Verde)
Scottish Whale & Dophin Project (Scotland)
Tethys Research Institute
Whale and Dolphin Project, La Gomera (Spain)
Whale Research in the St. Lawrence Estuary (Canada)
Whales and Dolphins off Côte d'Azur, France
Wild Dolphin Societies (USA)

Seals
Charles Darwin Foundation, Galapagos (Ecuador)
Ecovolunteer Network, the
Monk Seal Project, Turkey
Orkney Seal Rescue Centre (Scotland)

Other Marine Mammals
Friends of the Sea Otter (USA)
Earthwatch Institute
Manatee Research Project, Belize
Oceanic Society Expeditions

Sharks
Bimini Lemon Shark Project, Bahamas
Great White Shark Project (South Africa)

Corals
Cedam International
Coral Cay Conservation
Operation Wallacea
Reef Check Global Coral Reef Monitoring (USA)

Amphibians & Reptiles
ARCAS - Asociaciòn de Rescate y Conservaciòn de Vida Silvestre
ARFA - Asociacion de Rescate de Fauna (Venezuela)
Cano Palma Biological Station, Costa Rica
CARAPAX - European Center for Conservation of Chelonians
Charles Darwin Foundation, Galapagos (Ecuador)
CVA - Conservation Volunteers Australia
CVG - Conservation Volunteers Greece
Kanha National Park Ecosystem, the, India
Management Plan for Pilos Lagoon (Greece)
Rehabilitation and Release of Wildlife (Costa Rica)
Tambopata Resident Naturalist Program, Peru

Sea Turtles
ARCAS - Asociaciòn de Rescate y Conservaciòn de Vida Silvestre
Biosphere Expeditions
CARAPAX - European Center for Conservation of Chelonians
Caretta Research Project (USA)
Costa Rican Sea Turtles (Costa Rica)
CTS - Centro Turistico Studentesco e Giovanile
Dolphins and Sea Life Around the Maltese Islands (Malta)
Earthwatch Institute
Ecovolunteer Network, the
Leatherback Seaturtle Tagging Programme (Grenada)
Loggerhead Sea Turtles in Linosa (Italy)
Marine Turtle and Youth Environmental Education (Mexico)

Monitoring of Olive Ridley Sea Turtle Populations (Costa Rica)
Oneworld Volunteers
Punta Banco Sea Turtle Project, Costa Rica
Sea Turtle Conservation Program, Costa Rica
Sea Turtle Project, Rhodes Isalnd (Greece)
Sea Turtle Project, Thailand
Sea Turtle Rescue Centre, Greece
Sea Turtle Summer Field Work, Greece
Sea Turtles of the Pacific Coast of Costa Rica (Costa Rica)
Turtles of Tortuguero, Costa Rica

Birds

À Pas De Loup 'Volunteers For Nature'
African Conservation Experience
Amargal Tropical Rainforest Research, el (Colombia)
ARCAS - Asociaciòn de Rescate y Conservaciòn de Vida Silvestre
ARFA - Asociacion de Rescate de Fauna (Venezuela)
Assoclatlon for the Conservation of Southern Rainforests
Birds of Tortuguero, Costa Rica
Black Vulture Protection, Bulgaria
Bonelli Eagle Project, Portugal
BTCV
Cano Palma Biological Station, Costa Rica
Chocoyero - el Brujǫ Co-managemet Project, el (Nicaragua)
CVA - Conservation Volunteers Australia
Earthwatch Institute
Ecolodge San Luis & Research Station (Costa Rica)
Genesis II Cloudforest Preserve and Wildlife Refuge (Costa Rica)
Golden Eagles of Mull, the (Scotland)
Griffon Vulture Conservation Project (Croatia)
Hellenic Ornithological Society
Kanha National Park Ecosystem, the, India
LIPU - Lega Italiana Protezione Uccelli
Manga del Mar Menor Restoration and Research (Spain)
Monte Adone Wildlife Protection Centre (Italy)
Munda Wanga Wildlife Park and Sanctuary (Zambia)
Oceanic Society Expeditions
Oneworld Volunteers
Operation Osprey, Scotland
Rehabilitation and Release of Wildlife (Costa Rica)
Ringing Programme of Migratory Passerines (Spain)
RSPB - The Royal Society for the Protection of Birds

Birds, con't.
SANCCOB - South African Fundation for the Conservation of Coastal Birds
SCA - Student Conservation Association, Inc.
Scottish Wildlife Rescue (Scotland)
Sinai Wildlife Clinic (Egypt)
Sustainable Management of the Aguarongo (Ecuador)
Tambopata Resident Naturalist Program, Peru
Temperate Rainforest Research Project (Canada)
U.S. Fish and Wildlife Service
Wildlife Trauma Clinic and Rehabilitation Centre, South Africa
YCI - Youth Challenge International

Trees &Vegetation
À Pas De Loup 'Volunteers For Nature'
Acorus Restoration Native Plant Nursery (Canada)
Amargal Tropical Rainforest Research, el (Colombia)
ASVO - Asociacion de Voluntarios Para el Servicio de Area Protegidas
Bohorok Environmental Centre (Indonesia)
Cape Tribulation Tropical Research Station (Australia)
Chantiers de Jeunes Provence Côte d'Azur
Charles Darwin Foundation, Galapagos (Ecuador)
Chocoyero - el Brujo Co-managemet Project, el (Nicaragua)
CVA - Conservation Volunteers Australia
CVG - Conservation Volunteers Greece
Ecolodge San Luis & Research Station (Costa Rica)
Ecovolunteer Network, the
Europarc Deutschland
Forest Health Monitoring (New Zealand)
Forest Restoration (USA)
Genesis II Cloudforest Preserve and Wildlife Refuge (Costa Rica)
Global Service Corps
Golden Boomerang Landcare (Australia)
Hawaiian Forest Restoration Project (USA)
International Trust for Traditional Medicine (India)
Iracambi Atlantic Rainforest Research and Conservation Center, Brazil
Jatun Sacha, Ecuador
Libanona Ecology Centre, Madagascar
Living and Working within a Sustainable Village (Hungary)
Manga del Mar Menor Restoration and Research Project (Spain)
National Trust, the
NZTCV - The New Zealand Trust for Conservation Volunteers
PROVCA - Programa de Voluntarios para
    la Conservacion del Ambiente (Costa Rica)

Proyecto Campanario (Costa Rica)
Re-aforestation Project, Ghana
San Gorgonio Wilderness Association
Skaftafell National Park, Iceland
Sousson Foundation
Sustainable Management of the Aguarongo (Ecuador)
Talking Leaves Ranch, Inc. (USA)
Tambopata Resident Naturalist Program, Peru
Temperate Rainforest Research Project (Canada)
Treckforce Expeditions
Tree Planters Farm (Australia)
U.S. Department of Agriculture - Forest Service
U.S. National Park Service
Volunteer for Nature
Volunteers for Outdoor Colorado
WWF - Italy
YCI - Youth Challenge International

Various Species & Habitats
African Conservation Experience
Amargal Tropical Rainforest Research, el (Colombia)
American Littoral Society, New York Chapter
Appalachian Trail Conference
ASVO - Asociacion de Voluntarios Para el Servicio de Area Protegidas
Black Sheep Inn, Ecuador
Brathay Exploration Group
BTCV
BTCV Scotland
Chocoyero - el Brujo Co-managemet Project, el (Nicaragua)
CVG - Conservation Volunteers Greece
Coordinating Committee for International Volunteers
Cotravaux
Earthwatch Institute
Ecolodge San Luis & Research Station (Costa Rica)
Ecovolunteer Network
Frontier
Genesis II Cloudforest Preserve and Wildlife Refuge (Costa Rica)
Global Service Corps
Greenforce - Careers in Conservation
i to i
Involvment Volunteers Association, Inc.
Iracambi Atlantic Rainforest Research and Conservation Center, Brazil
IUCN - The World Conservation Union

Various Species & Habitats, con't.
Legambiente
Libanona Ecology Centre, Madagascar
NZTCV - The New Zealand Trust for Conservation Volunteers
Operation Crossroads Africa, Inc.
PROVCA - Programa de Voluntarios para
    la Conservacion del Ambiente (Costa Rica)
Proyecto Campanario (Costa Rica)
Siberian/East Russian Volunteer Program (Russia)
Southwestern Research Station (USA)
Trekforce Expeditions
United Nations Volunteer
U.S. National Park Service
Volunteer for Nature
Wilderness Trust, the
YCI - Youth Challenge International

COST INDEX

Note: costs may change without notice; travel costs are usually not included; see project or organisation description for details. Projects are listed in italics.

No cost or under US$100

À Pas De Loup 'Volunteers For Nature'
Acorus Restoration Native Plant Nursery (Canada)
American Bear Association
American Littoral Society
Appalachian Trail Conference
ARCAS - Asociaciòn de Rescate y Conservaciòn de Vida Silvestre
Arcturos
ARFA - Asociacion de Rescate de Fauna (Venezuela)
Association for the Conservation of the Southern Rainforests
Black Sheep Inn, Ecuador
Bonelli Eagle Project, Portugal
Cape Tribulation Tropical Research Station (Australia)
Centre for Alternative Technology
Charles Darwin Foundation, Galapagos (Ecuador)
Chocoyero - el Brujo Co-managemet Project, el (Nicaragua)
Coordinating Committee for International Volunteers
Cotravaux
Ecology & Conservation of Deer in Patagonia (Argentina)
Europarc Deutschland
Forest Health Monitoring (New Zealand)
Forest Restoration (USA)
Golden Boomerang Landcare (Australia)
Hawaiian Forest Restoration Project (USA)
Hellenic Ornithological Society
International Trust for Traditional Medicine (India)
IUCN - The World Conservation Union
Management Plan for Pilos Lagoon (Greece)
Marine Mammal Center, the (USA)
Marine Turtle and Youth Environmental Education (Mexico)
Monitoring of Olive Ridley Sea Turtle Populations (Costa Rica)
Monkey Sanctuary, the (UK)
Monte Adone Wildlife Protection Centre (Italy)
National Trust, the
Noah's Ark (Greece)
NZTCV - The New Zealand Trust for Conservation Volunteers
Operation Osprey, Scotland
Orkney Seal Rescue Centre (Scotland)
Pandrillus Foundation (Nigeria)

No cost or under US$100, con't.
*PROVCA - Programa de Voluntarios para
la Conservacion del Ambiente (Costa Rica)*
Proyecto Campanario (Costa Rica)
Rehabilitation and Release of Wildlife (Costa Rica)
RSPB - The Royal Society for the Protection of Birds
SANCCOB - South African Fundation for the Conservation of Coastal Birds
San Gorgonio Wilderness Association
SCA - Student Conservation Association, Inc.
SCI - Service Civil International
Scottish Wildlife Rescue (Scotland)
Sea Turtle Conservation Program, Costa Rica
Sea Turtle Rescue Centre, Greece
Sea Turtle Summer Field Work, Greece
Siberian/East Russian Volunteer Program (Russia)
Sinai Wildlife Clinic (Egypt)
Southwestern Research Station (USA)
Talking Leaves Ranch, Inc. (USA)
Tambopata Resident Naturalist Program, Peru
Tolga Bat Hospital (Australia)
Tree Planters Farm (Australia)
United Nations Volunteers
U.S. Department of Agriculture - Forest Service
U.S. Fish and Wildlife Service
U.S. National Park Service
Volunteer for Nature
Volunteers for Outdoor Colorado
YCI - Youth Challenge International

US$100–499
African Experience
ASVO - Asociacion de Voluntarios para el Servicio de Area Protegidas
Bimini Lemon Shark Project, Bahamas
Black Howler Monkey Project, Argentina
Black Vulture Protection, Bulgaria
Bohorok Environmental Centre (Indonesia)
BTCV
BTCV Scotland
Cano Palma Biological Station, Costa Rica
CARAPAX - European Centre for Conservation of Chelonians
CERCOPAN Forest Based Research and Education Centre (Nigeria)
Chantiers de Jeunes Provence Côte d'Azur
Cotravaux

US$100–499, con't.
CTS - Centro Turistico Studentesco e Giovanile
CVA - Conservation Volunteers Australia
CVG - Conservation Volunteers Greece
Ecolodge San Luis & Research Station (Costa Rica)
Galapagos National Park & Marine Reserve (Ecuador)
Genesis II Cloudforest Preserve and Wildlife Refuge (Costa Rica)
Grey Wolf Project (USA)
Griffon Vulture Conservation Project (Croatia)
Iracambi Atlantic Rainforest Research and Conservation Center, Brazil
Jatun Sacha, Ecuador
Kanha National Park Ecosystem, the, India
Legambiente
LIPU - Lega Italiana Protezione Uccelli
Loggerhead Sea Turtles in Linosa (Italy)
Manga del Mar Menor Restoration and Research Project (Spain)
Monk Seal Project , Turkey
Re-aforestation Project, Ghana
Reef Check Global Coral Reef Monitoring (USA)
River Otter Project, Brazil
Scottish Whale & Dolphin Project (Scotland)
Sea Turtles of the Pacific Coast of Costa Rica (Costa Rica)
Sousson Foundation
Sustainable Management of the Aguarongo (Ecuador)
Temperate Rainforest Research Project (Canada)
Wakuluzu, Friends of the Colobus Trust (Kenya)
Wilderness Trust, the
Wildlife Trauma Clinic and Rehabilitation Centre, South Africa
WWF - Italy

US$500–999
Adriatic Dolphin Project (Croatia)
African Conservation Trust, South Africa
Ayutthaya Elephant Camp, Thailand
Beluga Research Project, Russia
Bieszczady Wolf Project, Poland
Bottlenose Dolphin Project (Italy)
Brathay Exploration Group
BTCV
Caretta Research Project (USA)
Carpathian Large Carnivore Projectt (Romania)
Central Coast Cetacean Project (Canada)
CTS - Centro Turistico Studentesco e Giovanile

Dolphin Research Center (USA)
Ecovolunteer Network, the
Howler Monkey Project, Mexico
International Otter Survival Fund
Ionian Dolphin Project, Greece
Ischia Dolphin Project (Italy)
Living and Working in a Sustainable Village (Hungary)
Mediterranean Fin Whale Program (Italy)
Moray Firth Dolphin Monitoring Project (Scotland)
Munda Wanga Wildlife Park and Sanctuary (Zambia)
Oceania Research Project (Australia)
Oneworld Volunteers
Orangutan Foundation, the (Indonesia)
Project Tamar (Brazil)
Re-hydration of the Earth, Kenya
Rhino Rescue Project, Swaziland
Sea Turtle Project, Rhodes Island (Greece)
Sea Turtle Project, Thailand
Skaftafell National Park, Iceland
Tethys Research Institute
Tiger Project, the, India
Whale and Dolphin Project, La Gomera (Spain)
Whale Research in the St. Lawrence Estuary (Canada)
Whales and Dolphins off Côte d'Azur, France
Wolf Tracking, Slovakia
Wolves and Brown Bear Research, Russia

US$1000–1500

Biosphere Expeditions
Birds of Tortuguero, Costa Rica
Bottlenose Dolphin Project, Belize
Cetacean Research & Rescue Unit (Scotland)
Earthwatch Institue
Ecovolunteer Network, the
Fondo per la Terra - Earth Fund
Gibbon Rehabilitation Project (Thailand)
Golden Eagles of Mull, the (UK)
Great Whales in their Natural Environment (Canada)
Great White Shark Project (South Africa)
i to i
Involvement Volunteers Association, Inc.
Leatherback Seaturtle Tagging Programme (Grenada)
Mingan Island Cetacean Research Expeditions

US$1000–1500, con't.
Oceanic Society Expeditions
Orangutan Health (Indonesia)
Project Delphis (USA)
Przewalski Horse Reintroduction Project (Mongolia)
Punta Banco Sea Turtle Project, Costa Rica
Taita Discovery Centre (Kenya)
Turtles of Tortuguero, Costa Rica
University Research Expeditions Program
Wild Dolphin Societies (USA)

Over US$1500
African Conservation Experience
Amargal Tropical Rainforest Research, el (Colombia)
Black Rhino, Kenya
Brathay Exploration Group
CEDAM International
Cheetah Conservation Fund, Namibia
Coral Cay Conservation
Costa Rican Sea Turtles (Costa Rica)
Earthwatch Institute
Ecology of Common Dolphin in the Alboran Sea (Spain)
Frontier
Global Service Corps
Greenforce - Careers in Conservation
Humpback Research Project, Brazil
i to i
Leopards of Phinda, South Africa
Libanona Ecology Centre, Madagascar
Lifeline Cat Research and Rehabilitation Centre, Belize
Manatee Research Project, Belize
Operation Crossroads Africa, Inc.
Operation Wallacea
Projecto Jubarte do Cabo Verde (Cabo Verde)
Raleigh International
Trekforce Expeditions
University Research Expeditions Program

Cost Not Stated
American Littoral Society
Dolphins and Sea Life Around the Maltese Islands (Malta)
Friends of the Sea Otter (USA)
Ringing Programme of Migratory Passerines (Spain)

STANDARD APPLICATION FORM
Green Volunteers © 2003

(To be photocopied enlarged, retyped or downloaded from the **Green Volunteers** Network **Pages** at www.greenvol.com. This is not an official application form; many organisations have their own, others may accept this.)   (Please print)

Last name: .... First name: ....

Nationality: .... Date of birth: .... Passport n°:..............................

Occupation: ....

Address for correspondence: ....

Tel.: .... Fax: .... E-mail: ....

Next of kin (name, address and tel. number): ....
....

If you are a student, write the name and address of the school, College or University:
....

Mother tongue:.. Other languages spoken:
excellent:............................. very good:........................... good:........................... basic:.........................

Education:...

Indicate your experience in volunteering (also in other fields) or in participating in environmental projects, wildlife rescue centres, fieldwork, camping, backpacking or other outdoor activities:
....
....
....

Skills which may be useful to the project:
....
....
....

Are you a member of any environmental organization? If yes, specify:
....

Do you have any health problems? If yes, specify:
....

Indicate your preferences for project's dates and location:
....

Any additional relevant information (feel free to add additional pages):
....
....
....

Date: ..... / ..... /...... Signature: ....

From the same publisher

(available from your bookstore or from the website www.greenvol.com)

World Volunteers   The World Guide to Humanitarian and Development Volunteering

About 200 projects and organisations worldwide for people who want to work in international humanitarian projects but don't know how to begin. Opportunities are from 2 weeks to 2 years or longer. An ideal resource for a working holiday or a leave of absence. A guide for students, retirees, doctors or accountants, nurses or agronomists, surveyors and teachers, plumbers or builders, electricians or computer operators... For everyone who wants to get involved in helping those who suffer worldwide.

Price: £ 10.99   € 16.00 $ 14.95   Pages: 256

Archaeo-Volunteers   The World Guide to Archaeological and Heritage Volunteering

Over 150 projects and organisations in the 5 continents for those who want to spend a different working vacation helping Archaeologists. Placements are from 2 weeks to a few months. For enthusiastic amateurs, students and those wanting hands-on experience. Cultural and historical heritage maintenance and restoration and museum volunteering opportunities are also listed. The guide also tells how to find hundreds more excavations and workcamps on the Internet.

Price: £ 10.99   € 16.00 $ 14.95   Pages: 256